Gender & Pop Culture

TEACHING GENDER

Series Editor
Patricia Leavy
USA

Scope
The *Teaching Gender* publishes monographs, anthologies and reference books that deal centrally with gender and/or sexuality. The books are intended to be used in undergraduate and graduate classes across the disciplines. The series aims to promote social justice with an emphasis on feminist, multicultural and critical perspectives.

Please email queries to the series editor at pleavy7@aol.com

Gender & Pop Culture

A Text-Reader

Edited by

Adrienne Trier-Bieniek
Valencia College, Orlando, USA

and

Patricia Leavy

SENSE PUBLISHERS
ROTTERDAM/BOSTON/TAIPEI

A C.I.P. record for this book is available from the Library of Congress.

ISBN: 978-94-6209-573-1 (paperback)
ISBN: 978-94-6209-574-8 (hardback)
ISBN: 978-94-6209-575-5 (e-book)

Published by: Sense Publishers,
P.O. Box 21858,
3001 AW Rotterdam,
The Netherlands
https://www.sensepublishers.com/

Printed on acid-free paper

Praise for *Gender & Pop Culture*

"The timely, well-written pieces in **Gender & Pop Culture** manage to convey some of the intellectual excitement—and dare I say it, fun—that the best in media studies and feminism can stimulate. Students and scholars alike will appreciate how the wide-ranging chapters in this volume provide greater depth and context to some of the great debates of our time about the 'effects of media' that take place every day in university classrooms and around kitchen tables. This should be required reading for anyone who's ever watched TV, gone to a movie or put on a pair of headphones!"
Jackson Katz, Ph.D., creator of *Tough Guise 2: Violence, Manhood and American Culture* and author of *The Macho Paradox*

"An important addition to the fields of gender and media studies, this excellent compilation will be useful to students and teachers in a wide range of disciplines. The research is solid, the examples from popular culture are current and interesting, and the conclusions are original and illuminating. It is certain to stimulate self-reflection and lively discussion."
Jean Kilbourne, Ed.D., author, feminist activist and creator of the *Killing Us Softly: Advertising's Image of Women* film series

"An ideal teaching tool: the introduction is intellectually robust and orients the reader towards a productive engagement with the chapters; the contributions themselves are diverse and broad in terms of the subject matter covered; and the conclusion helps students take what they have learnt beyond the classroom. I can't wait to make use of it."
Sut Jhally, Professor of Communication, University of Massachusetts at Amherst Founder & Executive Director, Media Education Foundation

"*Gender & Pop Culture* takes no prisoners in describing the influences of patriarchy on a wide range of media. With up-to-date examples, strongly worded arguments, and ideas for resistance, these chapters are sure classroom conversation starters."
Lisa Wade, Founder of *Sociological Images* and Professor at Occidental College

"This important new book by Trier-Bieniek & Leavy bursts off the pages with a devastating combination of age-old statistics and shocking new examples of gender-based inequities in popular culture. Trier-Bieniek & Leavy take readers on a walk through the very real continuing gender inequalities upon which cultural knowledge is constructed, demonstrating the pressing need for new approaches to this area of study. This book provides not only up-to-the-minute worldwide pop culture exemplars, but a clear-eyed overview of methodological approaches and theoretical frameworks for studying gender and pop culture that will be useful for novices to expert researchers in a range of disciplines. In addition, teachers, scholars and researchers will be thankful for the book's pick-up-and-go approach which includes additional resources, suggested readings, links to digital assets, activities, and problem-based learning exercises. Buy this book now!"
Anne Harris, Filmmaker and Professor at Monash University

Adrienne's Dedication

For Angie Moe, the greatest mentor a girl could ask for. And for Catherine Kelly, an amazing nurse, an even better friend and the Amy Poehler to my Tina Fey.

Patricia's Dedication

For Madeline, the most amazing daughter any mother could hope for. You are so strong, talented, kind, smart and funny. I love you to bits and I'm bursting with pride.

Table of Contents

Acknowledgments

First and foremost we thank Sense Publishers. A huge thank you to owner Peter de Liefde for supporting this project and encouraging such groundbreaking work with the Teaching Gender series. Thank you to Paul Chambers for your marketing efforts, Bernice Kelly for your outstanding production assistance and the entire Sense Publishers team. We are also very grateful to our copyeditor, Betsy Dean. It's such a pleasure to work with you, Betsy! We thank every contributor for their time, energy, talent and sharing their expertise. We learned something new from each of you! We also thank our muse, Tori Amos, for being a wonderful model of a female cultural architect; thanks for the inspiration.

Adrienne's Personal Acknowledgements

This book is an example of what two driven feminist friends can do given a long weekend in Maine, g-free pastries, a mutual admiration of each other and a modern day pen-pal relationship fueled by consistent emailing, texting and Facebook. Thank you Patricia, I have learned so much from you and having you (and your family) in my life is amazing. I extend much gratitude to the students in my honors Introduction to Sociology class at Valencia College in the spring semester of 2013. Thanks to Rebecca Baque, Steven Forsyth, Lysette Guambo, Ivan Gutierrez, Zechariah Hilles, Lacey Kresen, Gabriella Lopez and Taylor Raines for the additional research on reading sources. I thank Dr. Angie Moe, the greatest dissertation chair a girl could ask for and my colleague and friend Dr. Carrie Buist whom I am lucky to have in my corner. I also thank my family, particularly the support of my parents Rick and Deanne Trier and my mini-me/budding feminist cousin Breanna Price. Finally, I thank my husband Tim Bieniek who encourages me to grow into the most amazing version of myself… And who leaves me alone to watch The Housewives, Homeland and Scandal without judgment. I love you.

Patricia's Personal Acknowledgements

Adrienne, working with you on this has been a blast. You're a wonderful friend and colleague and my little gang and I are grateful to have you and Tim in our lives. An enormous shout-out to Shalen Lowell, the world's best assistant. Thank you so much for your research assistance and all of your efforts. Mark, you are the most supportive partner anyone could have. Thank you for being you. And last but never least, Madeline, my heart… it isn't easy growing up in a world with media telling you how to behave, what to look like and what to think, but you are such a smart and cool girl, I know you'll be just fine, and you sure keep teaching me. Keep marching to your own beat.

Chapter 1
Introduction to *Gender & Pop Culture*
Patricia Leavy & Adrienne Trier-Bieniek

During the 2013 Academy Awards, filmmaker Brenda Chapman accepted the Best Animated Film award for *Brave*, the story of a Scottish girl who eschews a tradition that requires her to marry a suitor of her parents' choosing. *Brave* put a new spin on the contemporary princess story. Gone was the ideal of beauty found in many of Disney's princesses, the long flowing hair, big doe-eyed looks, hour-glass figure and perfect smile. Merida, *Brave's* princess, had curly red hair that was tangled more times than not, a freckled face free of makeup, and her dress was torn from days spent practicing archery, riding horses and climbing rocks. Merida's frame was gangly, awkward and everything a pre-teen and teen girl embodies. In short, for an animated character, she was realistic. Further, differing from most princess movies, her goal was not to find a husband but rather to find herself and mend her relationship with her mother.

A few months later, in the summer of 2013, Disney revealed a makeover for the character of Merida for her official induction as a Disney Princess. The makeover created a very different Merida. Gone were the tight curls of hair, the freckles and the gangly awkward smile. The new Merida had flowing red hair, large blue eyes which were highlighted with makeup and drawn with a distinct sensuality. Her bust was increased, her waist decreased and her dress was designed to flaunt her newly constructed figure. While some saw this as a necessary step in marketing a Disney Princess, many (including Chapman) saw the change as a concession to the unrealistic and homogenous standards of beauty which are consistently forced on girls. The backlash against the "new" Merida was swift. The website *A Mighty Girl* created a petition on Change.org titled "Disney: No to the Merida Make-Over! Keep Our Hero Brave!" Chapman herself wrote an open letter on the *Huffington Post* declaring,

> I created Merida for my daughter — inspired by her strong-willed spirit — of which I am in complete awe and very proud. But

A. Trier-Bieniek et al., (Eds.), Gender & Pop Culture, 1–25.

despite my best efforts to guide her away from what media images and female stereotypes say to our children, it breaks my heart when she thinks she is too fat or too ugly because she doesn't look like a certain TV star or that "other girl" who is so much more beautiful in her mind. The majority of our children feel that way, and lack self-esteem about their own looks because of issues exactly like this one. (Chapman, 2013 para 6)

The petition at Change.org received over a quarter of a million signatures, leading Disney to take down the re-designed Merida and issue a statement that the new Merida was only created as a limited edition image. They conceded that the original image of Merida would remain on Disney merchandise.

The example of *Brave*, Merida, and Disney Princesses reveals many issues relating to gender and pop culture. This brief example can be used to illustrate the social construction of gender, mass media's impact on gender, and the power of media activism. Therefore, we provide *Brave* as a jumping-off point for this text.

How can we understand gender?

It is important to begin by distinguishing sex and gender as those terms are often mistakenly taken as synonyms. Sex is biological; it is physiologically what prompts us to be assigned as male or female. Gender is socially constructed; it consists of the ideas we have about masculinity and femininity and how we apply these notions to people based on their designated sex assignment. Judith Lorber (1994; 2008) explains that gender is a set of culturally-specific meanings attached to a person because of their sex assignment. So, if your biological sex is male, you are expected to enact masculinity as defined by your society in a given historical time. To put it another way, the current fashion trend in the U.S. in 2013 is for women to wear "skinny jeans" while men's styles remain baggy. This is an acceptable way to display masculine and feminine traits. When the style is reversed with women in baggy clothes and men in tight jeans comments may arise which signal gender confusion, such as "Why are you wearing girls' pants?"

Keep in mind that we are presenting a binary view of sex for the sake of this discussion; however, it is important to acknowledge intersexuality and "intersexed bodies" (please see Anne Fausto-Sterling, 1993 and Suzanne Kessler's, 1997).

The social construction of gender is significant and perhaps the single agreed upon principle in feminism, an expansive field constituted by diverse thought. This can be difficult to fully grasp because, as Judith Lorber notes, "Talking about gender for most people is the equivalent of fish talking about water (1994 as quoted in 2007, p. 141)." Gender takes on the appearance of naturalness. Our environments are very difficult to perceive when we are inside of them and so it is difficult to recognize how our realities are socially constructed, especially with regard to gender because it becomes naturalized. Gender *appears* like we were just born that way, that sex and gender are the same. Because it is hard to see, it is important that we expand on what it means to claim gender is socially constructed. Stephen Pfohl (2008) theorizes the core of constructionism as follows:

> "Things are... partially shaped and provisionally organized by the complex ways in which we are ritually positioned in relation to each other and to the objects we behold materially, symbolically, and in the imaginary realm. The ritual historical positioning of humans in relation to cultural objects and stories that we both make and are made over by—this, perhaps, is the elementary form of an effective social construction. This elementary form casts a circle of believability around artificially constructed accounts of the world. At the same time, the believability of the social constructions that lie inside the circle depends on what the circle expels to the outside. In this sense, social constructions are, at once, constituted and haunted by what they exclude." (pp. 645-646)

Social constructions both include and exclude; they tell and show us what is normative and what is deemed deviant. The social constructions become like water to a fish, so much a part of our environment that they appear normal or just "the way things are" and are consequently taken for granted.

One dangerous part of social constructions is that phenomena can become oversimplified. For example, gender, (our ideas about masculinity and femininity), becomes stereotyped and overgeneralized. In our culture, social constructions create a *gender binary* where masculinity and femininity are seen as polar opposites. Some feelings, behaviors, preferences, and skills are attributed to females and others to males. When people cross those lines they can be subject to ridicule or worse. For example, there are often representations of males in situation comedies where male characters are shown to be incompetent in childcare or housework, and this in turn becomes the source of comedy. Another common example is that female characters in films are typically obsessed with their romantic relationships and can even appear "psycho" as they try to land a man (see, for example, the 2009 film *He's Just Not that into You*). In short, masculinity and femininity are often narrowly defined (and done so in heterosexual terms). To see this at play take a five-minute break from reading and come up with a list of traits for "masculinity" and those for "femininity." After you create your list, try to think of examples from pop culture, such as television, film, or advertising, that reinforce the stereotypes you have recorded.

How do we learn gender?

Since gender is socially constructed and not innate, we learn gender norms through interactions with people and cultural texts and objects. Socialization is the lifelong process whereby people learn the norms and values of the society they live in. Part of this process is gender socialization. The major agents of socialization–family, peers, education, religion, and media– teach us gender norms and the potential consequences if these norms are challenged. Let's take the colors pink and blue as a simple example of how gender is socially constructed and learned through the socialization process. We hope it's fair to assume that most people recognize there is nothing innately meaningful about colors, only the meaning we assign to them (and the history of pink itself is quite interesting as it was originally assigned as a color for males, see *Pink Think: Becoming a Woman in Many Uneasy Lessons* by Lynn Peril, 2002).

4

Notwithstanding this, if you had a son would you let him wear pink to elementary school? Think about this honestly. If you would not, why? If it's because you would be afraid he would be teased, why do you think that is and what can we learn from it? In 2011 a viral YouTube video called *Riley on Marketing* featured a four-year-old girl, Riley Maida, filmed in a toy aisle asking the camera, "Why do all the girls have to buy pink stuff and all the boys have to buy different colored stuff?" By demonstrating how gender is created and reflected by people who are socially constituted, Riley gets to the heart of gender socialization.

On a micro, or smaller scale, to consider gender socialization is to also consider *gender identity*. Gender identity is how a person views him or herself with respect to masculinity or femininity and how this view of the self leads to the enactment of, or resistance to, socially ascribed *gender roles*. Gender roles dictate what is considered acceptable for men and women in terms of behavior, career, parenting, style of dress, and so on. As we mentioned earlier with the social construction of gender, we often think boys and girls, and later men and women, simply have "preferences" that are gendered. In other words, we assume women like going shopping more or have a natural preference for romantic comedies. We assume men dislike those activities naturally, and instead prefer sporting events and action movies. Statistics are found to support these beliefs. However, what is vital to understand is that those preferences are themselves the effect of gender socialization over the life course (or a sequence of events that happen over a lifetime.) As Lorber beautifully explains, the term *human nature* is itself misleading: "The paradox of human nature is that it is *always* a manifestation of cultural meanings, social relationships, and power politics" (1994/2007, p. 143). Who we become as gendered beings is enmeshed in a social process.

One way to think about gender identity and gender roles is to consider the concept of *doing gender*, developed by West and Zimmerman (1987) which refers to the ways that people present themselves with respect to masculinity and femininity. As a jumping-off point to talk about doing gender West and Zimmerman cite Harold Garfinkel's 1967 case study of Agnes, a transsexual who was raised as a boy but became female-identified at the age of 17. Garfinkel chronicled the ways that Agnes adopted in order to pass as a woman. West and Zimmerman called this a "sex category," meaning that we categorize the gender of a person based on how they perform their gender. This can be achieved through items of clothing which are deemed "masculine" or "feminine," the way a person wears their hair or any other distinguishing characteristics that a culture has declared appropriate for men and women. To put it another way, even though a person's genitalia are hidden from public view, we presume that we can correctly identify their gender based on how they present themselves. Further, if people don't present gender in prescribed ways, we can mistake them for the wrong sex. For instance, a long-haired man may be assumed to be female from behind.

Judith Butler (1990) applied this research (as well as the work of Simone de Beauvior and Sigmund Freud) to create the concept of *gender performativity*. For Butler, gender is not something we have, it is something that we do and perform; it is a verb. By performing our gender we are reflecting cultural norms, or various expectations that our culture considers normal for men and women at a specific historical time. Butler takes the field further by explaining that these norms are *heteronormative*, or that heterosexual orientation is what is deemed normal for a society. For example, have you ever heard a relative say that a single man in your family "just hasn't found the right girl?" The insinuation is that the man is heterosexual and that dating women is what is normal for him. When we look at our pop culture, examples of heteronormativity abound from television shows which depict heterosexual parents, to pop songs where singers pine over the loss of an opposite sex partner, to children's books and animated films which portray heterosexual nuclear families (even when depicting animals or made up creatures). But there are also increasingly resistive counter narratives and herein we can see the potential of pop culture to challenge heteronormativity. For instance, one of the reasons the television show *Modern Family* is so successful is because there are two homosexual characters raising a daughter together and going through all the same trials that heterosexual parents face.

How does feminism relate to gender?

On the television series *Parks and Recreation* the main character, Leslie Knope, is played by comedienne Amy Poehler. Knope is driven to become a leader in government, beginning with her position as Deputy Parks Director in the fictional town of Pawnee, Indiana. A counterpart to Leslie Knope is the character of Liz Lemon, played by Tina Fey on the series *30 Rock*. Multiple times throughout the series we see Liz Lemon declaring that, "women can have it all!" as she strives to balance a career and a family. In many ways Leslie Knope and Liz Lemon represent what many would consider to be a new generation of women who have benefited from the work of their mothers and who are striving for professional and personal success (as defined by their culture). Characters like Liz Lemon and Leslie Knope (and the real-life actresses who portray them) exemplify the impact of the *waves of feminism*. The analogy of a wave is connected to feminism because, like a wave, feminism has ebbs and flows.

The first wave of feminism in the United States dates back to the Seneca Falls Convention of 1848 and was held, primarily, to discuss the rights of women. One takeaway from the event was the Declaration of Sentiments which is considered to be an introductory document that led to the path of women seeking the right to vote, and many participants at the Seneca Falls Convention became leaders in the women's suffrage movement. Susan B. Anthony, Elisabeth Cady Stanton, Lucretia Mott and Fredrick Douglass began a call for women's rights that was partially answered in 1920 when women received the right to vote via the 19th amendment. The passing of the 19th amendment was depicted in pop culture via the 2004 film *Iron Jawed Angels* which starred Hillary Swank.

The second wave of feminism refers to the women's movement in the 1960s and 1970s and is largely connected to the work of Gloria Steinem and Betty Friedan. Steinem was a reporter whose undercover work as a waitress at the Playboy Club exposed the harassment, terrible working conditions, and exploitation of the "Playboy Bunnies." Her article, titled "I was a Playboy Bunny," brought her national attention and led to Steinem founding *Ms. Magazine*, a magazine which is dedicated to national and international news about women and feminism. Betty Friedan was a college-educated housewife. During her time at home she began to feel restless and decided to ask her neighbors about what she called, "the problem that has no name." The result of those interviews was the 1963 book *The Feminine Mystique* in which Friedan combined research in psychology, media, and advertising to address that middle- and upper-class women were expected to find their identity in housework and child-rearing. However, many women were discontent in those limited roles and experienced various levels of dissatisfaction and depression as a result. The work of Steinem and Friedan was foundational for the women's movement in the 1960s and 1970s, a time when the second wave of feminism is credited with passing laws which protected abused or harassed women, brought sexual liberation in the form of the birth control pill, advanced the number of women seeking public office and/or graduate degrees, and saw the passing of Roe vs. Wade, enabling a woman's right to reproductive choice.

Just like a wave, feminism hit an ebb in the 1980s. The third wave of feminism was born in the early 1990s as a response to the backlash against feminism, particularly with people who believed that feminism was no longer necessary or that it was created for, and primarily benefited, White women. The lack of representation of women of color and international women in earlier feminist efforts contributed to dispiritedness, particularly with work like *The Feminine Mystique* with which critics argued that the middle-class, White women Freidan interviewed did not represent the experiences of lower-class and/or non-White women who had no choice but to work outside their homes. In 1992 Rebecca Walker wrote an op-ed for *Ms. Magazine* titled, "Becoming the Third Wave" in which she equated the confirmation hearings of Supreme Court Justice Clarence Thomas, who was also facing allegations of sexual harassment, to the need for a new movement of feminists. She also pushed for the experiences of women of color to be included in feminist agendas. Walker, along with the 2000 book *Manifesta* written by Amy Richards and Jennifer Baumgardner, is credited with shaping the third wave's agenda which focuses on the rights of women internationally, the acknowledgement and inclusion of women of color in feminism, and the use of popular culture and technology in feminist activism.

One way the third wave of feminism aims to include and acknowledge the varied experiences of women of color is through the concept of *privilege*. Privilege speaks to the "unearned privileges" (benefits) a person may be afforded on the basis of their race (or another status characteristic like sexual orientation or social class). Drawing on the ground-breaking work of Peggy McIntosh (1989), when we say "unearned," we mean these benefits are not merit based; that privilege is something that was simply given to a person. These privileges only exist within a stratified or unequal society. So, for example, a White person in the United States can turn on any of the major television networks and expect to see people that look like them. In an equal society this would be something everyone could do. People who benefit from unearned privileges often do so unknowingly; their advantage, which is inextricably bound to others' disadvantage, is unrecognized. That is a part of the privilege, the privilege of not seeing inequality (McIntosh, 1989). McIntosh defines privilege, in part, by writing: "As a white person, I realized I had been taught about racism as something that puts others at a disadvantage, but had been taught not to see one of its corollary aspects, white privilege, which puts me at an advantage" (1989, p. 9).

Patricia Hill Collins and bell hooks have also theorized extensively about privilege. Hill Collins (1990) developed the concept *matrix of domination* as a part of *intersectionality theory* which contends that race, class, gender, sexual orientation, and even age all serve as vectors of oppression and privilege. In other words, we don't just live in a body that is raced, it is also gendered, classed, and so on. Examining the concerns and situations of women of color has led to increased attention to the needs of international women and the development of non-western or critical indigenous feminism. Chandra Talpade Mohanty (2003) addresses the need for third world and western women to work together to advance the rights of women in the global south. Additionally Vandava Shiva, a physicist, has written extensively on the topic of ecofeminism, an approach which connects the domination of women to the desecration of the environment. Ecofeminism argues that Western patriarchal societies have contributed to the oppression of non-Western cultures via their treatment of women and the environment. Shiva explains this connection by giving the examples of farming communities in India which are generally farmed by women. Yet, women do not own the land-rights to the farms in which they labor and they are bound by regulations which have trickled down from Western legislation.

Another example of privilege being challenged in new approaches to feminism is *queer theory*. Queer theory is an umbrella term for a range of theories. For our purposes, queer theory links sexual orientation and gender by contending that the categories of sex and gender are not fixed, rather they are fluid and should not be limited to conventional ideas of gender. Moreover, like gender, sexual orientation is socially constructed. Pascoe (2007) explains that queer theory "… moves beyond traditional categories such as male/female, masculine/ feminine, and straight/gay to focus instead on the instability of these categories… Queer theory emphasizes multiple identities (p. 11)." Pascoe is contending that queer theory opens up gender categories and takes away gender roles and norms. This means that what is typically considered masculine can be applied to women and what is considered feminine can be applied to men. Perhaps the clearest illustration of queer theory comes from considering transgender individuals. As Nagoshi and Brzuzy point out, "The experiences of transgender individuals, those who do not conform to traditional gender identity binaries, raise compelling questions about the nature of socially defined identities. Does one's identity in a category, such as gender, require that this identity be fixed in a particular body" (2010, p. 431)?

Transgender theory, according to Nagoshi and Brzuzy, uses gender identity to understand the experiences of transgender and transsexual individuals, particularly the ways that transgender people embody their gender. It contends that being transgender challenges social norms about gender because trans people have lived life in both genders. Transgender people shine a light on the artificiality of the gender binary and can thus become the target of great prejudice.

An excellent example of queer and transgender theory is the character of Sophia, one of the prisoners in the Netflix series *Orange is the New Black.* Played by transgender actress Laverne Cox, Sophia represents not only what transgender people go through when placed in the prison system, but also the day-to-day challenges they face. For example, there is a scene where Sophia is purchasing shoes for her son and the sales person refers to her as "sir, ma'am, whatever you are." By directly addressing Sophia's transgender identity the sales person is illustrating Butler's point that gender is a social performance. Interestingly, because of our stringent binary, Hollywood seems to think that performing opposite gender expectations is particularly challenging and there is a long history of awarding actors and actresses who play transgender characters (for example; Dustin Hoffman in *Tootsie*, Hilary Swank in *Boys Don't Cry* and Felicity Huffman in *TransAmerica*).

How do feminist researchers study gender?

In order to study gender (as well as a host of other topics), feminist researchers have adapted and developed a wide range of research practices based on theoretical, methodological and activist principles. There is no one way to conduct feminist research and there are a range of theoretical frameworks feminists have adopted, so certainly this brief review can't cover all of them. We hope it will give you a flavor of some of the ways feminists build knowledge about social life. Theoretical frameworks include different approaches to the research process based on assumptions about what can be known, who can be a knower, and how research should proceed. The major approaches to research include: empiricism, standpoint epistemology, intersectionality theory, postmodern theory, and post-structural theory, but this list is far from exhaustive (for a full discussion of these theoretical perspectives see Hesse-Biber & Leavy, 2007).

Researchers combine a theoretical framework with research methods in order to develop a methodology, which is a plan for how a particular study will be carried out (Harding, 1993). Research methods are tools for collecting and analyzing data and should be selected in relation to the problem at hand (Hesse-Biber & Leavy, 2005; 2011). Feminist researchers may use a range of research methods in their work, including quantitative methods such as survey research using a Likert scale where respondents select among standard responses (such as *strongly agree, agree* and so on). Statistics can be formulated to show rates of responses. Qualitative methods can also be used, particularly when you are interested in gathering in-depth information from people and you are willing to give up some breadth of data (a large sample) for depth. Qualitative methods include strategies like interviews or observational research and allow you to go further into people's attitudes, beliefs, and their reporting of their behaviors and explanations.

Suppose you want to study media content itself, as opposed to how it impacts individuals. In this instance you conduct a content analysis of a sample of media (perhaps looking for themes or perhaps looking for instances in which something occurs). In a situation where your primary goal is to reach a diverse and public audience with your work, challenge stereotypes, and promote reflection, you may opt for an arts-based approach. For example, after conducting a literature review to see trends in media coverage of male and female candidates you could write two short stories, one that follows the media campaign of a male political candidate and one that follows that of a female.

This is just a small sampling of the approaches one could take. As you can see, there are countless methodological possibilities for researchers interested in studying gender and they are each useful in different contexts. It is important to understand how feminist research occurs as you read the essays that follow, which all refer to scholarly work. These essays represent more than "opinions," they are raising issues that have been well-researched.

We hope that these foundational concepts about gender and feminism are useful as we look more specifically at how popular culture serves as an agent of socialization, circulating social constructions of gender that in turn shape gender identities.

What is popular culture?

Popular culture generally refers to the images, narratives, and ideas that circulate within mainstream culture. They are "popular" in that they are known to the masses–most in a given society are exposed to the same dominant aspects of pop culture. Scholar John Storey (2003) traces the history of pop culture noting eight historical moments: folk culture, mass culture, high culture, hegemony, postmodern culture, cultural identities, and global culture. In this day and age there is little distinction between media culture and popular culture. Therefore, popular or media culture is also a part of commercial culture. From a social science perspective, pop culture includes both practices and products. Beginning with the former, there are a range of practices or rituals by which we produce and consume pop culture. There are also the cultural texts themselves, or the products of pop culture (using the word "text" in its broadest sense to include a range of objects, stories, and mediated images).

Media culture is one of the major agents of socialization through which we learn the norms and values of our society. It is not surprising that our socially constructed ideas about gender often originate in, and are reinforced by, dominant narratives in the popular culture. As a socializing force that most are exposed to, popular culture becomes a second skin and is taken for granted. Collectively, we learn a set of beliefs and values through images and narratives that take on the appearance of normality; however, there is nothing natural about media culture, pop culture texts have been constructed. This begs questions like: Who constructs them? Whom do they benefit (financially and/or with respect to power and cultural capital)? Whom do they harm? What ideas do they normalize? Media scholar Sut Jhally (1990; 1997) urges us not to lose sight of the commercial interests driving media culture. He warns that profit-driven media conglomerates monopolize the cultural space, creating and distributing dominant ideologies intended to sell everything from war propaganda to commodities.

As an agent of socialization, media culture differs from family, religion, and other socializing institutions because it of its far-reaching grasp or monopoly of the cultural landscape and also because we often elect to spend our leisure time participating in, generally consuming, pop culture. We are more likely to view it as fun and frivolous, and therefore may fail to interrogate the messages of pop culture and how they are impacting us. Media and gender scholar Jean Kilbourne explains this clearly in the well-known educational (1997) video *The Ad and the Ego*. She notes that everyone thinks they are personally exempt from the impact of advertising in pop culture and that she often hears, "I don't pay attention to that" and "It doesn't impact me." Kilbourne jokes that she mostly hears these statements from people wearing Budweiser caps, implying they are indeed impacted. Additionally, Jackson Katz (1999, 2013) explores a similar theme in his *Tough Guise* film series. In this series, Katz addresses the impact pop culture and media have on defining what men see as masculine. Katz's work is especially relevant when investigating how pop culture impacts our lives because it's important to understand there may be a disjuncture between perception and reality. This is one of the reasons feminist scholars employ a range of research methods in their studies, some that are better suited to assess attitudes, others behaviors, and others the content of pop culture texts themselves.

What are the stories, images and ideas about gender that circulate in pop culture?

There are three main dimensions when trying to understand the relationship between gender and pop culture texts: production, representation, and consumption (Milestone & Meyer, 2012). Posed as questions we can ask:

- Who produces pop culture texts?
- What representations of gender circulate in dominant pop culture?
- What about resistive or counter-dominant representations of gender?
- What is the relationship between gender and the consumption of pop culture texts?

Who produces pop culture texts?

In Western culture, popular or media culture dominates the cultural landscape. There is hardly anywhere to look where you won't see the impact of media, whether it is advertisements on the side of buses, billboards down the highway, magazines at the grocery store checkout, or CDs for sale at the counter of Starbucks. Bear in mind these examples say nothing of the pop culture we choose to consume– television, movies, social media, concerts, sporting events and so on. Because pop culture dominates the cultural space, the creators behind the scenes are cultural architects, building our environment. Arguably the role of the makers of pop culture is as great in society as the role of architects who design homes, buildings, and public spaces. The creation of popular culture becomes the fabric of society–who we are as people and who we think we can become, including powerful ideas about gender.

When we look at who produces pop culture the gender disparity is overwhelming. In the 2011 film, *Miss Representation*, the filmmaker presents some shocking statistics about the roles of women in entertainment.

- Women are 17% of all executive producers
- Women are 13% of all film writers
- Women are 7% of all film producers
- Women are 2% of all cinematographers
- Women are the authors of 20% of all op-eds in American newspapers
- Women are 3% of all creative directors in advertising
- Women hold 3% of all clout positions in media

This list could go on and on. Media culture is overwhelmingly produced by men.

There is also a lesson here to be learned about the "unearned privileges" we mentioned earlier. When we think about gender inequality we often think "girls and women" and therefore focus on the disadvantages to girls and women (Katz, 1999). However, disadvantage is only one side of the coin. There is also the side of privilege and unearned benefits. Let's look at the other, often invisible side of these statistics.

- In 2011 men are 83% of all executive producers
- In 2011 men are 87% of all film writers
- In 2011 men are 93% of all film producers
- In 2011 men are 98% of all cinematographers
- In 2011 men are the authors of 80% of all op-eds in American newspapers
- In 2011 men are 97% of all creative directors in advertising
- In 2011 men hold 97% of all clout positions in media

What representations of gender circulate in dominant pop culture?
What about resistive or counter-dominant representations of gender?

Given that males are the primary writers of popular culture, and that this is a commercial industry unlikely to challenge the status quo for economic reasons, it is not surprising that we often see stereotyped portrayals of femininity and masculinity. To consider this issue, let's turn to a parody written by Martha Lauzen titled *If Women Ran Hollywood... 2012*. After recounting the stark gender imbalance in Hollywood as evidenced by gender inequity behind the scenes and on-screen, Lauzen muses about what would happen if women ran Hollywood instead of men and lists 14 "what ifs." Here are a couple examples from her list (you can read Lauzen's entire list at http://www.womensmediacenter.com/feature/entry/if-women-ran-hollywood-.-.-.-2012):

- "Cable television networks targeting a male audience with moniker's such as Men's Entertainment (or ME) would traffic in the most heavily prescribed social roles imaginable, encouraging men to stay in their proper place."
- "The *Real Husbands of* (*fill-in-the-blank*) would be a successful reality show franchise for Bravo featuring males in manufactured situations and reinforcing the worst possible stereotypes."

The point is clear: sexism in the production of popular culture leads to sexist representations within popular culture. Put more gently, having fewer perspectives behind the scenes will lead to a more limited pool of representations and less diversity in storytelling style and content.

The contributors throughout this volume examine representations of femininity and masculinity within particular genres of pop culture. As context for those discussions, here are some general statistics from 2011 that highlight persistent gender inequity:

- Male characters were more likely to be shown at their job than female characters, 41% to 28% (http://www.missrepresentation.org/about-us/resources /gender-resources)
- Men on television were more likely to talk about work than women, 52% to 40% (http://www.missrepresentation.org/about-us/resources/gender-resources)
- Women on television were more likely to talk about relationships than men, 63% to 49% (http://www.missrepresentation.org/about-us/resources/gender-resources)
- Males outnumber females in family films three to one (a statistic that has held steady since 1946) (http://www.missrepresentation.org/about-us/resources/gender -resources)
- Only 16% of protagonists in film were female (making 84% male) (http://reelgirl .com/2011/10/stats-from-miss-representation/)

These trends hold true across media, even the news:

- Women and girls are the subject of less than 20% of all news stories (http://reelgirl.com/2011/10/stats-from-miss-representation/)
- Women make up 14% of the guests on influential Sunday television talk shows and only 7% of repeat guests (http://reelgirl.com/category/statistics/)
- In 2010 *The New York Review of Books* had a six to one ratio of male to female bylines. There was also glaring gender imbalance in *The New Republic* and *The Atlantic* (http://reelgirl.com/category/statistics/)
- In 2010 *The New Yorker* reviewed 36 books by men and nine by women. There was also stark gender imbalance in book reviews in *Harper's* and *The New York Times Book Review* (http://reelgirl.com/category/statistics/)

What we see from these statistics is that who produces popular culture impacts who is represented and in what manner. In the preceding lists we can see implications for gender roles and gender identity, power and world-making activities, and professional development and influence over others.

It is important to remember that narrow and binary constructions of gender are harmful to everyone in society. The media consistently define masculinity in narrow and heterosexist ways making it difficult for many real boys and men to exhibit characteristics associated with femininity or embody roles commonly identified as female, such as that of nurturer. Males who exhibit these important human qualities may be bullied and called "sissy" among other terms. These dualistic constructions are so engrained in the culture that they affect both males and females. For example, on a recent episode of *Project Runway*, one female contestant critiqued another for being too emotional. She said her competitor should "take it like a man."

Despite the dominant narratives about gender, popular culture is not homogenized and increasingly we see resistive or counter representations. For example, some of the contributors in this book discuss how television shows like *Modern Family* are offering alternative representations of gender and family, and advertising campaigns like "Real Beauty" by Dove are expanding representations of femininity. There are individuals posing challenges too. For example, in 2012 musician Frank Ocean posted an open letter on Tumblr explaining that he had been in a relationship with a man who was the first person he ever truly loved. Ocean's blog went viral and was commented on widely by supporters such as Russell Simmons, Beyoncé, and Jay-Z as well as those making homophobic public outbursts, like Chris Brown.

What is the relationship between gender and the consumption of pop culture texts?

While media images are so ubiquitous there are many we are all exposed to simply by going to the grocery store, we also engage in a *selection* process. Our gender identity may impact what pop culture texts we choose to consume. For example, many college students place ads and clippings from magazines on their dorm walls. How do they select what images to display?

There are also the issues of *internalization* and *effects of media representations*. Beginning with the former, not everyone will internalize the messages of popular culture in the same ways. For example, two college-age women may avidly read women's fashion magazines and consume other hyper-feminine media content and their psyches won't necessarily be impacted in the same way. One woman may develop a poor body image, low self-esteem, and may engage in any number of behaviors as a result, from cosmetic surgery to developing an eating disorder or disordered eating. The other woman may be less deeply impacted; however, there is no telling the extent to which that media still shapes her beauty or relationships ideals. Although we don't all internalize gender constructions the same way, we all live in a society in which there are widespread effects of media representations. Here are a few examples:

- Girls' self-esteem decreases in adolescence as compared with their male counterparts and this can lead to lowered ambition (*Miss Representation*)
- The routine objectification of women's bodies has led to what the American Psychological Association (APA) has deemed a

national epidemic of self-objectification http://www.forbes.com/sites/samanthaettus/2011/10/21/25-alarm -bells-for-women-sounds-from-miss-representation/
- The APA, CDC, and National Institutes of Health (NIH) show a clear link between media violence and real-world violence, which is gendered (*Miss Representation*)
- Some women experience "role strain" or "role conflict" as they struggle to "do it all" as media has prescribed (*Miss Representation*)
- In the United States, 20 million women and 10 million men suffer from a clinically significant eating disorder at some time in their life (http://www.nationaleatingdisorders.org/get-facts-eating-disorders)

While we are not all impacted equally by the pop culture environment, and can exercise some agency in what media we consume, there is no doubt that the personal and social effects of media culture are far reaching.

Organization of the book

The pages that follow offer a range of contributions on the major genres of pop culture. We have invited authors with different backgrounds and writing styles to share their expertise. We hope the readings not only provide information and frameworks for understanding gender and pop culture more critically, but also stimulate lively discussion, debate, and personal and social reflection.

Before beginning the readings that will you take you through *Gender and Pop Culture: A Text-Reader*, we offer this summary of each chapter. Please note, the chapters need not be read in sequence. Following this introduction to the text is Chapter 2 "Blurred Lines of a Different Kind: Sexism, Sex, Media and Kids," Scott Richardson's exploration of the impact of media on children. Through re-creations of dialogue with his students and children, Richardson addresses how the most well-known images and music in pop culture continue to provide children with gender roles steeped in patriarchal traditions. Richardson uses the Disney princesses and the 2013 song "Blurred Lines" by Robin Thicke as two of many examples which demonstrate the messages of sex and sexuality children receive.

Chapter 3 is Patricia Arend's fascinating review of the impact of advertising on gender. Arend draws from advertising media such as Danica Patrick's GoDaddy.com sexy ad campaign, the ways masculinity is depicted in commercials for pick-up trucks, and the links to violence against women in Dolce and Gabanna's images. Through a conversation of advertising's use of gender roles as a framework for masculinity and femininity, Arend applies concepts, like doing gender, and theorists, like Erving Goffman, to contemporary advertising campaigns.

Themes of patriarchy, music, and activism can be found in Chapter 4, "From Lady Gaga to Consciousness Rap: The Impact of Music on Gender and Social Activism." Adrienne Trier-Bieniek and Amanda Pullum analyze songs by Beyoncé, Lupe Fiasco, and Ani DiFranco in order to demonstrate the ways music has become a tool for feminist consciousness-raising. Counter to Thicke's "Blurred Lines, the artists covered in this chapter seemingly want to create music that will challenge patriarchal standards while also being aesthetically pleasing to listen to.

Chapter 5, "As Seen on TV: Gender, Television, and Popular Culture" bridges the history of television's depiction of gender via shows like *I Love Lucy* or *Maude* with contemporary reality television such as *The Real Housewives* franchise and *The Jersey Shore*. Jenn Brandt incorporates recent television situation comedies like *Two and a Half Men* and *The Big Bang Theory* as examples of how television assigns gender roles to characters, perhaps sometimes without questioning the impact of their caricature of what it means to be male or female. This is a theme which carries into Chapter 6 "Popular Movies that Teach: How Movies Teach about Schools & Genders." In this chapter, Adam Greteman and Kevin Burke also draw from historical-to-contemporary examples of how gender has been portrayed in film, but they do so through looking at how the education system is presented in the movie. By looking at films like *Grease*, *Hairspray*, *Dangerous Minds,* and *High School Musical*, Greteman and Burke direct our attention to the ways gender "goes to school" by combining a history of film with gender stereotypes and pop culture's fascination with youth.

With Chapter 7, "Gender, Sport and Popular Culture," Emily A. Roper and Katherine M. Polasek, combine a discussion of women's history in sports with a sociological interpretation of how gender is connected to and constructed by sports. Roper and Polasek make the compelling argument that while sports do tend to further engender ideas about femininity, they also trap men into strict ideas about what masculinity is and how they should perform as men. Finally, in Chapter 8 "Gender and Technology: Women's Usage, Creation and Perspectives" Cindy Royal addresses the relationship between women and technology. Even though women have been the primary users of the telephone and the first computer programmer was a woman, technology has always been a male-dominated field. Royal chronicles this gender disparity and the impact on women in tech-related fields.

In the final chapter, "Using the Lessons Outside of the Classroom: In Other Words, Now What?" we suggest several ways that students can apply what they have learned in this book to their own lives and the communities in which they live. Following the concluding chapter we provide additional resources, such as suggested readings for each of the topics covered in this book as well as topics beyond the scope of the book, such as international studies in popular culture. We hope this text provides a strong base to interrogate gender and popular culture, and that you have some fun along the way.

Pedagogical Resources

Questions for Class Discussion

1. How do you present your gender? Have you ever been mistaken for the opposite gender?
2. Which form of media do you use most consistently? What would happen if you stopped using it?
3. Consider and discuss the statistics of women's participation in the entertainment industry. Why do you think women are largely invisible?
4. Discuss the waves of feminism and create an outline for what you think the fourth wave of feminism should look like. What role will media and pop culture play in its foundation? What issues do you think should be front and center?

Class Activity

Bring one or two pieces of pop culture to class. This can be anything from a magazine, newspaper, laptop or tablet. Perform a content analysis on the media by finding common themes related to gender and talking about them. For example, if you use your laptop you could go to a page like Twitter or Facebook and analyze the ads which pop up on the page. You can also count the times a certain kind of image or text appears. For instance, if you are content analyzing a newspaper for coverage of male and female political candidates, how many times are issues like family or clothing mentioned?

Class Activity with Supplemental Reading

Have students read the novel research-informed *Low-Fat Love* by Patricia Leavy. They should highlight all of the pop culture references while reading. Break students into small groups (3-5 students) and ask them to explore the following issue: *Low-Fat Love* can be used to explore the social construction of femininity and masculinity. Have a discussion about how the characters in the book illustrate some of the ways we construct and perform gender identities. What is the role of pop culture in how the characters construct their identities? The class can reconvene and students can share some of their ideas which you can write on the board (creating two columns for femininity and masculinity).

Problem-Based Learning Exercise

Problem-based learning assumes that students learn together by doing– by engaging in research and problem-solving. The following PBL is divided into four parts which can be spaced out over a few weeks or over the entire semester. Randomly divide students in groups of 3-5.

To begin. Each group should talk about their goals for group work and then pick an area of popular culture they you are interested in learning more about this week and then select a genre within that area. Examples includes: film (some example genres are: romantic comedies, westerns, horror, children/animation, foreign, action-adventure); magazines (women's fashion, men's, fitness); television (sitcoms, dramas, children's shows/cartoons, tween shows, game shows, talk shows); fiction (novels, comics, graphic novels, children's books); etc. Students will be studying the genre they select all week so groups should spend some time deciding what everyone is interested in learning about.

PBL1

Learn some general scholarly information about your topic—what kind of social research has been done on your topic and how do sociologists frame your topic (how do they talk about it)? Bring a sample of articles to class tomorrow and be prepared to briefly talk about your answer to this question.

PBL 2

What are the dominant ideas about masculinity and femininity put forth in the genre of pop culture you selected? How are "maleness" and "femaleness" predominantly presented/defined within this genre? Look for some research to address this question (you may also come up with some examples to illustrate your points).

PBL 3

One of the ways to combat the gender stereotyping children and young adults learn through the socialization process is through "media literacy" education. Arguably in our media saturated society this kind of learning can be viewed as vital for overall (psychological) health and well-being (just like health education is). Find scholarly literature that explains what media literacy education is and then think about how it can be constructed in relation to your genre.

PBL 4

Take what you have learned this week and put together a 15-20 minute presentation for the class on your topic. To take it to another level, as a part of your presentation create an arts-based piece (for example a short story, a series of poems, a script, etc.) that enhances your presentation. Please write up a one-page artist-researcher statement that you will hand in.

Additional Sources for Class Activities

The Geena Davis Institute on Gender in Media (www.seejane.org)
Media Education Foundation (www.mediaed.org)
Women's Media Center (www.womensmediacenter.com)

References

Boihem, H. (Producer & Director). (1997). *The ad and the ego.* US: Parralax Pictures, Inc.

Butler, J. (1999). *Gender trouble: Feminism and the subversion of identity.* London, UK: Routledge.

Chapman, B. (2013). *Staying true to Merida: Why this fight matters.* Retrieved from http://www .huffingtonpost.com/brenda-chapman/staying-true-to-merida_b_3322472.html

Collins, P. H. (1990). *Black feminist thought: Knowledge, consciousness, and the politics of empowerment.* London, UK: HarperCollins.

Harding, S. (1993). Rethinking standpoint epistemology: What is strong objectivity? In L. Alcoff & E. Potter (Eds.), *Feminist epistemologies* (pp. 49–82). New York, NY: Routledge.

Hesse-Biber, S. N., & Leavy, P. (2005). *The practice of qualitative research.* Thousand Oaks, CA: Sage.

Hesse-Biber, S. N., & Leavy, P. (2007). *Feminist research practice: A primer.* Thousand Oaks, CA: Sage.

Hesse-Biber, S. N., & Leavy, P. (2011). *The practice of qualitative research* (2nd ed.). Thousand Oaks, CA: Sage.

Jhally, S. (1990). *The codes of advertising: fetishism and the political economy of meaning in the consumer society.* New York, NY: Routledge.

Jhally, S. (Producer and Director). (2013, 1999). *Tough guise.* US: Media Education Films.

Lauzen, M. (2012). *If women ran hollywood... 2012.* Retrieved from http://www.womensmediacenter.com/feature/entry/if-women-ran-hollywood...2012

Lorber, J. (1993). Seeing as believing: Biology as ideology. *Gender and Society, 7*(4), 568–581.

Lorber, J. (1994). *Paradoxes of gender*. New Haven, CT: Yale University Press.

Lorber, J. (2008). Constructing gender: The dancer and the dance. In J. A. Holstein & J. F. Gubrium (Eds.), *Handbook of constructionist research* (pp. 531–544). New York, NY: Guilford Press.

McIntosh, P. (1989). White privilege: Unpacking the invisible knapsack. *Peace and Freedom* (July/August), 9–10.

Milestone, K., & Meyer, A. (2012). *Gender and popular culture*. Cambridge, UK: Polity.

Mohanty, C. T. (2003). *Feminism without borders: Decolonizing theory, practicing solidarity*. Durham, NC: Duke University Press.

Nagoshi, J. L., & Brzuzy, S. (2010). Transgender theory: Embodying research and practice. *Affilia: Journal of Women and Social Work, 25*(4), 431–443.

Newsom, J. S., & Acquaro, K. (Director & Producer). (2011). *Miss representation*. USA: Girls Club Entertainment.

Pascoe, C. J. (2007). *Dude, you're a fag: Masculinity and sexuality in high schools*. University of California Press.

Pfohl, S. (2008). The reality of social constructions. In J. A. Holstein & J. F. Gubrium (Eds.), *Handbook of constructionist research* (pp. 645–668). New York, NY: Guilford Press.

West, C., & Zimmerman, D. (1987). Doing gender. *Gender & Society, 1*, 125–151.

Chapter 2
Blurred Lines of a Different Kind: Sexism, Sex, Media and Kids
Scott Richardson

"Dr. Richardson, you're perverted."

"What?"

"I'm sorry if I'm out of line, but how can you possibly think like *that*?"

Allison Baker, a kind and thoughtful sophomore stood between me and the classroom door. Class had just ended.

"I think you're perverted."

I began to blush. Her classmates circled us as though we were middle schoolers, clenching our fists and yelling insults. They wanted to see blood.

"I'm sorry, Allison, I'm not following you."

She glared at me, now teary eyed, terribly irritated, and pressed once again, "How can you think like that?"

I must have looked baffled. Brianna, another student, and Allison's roommate clarified, "She loves Disney. Everything is Disney in her room. She has posters everywhere."

This was not the first time that I encountered women (or men) in love with Disney movies. These fairytales were deeply significant to their childhood. Many were raised on a Disney diet.

Frustrated, I wanted to say, "Allison… use your brain," but I recognized that this approach would be unproductive and perceived as simple insult. So instead, I went into teacher mode.

"What do you mean by perverted?"

"I mean, that it's not about sex or gender or whatever you were saying in class. Disney stories are about happiness, fantasy, and love."

"Interesting. I could argue otherwise. But still…what do you mean by perverted?"

Allison paused, wiped a tear from her cheek, and looked to her friend for help. "Don't look at me," Brianna responded.

I tried to bring her to a thoughtful state and said, "I'm not trying to be smart, Allison, I just want to understand you better. Help me to understand."

A. Trier-Bieniek et al., (Eds.), Gender & Pop Culture, 27–52.

After another long pause she responded, "Ok, I don't know what I meant by perverted. I guess I'm upset because why would you, I mean anyone, ever do some quote-unquote analysis on Disney movies…just to tell us how horrible they are?"

"Well, I think you have two questions here. The first is why people have looked at Disney culture and what it represents. The second is why am I 'ruining it' for you…"

"Exactly!" Allison interrupted, "It feels like you are trying to ruin it for me. Like you're attacking me!"

Allison, and probably others too, felt violated about what transpired in class that day. I had given a brief talk about how kids are socialized to perform masculinity and femininity. I made it a point to demonstrate that these forces of socialization, which teach us the norms and values of our culture, bombard children from all angles. School, friends, parents, media, and elsewhere, work to tell, and at times monitor, how children perform (Butler, 1990) gender and sexuality. More times than not, these performances uphold what bell hooks (1981) calls our "white supremacist capitalist patriarchy"— "the interlocking systems of domination that define our reality" (as quoted in Jhally, 1997). "White," "supremacist," and "capitalist" are adjectives modifying "patriarchy," the noun, which she defines as, "a political-social system that insists that males are inherently dominating, superior to everything and everyone deemed weak, especially females, and endowed with the right to dominate and rule over the weak and to maintain that dominance through various forms of psychological terrorism and violence" (hooks, 2004, p. 18). This is strong wording. It may be difficult to "see" psychological terrorism and violence in most of our everyday lives because patriarchy does not always (need to) explicitly employ it. What this means to me is that psychological terrorism and violence is often implicitly present, and ready to be unleashed if white men begin to lose their dominant status in our society.

Citing Disney movies as a media example—the equation of a beautiful (often helpless or flawed) princess and a handsome savior prince—was an easy one. Female Disney characters always demonstrate, to some degree, that they are in need of a man. Never are these characters like, "Well… I think I'm going to take some time to pursue my career goals," or "I'm interested in keeping my dating options open. So, yes, I'll date you but it's not an exclusive thing." Male Disney characters always oblige the "needs" of the woman. Never does Prince Charming say, "Well… you're nice and all, but I'm really into headsy kinda gals," or "Do you know Prince Romero? He's exactly my type!"

There are only a few Disney films that try to feature storylines that are not romantically or sexually based. But most times, the primary characters are always males. For example, *Monsters University*, a Pixar/Disney film featured a green one-eyed monster, Mike Wazowski, and a large blue and purple polka dotted monster, James P. Sullivan, as they attended MU to fulfill their dreams of becoming a "scarer." The film offers a non-typical Disney storyline, however, the writers could not resist embedding a scene where James ogles a few "Python Nu Kappa" (PNK) sorority sisters, who despite the third eye and their purple, pink and aqua skin colors, are most human-like and sexualized: thin, long batting eyelashes, lipstick, and mini-skirted. It is important to wonder, what does this add to the story? Additionally, what message does this short scene deliver to kids? To me, it demonstrates that girls should be perceived as sexual objects and should look "hot" while the boys should be predators.

In other words, it is the same formula, or narrative, over and over again. Disney tales are heteronormative and implicitly based on sexuality. Why bother making multiple movies—if not practically every movie—with this same narrative? On a whole other level, why do we not wonder if love stories are even appropriate for young children? After all, what does or should a five-year old know about the complicated world of dating, sex, marriage, and adult romance? And why does the story almost always end with a wedding, a highly anticipated kiss, or something of this nature? Meaning, Disney fantasies end with bagging the guy/girl but we rarely see what comes next: sex, kids, marital strife, divorce, infidelity, balancing family and work, and so on. Okay, maybe these themes need not be primary narrated in movies either, but we are selling our kids short if Disney, and other media forms/outlets, cannot be creative enough to develop entertainment about anything, literally anything else at all, except heterosexual romance? Effectively, I'm calling Disney perverted.

Why mix kids, sex, and gender so much? So my question is: What is *their* hang up?

My point in class that day was that we, as a society, have largely become mindless consumers of media that constantly socialize children to understand, embody, and perform gender and sexuality in early and narrowly defined ways. The argument I was making was not some earth shattering new critique. In fact, for decades researchers have understood the perils of sexist and sexualized media and its impact on children. As a society, we have just mostly ignored it.

A Brief Primer on Gender & Sexuality

Before moving on, it is important to understand that gender is socially constructed (Butler, 1990) and is multiple and flexible in nature (Connell, 2005). Though many of us were born with some sort of biological orientation (male or female) none of us were born "masculine" or "feminine." We were also not born "boy" or "girl." Baby banners announcing, "It's a boy!" or "It's a girl!" should read, "I'm ascribing this baby boyhood" or "I'm socially constructing this baby as a girl." Masculinity and femininity are constantly performed and (re)constructed throughout our lives. How "masculine" or "feminine" these performances are deemed mostly depends on how they are judged by others. Where and with whom these performances take place also matters. Take for example, the male-to-male butt slap. The butt slap is often a hyper-masculine performance. One could imagine that a group of guys playing flag football might reward one another with hugs and butt slaps after touchdowns and interceptions. These men, and their performances, would be perceived as extremely masculine. Now let's imagine a group of men who got together for their weekly book club. If Joe had a brilliant insight regarding a difficult-to-understand passage and Bob rewarded him by slapping him on the butt...would that be perceived as masculine? The same kind of "masculinity" that the football players portrayed?

Most of us learn to perform gender in various ways—we code switch depending on our social situation and environment. Many times how "masculine" or "feminine" our performances are changes minute to minute. For example, I am a fan of good books and coffee. I like to sit in quaint cafés, legs crossed, sipping on a latte while devouring some new cutting edge feminist text. Most times, the cafés I visit are filled with women and a few other men like me, and so, I am probably perceived as one of the most masculine figures in the room. However, when a construction crew on break walks through the door, I (and my gendered performance) becomes instantly "feminine."

Sexuality, most believe, is simple biological determination, but the truth is that sexual manifestation is a cocktail of biology and social construction. Biology helps determine some of what one is able to do—meaning, depending on your physical "parts," you are able to "do" certain sexual acts, or represent sexuality in certain ways. But how and what people decide is pleasurable is often socially constructed between partners who have been socialized in a larger, media-rich environment. An easy way to illustrate this is to think about heterosexual practices. The range of how heterosexual couples "have sex" is vast and varies tremendously between couples. Sexual experience even varies between partners who are engaging in the act with one another. One individual's experience is not the same as the others.

So what? Well… believing masculinity and femininity are inherent male and female traits respectively is a mistake. It is also a mistake to believe that sexuality of any kind can be consistently portrayed in one way or another. The media, however, works terribly hard to tether American men to "masculinity" and women to "femininity" by employing consistent heterosexual sexist and sexualized entertainment, advertising, and news. In other words, the media are working to sell us a myth: that boys and girls are born so completely different from one another that when they grow old enough to sit in front of the television or listen to the radio, they will desire different programming. A great deal of research has determined that "male" and "female" brains are more similar than dissimilar, and these differences do not result in behavioral differences or preferences (Fine 2010; Eliot, 2009). Lombardi (2012) tells us, "Much of what we assume to be differences in the brain—distinctions that would cause boys and girls to relate differently or learn differently—are simply reflections of how parents unconsciously socialize their children about gender at an early age"

(p. 47). Parents often socialize their kids with sexist and (hetero) sexualized media, even if unintentionally. Sure the media presents "outliers"—think, Lady Gaga, Adam Lambert, *Will & Grace, Modern Family,* and *Glee*—every now and again, but are often stereotyped as the "other" version of sexuality (in a binary, rather than a spectrum). Often non-heteronormative characters are used for comedic relief and not much more. The media makes little attempt to develop characters (in films, television, cartoons, ads, music, on stage etc.) as complex human beings capable of a full range of emotions, actions, and ideas— representative in various, flexible, and multiple sexual and gendered performances. This is most clearly illustrated by the Disney Princess movies that have by and large not changed intrinsically in decades despite claims to the contrary.

Historical Context

The media has peddled sex and gender stereotypes generation after generation and Americans, as well as others across the world (Holmes, 2012) have been steady consumers. The sexist and sexualized media, ever present in daily life, becomes an integral part of individuals' identities that when challenged—like I did for Allison—people become defensive. It is perceived as an attack on how they've been raised, their cultural traditions, and identities. And to an extent, they are correct. The reality is that we have all become products of our media-rich environment to one extent or another. We have implicitly and explicitly learned about what it means to be "masculine," "feminine," and heterosexual to the point that we often forget these portrayals are deeply stereotypical and limiting, and we actually begin to believe that media represents real life.

To be fair, there are some people who seem more informed. These individuals recognize some of the dangers of popular media. In a Kaiser Family Foundation report (2007), most parents surveyed reported that they "aren't very happy with the amount of sex or violence in the media today" with about two-thirds saying that they are "*very* concerned about the amount of inappropriate media content children in this country are exposed to" believing that "media is a major contributor to young people's violent or sexual behaviors" (p. 1). However, only a fraction of these same parents (20%) believe that *their* children are exposed to "a lot" of inappropriate content—that inappropriate media is primarily "someone else's problem" (p. 1).

Most parents are a mix of those who are like Allison—they don't "get it"—and those in the Kaiser report who perceive American media as harmful but are in denial about how much content their kids consume. Either way, it is alarming because over the past several decades research on the perils of sexist and sexualized (as well as racist, violent, and xenophobic) media has been well documented. And the debate over censorship has been going on for centuries.

Research

We need no more "wardrobe malfunctions" at the Super Bowl to provide insight that we live in a hypersexualized and sexist world thanks to media. Rather, we just need to pay attention to the research available. The Geena Davis Institute on Gender in Media, The Kaiser Family Foundation, and academics across the world have consistently conducted research on the kinds of sexist and sexualized media exposure kids receive. The following is just a sample of some of this research.

Sexual Risks/Sexual Responsibilities

Early research demonstrated that in 1976, just one television scene, "of 27 involving sexuality (3.7%) addressed any risk or responsibility topic, and that involved a humorous remark about abortion. In 1986, again only a single scene out of 48 (2.1%) was observed, and this comprised a discussion about a possible abortion" (Gunter, 2001, p. 88). In 1988, Lowry & Towles sampled prime-time television shows that portrayed 722 sexual interactions. Of these interactions only 14 considered pregnancy prevention and 18 considered sexually transmitted disease prevention. Kunkel, et. al. (1999) sampled 1,170 television programs and found that although 56% of them contained sexual interaction—an average of 3.2 scenes of sex occurring per hour, totaling 420 scenes all together,—only 9% of these scenes made any mention of potential risks or consequences. In this same study, 76% of teenagers indicated that a reason they have sex is because television shows and movies normalize it for them.

Television in particular has been studied, beginning decades ago, as a sexual socialization agent (e.g., Baran, 1976a, 1976b; Courtright & Baran, 1980). Many more have studied the impact sex in media has on perceptions, values, beliefs, and sexual behaviors (Baran, 1976a; Buerkel-Rothfuss & Strouse, 1993; Newcomer & Brown, 1984; Peterson, Moore & Fursenberg, 1984; Walsch-Childers, 1991; Klein et al., 1993; Gruber & Grube, 2000; Villani, 2001; Ward, 2002; Collins et al., 2004; Lenhart, 2010). Interestingly, the earliest of these studies reported that sexual content predominantly impacted kids' *perceptions*, while the most recent studies indicate that this content now supports and impacts kids' *behaviors*, including an accelerated on-set of risky sexual activity.

Embodiment of Gender

As we previously learned, sexuality is tangled with gender and the media presents us with heteronormative and narrow portrayals that girls/women should sexually perform in particular ways (perceived feminine) and boys/men should sexually perform in other ways (perceived masculine). These over-sexualized and stereotyped gender portrayals have been existent since the inception of modern media (e.g., *Leave it to Beaver; Gone With the Wind; I Love Lucy)* and have only worsened in content and scope (e.g., *The Big Bang Theory; American Pie; Magic Mike; Two and a Half Men; The Bachelor; The Bachelorette; Here Comes Honey Boo Boo; The Real Housewives of Orange County*). Entertainment explicitly marketed toward younger children (e.g., *Max & Ruby; Smurfs; Bob the Builder; Lalaloopsy; Mike the Knight*) while not usually sexually explicit, helps groom children to recognize particular gendered roles. Boys are generally portrayed as more adventurous and engaged in physical activities, acting goofy, and taking more risks. Girls are generally more passive, play secondary characters, and are almost always "pretty." The Geena Davis Institute on Gender in Media notes that:

- "Males outnumber females 3 to 1 in family films" and astonishingly this ratio "is the same as it was in 1946"
- "Females are almost four times as likely as males to be shown in sexy attire"
- That their general appearance physical appearance is sexier (male characters are more acceptably any size and appearance while even in family films, female characters "serve primarily as eye candy")
- "From 2006 to 2009, not one female character was depicted in G-rated family films in the field of medical science, in law, politics, or as a business leader…80.5% of all working characters are male and 19.5% are female"
- Generally, "messages that devalue and diminish female characters are still rampant in family films…statistically, there has been little forward movement for girls in media in six decades…gender inequality on screen has remained largely unchanged and unchecked."

This portrayal and subsequent embodiment of gender (Kilbourne, 1999; Lamb & Brown, 2006; Brown, Lamb & Tappan, 2009; Orenstein, 2012; Geena Davis Institute on Gender in Media, 2013) has dire consequences, not only sexually but also on kids' self-esteem (Orenstein, 1994; Kilbourne, 1999; O'Keeffe & Clarke-Pearson, 2011; Holmes, 2012;), and increases their tendency toward sex-based bullying and sexually violent acts (Lenhart, 2010; Malamuth & Huppin, 2005; Malamuth, Addison & Koss, 2000) for both boys and girls. Lamb & Brown (2007) confirm that sexualized images are linked to depression, eating disorders, and low self-esteem but that television shows and movies are not the only ways kids are damaged. That is, print, Internet, and television advertising has an equally damaging impact. Lamb warns that, "boys have journeys, girls have makeovers" (Munsey & Meyers, 2007). The media, whether in the form of a major motion picture or a small ad on the side of a webpage, all teach and groom our children to embody gender and sexuality regardless of consequence. In their book *So Sexy So Soon* (2009) Levin & Kilbourne state, "Children are paying an enormous price for the sexualization of their childhood…A narrow definition of femininity and sexuality encourages girls to focus heavily on appearance and sex appeal… And boys, who get a very narrow definition of masculinity that promotes insensitivity and macho behavior, are taught to judge girls based on how close they come to an artificial, impossible, and shallow ideal" (p. 5).

Censorship

Every day, from dusk to dawn, we are exposed to the media. To avoid it we have to take considerable measures to remove ourselves from any sign of civilization, which is usually not an option. So instead, we carry on with our normal lives and become complacent about the kinds of messages we and our children internalize from our media-rich environment. At times, because of our complacency, the media devises plans to get our attention through a shockingly sexy ad or with some super sexualized lyrics. And other times, the media capitalizes on our complacency by pumping us full of the same old messages that build narratives about the way we should look, act, and consume. It's rare that we get upset by this bombardment, but every now and again we just can't take it anymore. We wonder why it's okay for us, and our kids in particular, to be bathed in the media's messages. What is interesting, however, is that we rarely turn to censorship, a mechanism already in place, and that has played a role in monitoring media for thousands of years, to possibly alleviate our concerns. Let's be clear here, this is not my personal plea for extreme or lax censorship, but rather it is a way to a way to explore how we might regulate the exposure and impact of media.

In Plato's *The Republic* (approx. 380 BC), he argued that children's engagement in visual and performing arts should always be representational of beauty and good. Literary materials in particular came under strict scrutiny—especially poems and drama. Plato was concerned that if children engaged in too much fantasy, or were exposed to the ugly forms of humankind, they would grow disconnected with reality, participate in self-deception, and might emulate bad behaviors (observed in characters such as those in many classic Greek tragedies). Therefore, Plato begged that as people considered performing in the arts that:

Any representational roles they do take on, from childhood onwards, be appropriate ones. They should represent people who are courageous, self-disciplined, just, and generous and should play only those kinds of parts; but they should neither do nor be good at representing anything mean-spirited or otherwise contemptible, in case the harvest they reap from representation is reality. I mean, haven't you noticed how if repeated representation continues much past childhood, it becomes habitual and ingrained and has an effect on a person's body, voice and mind? (Plato, 395c)

Plato and ancient Greeks, however, disagreed. Athenians' highest prized sexual relationship was between an adult male and an adolescent boy. This relationship was viewed important to male socialization (Gagnon, 1977). Children were not to be protected from sex or realness of the world. In ancient Rome, boys were also often sexual partners to adult men. A male child's first ejaculation was even "celebrated by his family at the feast of the Liberalia" (Brown, 1998, p. 79). Although girls were not allowed to be promiscuous, they were often married by 12 or 14 years old, and so they were not shielded from early sexual activity either (Heins, 2001). It is important to note that ancient Athenians and Romans perceived sexuality (and gender variation) to be normal, and so there was no need to make sexuality or gender expression "taboo" via censorship. It was in large part due to Eurocentric religious practices that censorship was institutionalized—which of course, only sensationalized sex and gender.

Censorship of sexual expression became a reality and was "primarily a function of the Church" (Heins, 2001, p. 18) in the late-15th century. Censorship not only attempted to protect children but adults too because, according to the Church, they should be concerned with being "moral" Christians. Censorship initiatives were later translated into law, particularly in Europe, and eventually the colonial United States. Massachusetts passed a law in 1711 that banned "any filthy, obscene, or profane song, pamphlet, libel, or mock sermon" (Prov. St. 1711-12, c. 6, §19, 1 Prov. Laws). Later, in 1842, the first federal sex-censorship law authorized the U.S. Customs Service to "confiscate 'obscene or immoral' pictures or prints and bring judicial proceedings for their destruction" (Heins, p. 25). In centuries to come, the U.S. enacted several laws aimed at protecting the sexual innocence of children. The Federal Communications Commission (FCC) was established by the Communications Act of 1934 and has been the primary governmental body regulating communications of all kinds to a great degree (with some exception to the Internet). The FCC's impact is evidenced by contemporary movie and television ratings (G – MA/X), schools' anti-pornography/indecency Internet filters, music ratings (explicit), and when (time of day) certain radio and cable Internet shows are aired.

All of this censorship assumes that certain representations of sexuality (and to a lesser extent, gender) are damaging to children. I imagine that the FCC would argue that media is an agency of socialization, and as such it "implies a definite script, a charter under which the agency acts on behalf of the society, and a degree of consensus about what it is to do and how to do it" (Connell, 1987, p. 192). The opportunity to have conversations about censorship would do us well. Even if we would not change the manner in which media currently operates, it would still provide us the opportunity to step back and become better, more critical consumers.

A Contemporary Example

Recently, I was very upset. But before I tell you why, I want to disclose that I'm a pretty open-minded person; I would, for the most part (minus the adult/child sexual relationships), do okay in ancient Athenian society. I understand that gender and sexuality can be a smorgasbord of awesomeness and so I have a problem with how 1) binary (male and female/heterosexual and homosexual) representations in media continually work to reify stereotypes, and 2) how invasive media has become that we can hardly avoid it. Take for example—the reason I'm still upset—a "hot" 2013 summer hit, "Blurred Lines," by Robin Thicke, featuring T.I. and Pharrell Williams. The song's lyrics are focused on trying to convince a woman, or in Thicke's words, a "bitch," that she—whether she knows it or not—wants to have sex with him. This woman apparently has a partner, but Thicke and pals are convinced that he does not sexually satisfy her. In between the song's hook, "I know you want it," Thicke tells this "bitch" that he can sexually "liberate" her while T.I. raps that he would have rough sex with her (that this is what she needs) to the point where his large penis would tear her anus. This song is (stereo)typical, demeaning, and scary. It provides the same old, sad, uninventive narrative of the conquering male and sexpot girl waiting to be called upon and used for sex, as an object, a thing, and disregards whether she actually "wants it."

I first learned about this song while preparing breakfast for my kids (Maria, six and Mali, eight) as the pseudo-news of the *Today Show* played on the kitchen television. They did a segment called the *Hottest Songs of Summer* in which they played clips of music videos that dominated the summers of years past (like Will Smith's "Summertime," Nelly's "Hot in Herre," and Sir Mix-a-Lot's "Baby Got Back") and new songs of this summer including Thicke's "Blurred Lines." Besides girls in bikinis and thongs in Smith's, Nelly's, and Mix-a-Lot's videos, sexy models in the "Blurred Lines" video danced rubbing their half-naked bodies against the fully clothed (literally head to toe) male performers. "What the hell!" I thought, "… it's seven something in the morning… I just wanted to watch the news." I should have been a better, more critical consumer, and recognized that the *Today Show* is sharply steeped in sexism and sexuality and that the "news" portion is limited to scarcely a few minutes, including Al Roker's chuckling outside with visitors as he reports on the weather. The *Today Show* frequently invites quintessential stereotypical actors and singers to perform, features beauty, fashion and weight loss segments, and gossips about celebrity relationships. So, yes, it was my fault, but damn! After Thicke's video, Matt Lauer gave his stamp of approval, exclaiming, "It's just fun!" Programs like the *Today Show* are the meat and potatoes of pop culture, and I theorize, are more dangerous to kids and families because they import and normalize sexism and sexuality by featuring extreme, drastic, and graphic images, lyrics, and ideas present in the entertainment world elsewhere. Also, they too implicitly establish gender and sexual "normalcy" and boundaries by the language they choose when describing stories, the way they dress their anchors, and the stories they decide to cover. Because parents like me have the *Today Show* playing during breakfast, kids receive the message that this is normal—this is their culture.

Later, as I drove Mali to camp, I flipped through radio stations to (again) catch a bit of news. As the radio host fades out and "Blurred Lines" fades in. Mali said, "That's the song that was on TV."

"Mmm, hmm," I responded, quickly changing the station.

Before dropping Mali off, we made a stop at a coffee shop. The male barista wore a cancer fundraiser bracelet—"Feel Your Boobies"— which Mali read, and I doubt understood. Sitting at a table, a man watched the Thicke video on his iPad, which I'm sure Mali noticed too.

When we arrived at camp, Mali and I stood next to two moms.

"Emma found the perfect match for Katie," said one to the other.

Katie, who looks about nine, stood with her mom who smiled and responded with much enthusiasm, "Really? Who?!"

"We thought she should hook up with Max. They both like the same things and he's super cute."

"Huh?" I interjected, stunned. "I'm sorry, I know this isn't my conversation, but I don't understand... why are you sexualizing your kids?"

Emma's mom tells me to "F-off."

I'm sure they thought *I* was "taking it too far" but where does the encouragement of these junior sexualities lead? (I also find it odd when grown women sexualize male babies by saying things like, "Oh, look at those eyes...you're flirting with me, aren't you?" Just...um... creepy.)

Later that day, and still licking my wounds from being told to "F-off," I relaxed with Maria by watching some *Spongebob Squarepants*. Between episodes, commercials attempted to groom her for "tween" shows like *Drake & Josh,* have her nag me to buy products like Cinnamon Toast Crunch and Go-Gurt, and yes, to prepare her as an American woman (or sell speakers) by airing a Radio Shack ad featuring a version of "Blurred Lines" with set and dance simulating the music video except that the models sensually carried around "Beats Pills" as though they were weights and sex toys. Maria found it absurd, giggled and said, "What the?!" I echoed her sentiment.

In the evening, we went to a friend's house so that our kids could play. They had one elementary aged kid, and one son in tenth grade, Zach.

"Hey Zach, how are you?" I asked.

In response, he nodded his head and walked by. Like many high schoolers, he is constantly plugged in to his iPod which apparently disables him from human conversation. The kids went off to play and we sat and talked over a few beers. After an hour or so we moved into the living room to find Zach's open laptop on the couch. It was in sleep mode, but turned on when Zach's mom picked it up to move it out of the way. Paused was the music video "for the uncensored version of "Blurred Lines." The models in this version were no longer just scantily clad, but were actually topless without any use of concealing props. Their breasts were completely exposed. Toward the end of the video balloons were used to spell out "Robin Thicke has a big dick."

"Zach!" his parents called.

He came bounding down the stairs, annoyed. "What?"

"What have you been watching? We talked about this!"

"What, I wasn't doing anything. It's a song on the radio. You said songs on the radio are OK. I just looked it up."

Zach was right. It was the exact song on the radio, and it was being played non-stop. Everyone has been watching the videos, viewing the commercials, and listening to Matt Lauer think it's fun. The mainstream media was bombarding us with "Blurred Lines" literally and figuratively. The mainstream media also ensured that this song would, without concern regarding musical talent, be a pop hit. What's more is that media like this are essentially dictating what is (and is not) American culture. And if children like Mali and Maria, or teenagers like Zach, tune out "Blurred Lines" or whatever else media consistently presents them, they may feel "left behind," assuming it's even possible to tune it out. Yes, Maria, "What the?!"

What Does the Future Hold?

Well, for every step forward we take several steps back. For every Lady Gaga chanting, "We are born this way," there's a Kanye rapping, Eatin' Asian pussy, all I need was sweet and sour sauce," Beyoncé claiming her dominance by singing, "Bow down bitches…," and films/shows like *Fast & Furious I-VI, Big Time Rush, Wendell & Vinnie, Teen Mom, Real World, Jersey Shore, Today Show,* and even innocuous seeming kids shows like *Pound Puppies, Curious George,* and *Fairly Odd Parents* that peddle a stale gender script, sexuality, and sexism at every corner. This kind of media is simply overwhelming in mass, distribution, and message. So, unfortunately, I think the future looks bleak. I think media's ability to 1) bombard the American public, 2) turn a profit and reward top executives, 3) and play up patriarchy will not foster any significant change in the near future.

Bombardment

One problem is that more than ever, kids are being bombarded (turning them into unconscious consumers) by the world around them, and by the world they consciously "plug in" to. According to a Kaiser Family Foundation report (2010), children are dedicating on average more than seven hours of their day to screen time. That's likely more time than they devote to any other activity except for sleep. Access to media has increased drastically thanks in part to technological advances: "With the launch of the iPod, the explosion in instant messaging, the birth of mobile video and YouTube, and the advent of social networking sites…young people are rarely out of contact, or out of reach of the media" (Kaiser Family Foundation, 2007, p. 1).

Smartphones have also increased access to media. Currently, 37% of all teens in the U.S. have a cell phone. And of these teens, their mobile devices act as the primary source of accessing the Internet (Pew Research Center, 2013). Smart phone ownership and dependence is only destined to grow among children and teens and this brings a unique problem to parents that they have not had to consider in the past—their child's media consumption is becoming a mostly private ordeal. Teens have long attempted to sneak into R-rated movies, befriend older teenagers for their porn stashes, and so on, but now there is no need. The whole world, the good, the bad and the stereotypical of it, is readily at their fingertips.

Smartphone savvy kids have learned to successfully stay connected to media, particularly social media, throughout the day and while in the company of their parents, teachers, and in other spaces that ask for face-to-face interaction. Because this on-going and private consumption of media happens in this "from pocket, to hand, back to pocket" kind of way, it is practically impossible for adults to monitor, or to help mediate and process their children's online interactions. This not only includes their social interactions between friends, but also their interactions with intended and collateral information. Intended information includes websites, videos, and sources that kids are deliberating searching. Collateral information includes advertising, search engine suggestions, and other material that confronts kids while they are searching and accessing intended information. Kids' use of cell phones has also increased the manner in which they "broadcast" their lives. Numerous social media sites allow kids to create online identities (often different than their in-person identities) in public ways that attempt to gain them popularity. These sites "stimulate the urge" to post videos, photos, texts, updates, and so on that reach typically hundreds of others (Manago, Taylor, & Greenfield, 2012). Uhls & Greenfield (2011), in an extensive study of preadolescent perceptions of popular media and fame, conclude that "developing an audience of 'friends' on social network sites make the concept of fame highly accessible to children, [and] these tools may be cultivating a culture of reward from a virtual audience, amplifying a desire for fame and public recognition for any and all actions" (p. 324). A "large part of this generation's social and emotional development is occurring while on the Internet and on cell phones" (O'Keeffe & Clarke-Pearson, 2011, p. 800).

Print media (e.g., books, magazines, comics, and so on) are rapidly transitioning to ebook formats. According to a study conducted by Scholastic Inc. and the Harrison Group (2013), 46% of children (age 6 – 17) have read an ebook in 2012. This figure is up from 25% in 2010. eReading has increased at home, school, the library, and friends' houses. eBook formats can be accessed via electronic tablets, computers, handheld devices, game consoles, and of course specially designed eReaders. All of these devices are Internet capable, and so although books may be read, they also provides yet additional unfiltered and secretive portals to Internet media. It is safe to say that children are consuming more media than ever before, and in more independent ways.

There are voices seeking to offer a fair and critical perspective of songs and videos like that of "Blurred Lines," but they are ultimately not taken very seriously. Katie Russell, a spokeswoman for Rape Crisis, told *The Independent,* "Both the lyrics and the video seem to objectify and degrade women, using misogynistic language and imagery that many people would find not only distasteful or offensive but also really quite old fashioned…More disturbingly, certain lyrics are explicitly sexually violent and appear to reinforce victim-blaming rape myths, for example about women giving 'mixed signals' through their dress or behavior, saying 'no' when they really mean 'yes' and so on." Thicke responds to some of this initial criticism with what I perceive as fake disgust, "I can't even dignify that [the critique] with a response" (Us Weekly, 2013). Even more amazingly, Thicke later claims, in an interview on the *Today Show*, that his song, "is a feminist movement within itself" (Huffington Post, 2013). Really?! Are we supposed to actually believe this? Thicke and friends take us for fools. And maybe we are—"Blurred Lines" enjoyed long stays at the top of the charts in the U.S., Canada, Australia, New Zealand, Ireland, the Netherlands, Spain, Germany, Italy, the UK, and other countries. It set new all-time records for airplays, all-format audience impressions, and for the most weeks with over 400,000 downloads sold (Billboard, 2013). Translation: cha-ching!

Big Business

Below are some figures demonstrating "big business" in the entertainment world. CEOs for four entertainment companies (Walt Disney, Time

Warner, CBS, and Viacom) that heavily rely on "youth programming" earned a total of approximately $132 million dollars in 2012 alone.

Fortune 500 Top Companies List in 2013

Rank	Company	Revenue ($b)	Profits ($mm)
66	Walt Disney	42.3	5,682
105	Time Warner	28.7	3,019
186	CBS	14.7	1,574
198	Viacom	13.9	1,981

source: http://money.cnn.com/magazines/ fortune/fortune500/

CEO Compensation Packages in 2012

Company	CEO Name	Compensation 1 yr ($m)
Disney	Bob Iger	39.83
Time Warner	Jeff Bewkes	19.79
CBS	Leslie Moonves	41.48
Viacom	Philippe Dauman	30.89

source: http://www.forbes.com/lists/2012/12/ ceo-compensation-12_rank.html

With this kind of money involved, there seems to be little concern about how their programming may impact kids. With these profit margins, companies are not looking to disrupt "what works"—patriarchy.

Patriarchy

It is important to note that because we are consuming media—and paying for much of it—does not mean that we prefer sexist, heteronormative messages or that sex just sells. Lisa Wade (2009) notes, "If it was simply 'sex sells,' we'd see an even pattern of sexualization. But we don't. More often than not, it is women who are sexualized. What is being sold, *really*, isn't sex, but the legitimation and indulgence of (supposedly heterosexual) men's sexual desires (para 8)." Male desires are not only legitimized by media, but media employs male desires to legitimize their enterprises. Meaning, masculine (heterosexual) desire affirms patriarchy which is a construct that centers our universe. If media violates patriarchy, many would likely feel "uncomfortable" and view such films, advertisements, music, etc. as "queer," "illegitimate," or afford it to a "minority population."

An easy way to test how patriarchy (and male heterosexual eroticism) remains a centering and important construct is to think about how parents might react to their children when they "border cross" (Thorne, 2005) the perceived boundaries of gender. Girls are afforded much more leniency at dressing in "masculine" clothes, engaging in activities that used to be reserved just for boys (especially certain sports) and to identify as a "tom boy." In many cases, girls are deemed "cute" for these behaviors—except when they consistently demonstrate no "feminine" qualities. However, it is much "riskier" for boys to dress in pink, purple, or feminine cut clothing, to engage in perceived feminine activities (e.g., playing with dolls or dress up like mom), and to identify as a "mama's boy." This also applies to the consumption of media. Girls who watch *Teenage Mutant Ninja Turtles* (like my two daughters) are deemed "cool," but boys who watch *Winx Club* are deemed "sissy." The reason why girls can cross the borders of femininity is because it pays homage to patriarchy. But boys who cross the borders of masculinity violate something sacred; they threaten the value, currency, and importance of patriarchy.

Patriarchy sells because we are dependent upon it; it is what we see as "normal." Of course, patriarchy rarely serves *anyone*—even White males —but patriarchy is what we know. It is our allegorical cave. Therefore, it is only until we come out of the cave that we can begin to make sense of our dependence on patriarchy and the sexual and gendered complexity of ourselves, others, and kids. The overthrow of patriarchy is our only true hope of demanding media change.

Advice

Many books and articles end by providing some suggestions to "right the ship." I, too, have some advice but I'm keeping it concise so it does not become unnecessarily complicated. Partner with kids and dare to "unplug" as much as possible, stop paying for sexist and sexualized media, talk about how the media gets it wrong, swear not to be a mindless consumer any longer, and reimagine the traditional roles and boundaries of masculinity and femininity. Oh, and with all you might, defeat patriarchy. That is all. Now get to work.

Questions for Class Discussion

1. Are you or do you know an "Allison"? How do we help teach people like Allison about sexism and sex in media without her feeling like we are attacking her, her upbringing or her culture?
2. Can you think of some instances from your childhood which taught you how to be "masculine" or "feminine?" What examples do you recognize in today's media? What do you think might be some of the consequences due to these implicit messages?
3. Heterosexual/heteronormative characters and narratives dominate the media. Can you identify characters and narratives in the media that identify as homosexual, transgender, pansexual, queer, asexual, gender, queer, androgynous, etc. portrayed in meaningful ways? Meaning, that their orientation/ identification aren't simply a source of comedy or novelty?
4. What are some simple things you can *consistently* do to bring attention to/make changes in the way media presents sexism and sex? What might be some obstacles? How can you overcome these obstacles?

References

Baran, S. (1976a). How TV and film portrayals affect sexual satisfaction in college students. *Journalism Quarterly, 53*(3), 468–473.
Baran, S. (1976b). Sex on TV and adolescent sexual self-image. *Journal of Broadcasting, 20*, 61–68.

Billboard. (2013, August 7). Robin Thicke extends hot 100 run to nine weeks, setsaudience and sales records. Retrieved August 19, 2013, from http://www.billboard.com/articles/news/5638328/robin-thicke-extends-hot-100-run-to-nine-weeks-sets-audience-and-sales-records

Brown, L., Lamb, S., & Tappan, M. (2009). *Packaging boyhood: Saving our sons from superheroes, slackers, and other media stereotypes.* New York, NY: St. Martin's Press.

Butler, J. (1990). *Gender trouble.* London, UK: Routledge.

Buerkel-Rothfuss, N., & Strouse, J. (1993). Media exposure and perceptions of sexual behaviors: The cultivation hypothesis moves to the bedroom. In B. Greenberg, J. Brown, & N. Buerkel-Rothfuss (Eds.), *Media, sex and the adolescent* (pp. 225–247). Cresskill, NJ: Hampton Press.

Collins, R. L., Elliot, M. N., Berry, S. H., Kanouse, D. E., Kunkel, D., Hunter, S. B., & Miu, A. (2004). Watching sex on television predicts adolescent initiation of sexual behavior. *Pediatrics, 114*(3), 280–289.

Connell, R. (2005). *Masculinities.* Berkeley, CA: University of California Press.

Connell, R. (1987). *Gender and power: Society, the person, and sexual politics.* Stanford, CA: Stanford University Press.

Courtright, J., & Baran, S. (1980). The acquisition of sexual information by young people. *Journalism Quarterly, 57,* 107–114.

Eliot, L. (2009). *Pink brain, blue brain: How small differences grow into troublesome gaps—and what we can do about it.* New York, NY: Houghton Mifflin Harcourt Publishing.

Fine, C. (2010). *Delusions of gender: How our minds, society, and neurosexism create difference.* New York, NY: W. W. Norton & Company.

Gagnon, J. (1977). *Human sexualities.* New York, NY: Scott Foresman.

Geena Davis institute on gender in media. (2013). Retrieved July 12, 2013, from http://www.seejane.org/research/

Gruber, E., & Grube, J. (2000). Adolescent sexuality and the media: A review of current knowledge and implications. *Western Journal of Medicine, 172*(3), 210–214.

Gunter, B. (2001). *Media sex*. (2nd ed.). Mahwah, NJ: Routledge.

Heins, M. (2001). *Not in front of the children, indecency, censorship, and the innocence of youth*. New York, NY: Hill & Wang.

Holmes, K. (2012). Media impact on girls in the US, China and India through a gendered filter. *Forum on Public Policy Online, 1*.

Hooks, B. (1981). *Aint I a woman: Black women and feminism*. Boston, MA: South End Press.

Hooks, B. (2004). *The will to change: Men, masculinity, and love*. New York, NY: Atria Books.

Huffington Post. (2013, July 31). Robin Thicke: Blurred Lines is a feminist movement, lyrics got misconstrued. Retrieved August 3, 2013, from http://www.huffingtonpost.com/2013/07/31/robin-thicke-blurred-lines-feminist-movement_n_3682209.html

Jhally, S. (1997). *Bell hooks: Cultural criticism & transformation*. [DVD]. Retrieved from http://www.mediaed.org

Kaiser Family Foundation. (2010). *Generation M²: Media in the Lives of 8- to 18- yearolds*. Menlo Park, CA.

Rideout, V., Foehr, U., & Roberts, D.; Keiser Family Foundation (2007). *Parents, children & media*. Retrieved from http://kaiserfamilyfoundation.files.wordpress.com/2013/01/7638.pdf

Kilbourne, J. (1999). *Can't buy my love: How advertising changes the way we think and feel*. New York, NY: Touchstone.

Klein, J., Brown, J., Childers, K., Oliveri, J., Porter, C., & Dykers, C. (1993). Adolescents' risky behavior and mass media use. *Pediatrics, 92*, 24–31.

Kunkel, D., Cope, K., & Calvin, C. (1996). *Sexual messages on family hour television: Content and context*. Menlo Park, CA: Kaiser Family Foundation.

Kunkel, D., Cope, K., Farinola, W., Biely, E., Roth, E., & Donnerstein, E. (1999). *Sex on TV: Content and context*. Menlo Park, CA: Kaiser Family Foundation.

Lamb, S., & Brown, L. M. (2006). *Packaging girlhood: rescuing our daughters from marketers' schemes*. (1st ed.). New York, NY: St. Martin's Press.

Lenhart, A., Purcell, K., Smith, A. Zickuhr, K. (2010). Social media and mobile Internet use among teens and young adults. *Pew Internet & American Life Project*.

Levin, D., & Kilbourne, J. (2010). *So sexy so soon: The new sexualized childhood and what parents can do to protect their kids*. New York, NY: Ballantine Books.

Lombardi, K. (2012). *The mama's boy myth: Why keeping our sons close makes them stronger.* New York, NY: Avery.

Lowry, D., & Towles, D. (1988). Prime time TV portrayals of sex, contraception, and venereal diseases. *Journalism Quarterly, 66,* 347–352.

Malamuth, N., Addison, T., & Koss, M. (2000). Pornography and sexual aggression: Are there reliable effects and can we understand them? *Annual Review of Sex Research, 11*(1), 26–91.

Malamuth, N., & Huppin, M. (2005). Pornography and teenagers: The importance of individual differences. *Adolescent Medicine, 16,* 315–326.

Manago, A., Taylor, T., & Greenfield, P. (2012). Me and my 400 friends: The anatomy of college students' Facebook networks and its relationship to communication patterns and well-being. *Developmental Psychology, 48*(2), 369–380.

Martel, D. (Director). (2013). *Blurred lines.* [Music Video]. US: Black Dog Films.

Munsey, C., & Meyers, L. (2007, October). U.S. children: Overweight and oversexed? *Monitor, 38*(9), 58.

National Committee on Pay Equity. (n.d.). Retrieved July 15, 2013, from http://www.pay-equity.org/

Newcomer, S., & Brown, J. (1984, August). *Influences of television and peers on adolescents' sexual behavior.* Paper presented at the 92nd annual convention of the American Psychological Association, Toronto.

O'Keeffe, G., Clarke-Pearson, K., & Council on Communications and Media. (2011). The impact of social media on children, adolescents, and families. *Pediatrics, 127*(4), 800–804.

Orenstein, P. (1994). *Schoolgirls: Young women, self-esteem, and the confidence gap.* New York, NY: Anchor Books.

Orenstein, P. (2012). *Cinderella ate my daughter.* New York, NY: Harper.

Peterson, J., Moore, K., & Furstenberg, F. (1984, August). *Television viewing and early initiation of sexual intercourse: Is there a link?* Paper presented at the annual meeting of the American Psychological Association, Toronto.

Pew Research Center. (2013). Retrieved July 12, 2013, from http://www.pewresearch.org/daily-number/a-quarter-of-teens mostly-access-the-internet-using-their-cell-phones/

Plato. (n.d.). *The republic.* [Translation by Robin Waterfield, 1993]. Oxford: Oxford University Press.

Prov. St. 1711-12, c. 6, §19, 1 Prov. Laws, 682; see Grant, S. & Angoff, S., (1930). *Massachusetts and censorship.*

Richardson, S. (2012). *Elementary school: (Hyper)masculinity in a feminized context.* Boston, MA: Sense Publishers.

Scholastic & Harrison Group. (2013). *Kids & family reading report,* (4th ed.). Retrieved July 14, 2013, from http://mediaroom.scholastic.com/files/kfrr2013-wappendix.pdf

The Independent. (2013, June 21). *Robin Thicke's number one single 'Blurred Lines' accused of reinforcing rape myths.* Retrieved July 11, 2013, from http://www.independent.co.uk/arts-entertainment/music/news/robin-thickes-number-one-single-blurred-lines-accused-of-reinforcing-rape-myths-8667199.html

Thicke, R., Williams, P., & Harris, C. (2013, March 26). *Blurred lines* [Recorded by Robin Thicke, T. I., & Pharrell]. Producer Pharrell Williams.

Thorne, B. (2005). *Gender play: Girls and boys in school.* Piscataway, NJ: Rutgers University Press.

Uhls, Y., & Greenfield, P. (2011). The value of fame: Preadolescent perceptions of popular media and their relationship to future aspirations. *Developmental Psychology, 48*(2), 315–326.

Us Weekly. (July 10, 2013). *Robin Thicke slams Blurred Lines criticism: I can't even dignify that with a response.* Retrieved July 11, 2013, from http://www.usmagazine.com/celebrity-news/news/robin-thicke-slams-blurred-lines-criticism-i-cant-even-dignify-that-with-a-response-2013107

Villani, S. (2001). Impact of media on children and adolescents: A 10-year review of the research. *Journal of the American Academy of Child & Adolescent Psychiatry, 40*(4), 392–401.

Wade, L. (2009, March 2). Sex sells. *Sociological Images.* Retrieved July 9, 2013, from http://thesocietypages.org/socimages/2009/03/02/sex-sells/

Walsch-Childers, K. (1991, May). *Adolescents' interpretations of the birth control behavior of a soap opera couple.* Paper presented at the meeting of the Health Communication Division of the International Communication Association, Chicago.

Ward, L. (2002). Does television exposure affect emerging adults' attitudes and assumptions about sexual relationships? Correlational and experimental confirmation. *Journal of Youth and Adolescence, 31,* 1–15.

Chapter 3
Gender and Advertising
Patricia Arend

Introduction

The scene opens with race car driver Danica Patrick in a tight, black leather outfit and heels standing next to two seated individuals. She states: "There are two sides to GoDaddy: the sexy side represented by Bar Rafaeli [a blond, blue-eyed, normatively beautiful Israeli model], and the smart side that creates a killer website for your small business, represented by Walter [a White, overweight, curly-haired male geek in glasses working on a laptop]. Together, they're perfect." Patrick pauses and the camera zooms in to capture the model and the geek kiss for a full 10 seconds, an eternity in Super Bowl commercial time. Across the screen we see the words, "When sexy meets smart, your small business scores." Patrick chimes back in: "Get your domain and website at Go Daddy.com."

This commercial, which ran during Super Bowl XLVII in February 2013, was GoDaddy.com's latest tongue-in-cheek advertising campaign for a business that uses sexism, stereotypes, and sex appeal to register domain names and develop websites. *Ms. Magazine* blogger Anita Little (2013) dubbed it number one on her list of the "Top Five Most Sexist Super Bowl Ads, 2013" stating, "Once again, we have the recurring male gaze-y fantasy of the nerd landing the supplicant bombshell. Plus, the man is the smarts of the operation, whereas the woman just needs to sit there and be flawless." Just 30 seconds introduces viewers to multiple important themes in advertising: women must be beautiful to a heterosexual male viewer above all else; beauty is usually represented by a thin, White woman; if women are athletes or breaking barriers in a male-dominated field they must also be sexy; men who appear should be active and their appearance should matter less.

Advertising is the art of persuading people to buy a product. It includes any method used to this end, in any medium, such as film,

A. Trier-Bieniek et al., (Eds.), Gender & Pop Culture, 53–79.

television, radio, the Internet and print, from billboards to magazines and newspapers. Advertising works (or attempts to work) in a variety of ways which are often dependent on the type of product that is being offered. It can provide straightforward information about a good or service meant to convince the consumer of its quality or usefulness, such as describing how a dishwashing detergent performs. It can also establish and control brand identity. For example, Pepsi's "The Choice of a New Generation," "Next," and "Now" campaigns associate the beverage with youthfulness and teen culture, in the hopes that new consumers will displace the market dominance of Coca Cola. Stimulating desire in the consumer is yet another method advertisers employ to sell products. This can be achieved through convincing the consumer that without the product they will *lack* something personally or socially important, such as the shoes the popular crowd is wearing at school or the thick, lustrous hair displayed by normatively beautiful women. Similarly, desire can also be stimulated by showing people what having a product might bring to their lives, whether it be adventure associated with the most durable sport utility vehicle or romance fostered by sexy undergarments. Appeals to nostalgia, associations with admired celebrities and other "role models," and many more strategies exist to sway consumers to open their wallets and pocketbooks.

According to feminist media critic Jean Kilbourne (1999), many people claim that advertising has no effect on them. However, companies would not spend over $250,000,000,000 per year on advertising if it were not at least somewhat successful. One iconic advertising campaign illustrates this point. In 1999 *Advertising Age* named "A Diamond is Forever" the "slogan of the century." Written by copywriter Frances Gerety of the N.W. Ayers advertising agency, this campaign for De Beers Diamonds (and other campaigns that followed– such as the introduction of the four C's: color, cut, clarity, and carat) dramatically increased sales of diamonds in general and diamond engagement rings in particular in the U.S. Essentially what these campaigns did was convince individuals that these rocks—plentiful in nature and mined under slavery and later slave-like conditions in Africa—were rare, precious symbols of romantic love.

That advertising has the potential to persuade does not mean it is all powerful, all of the time. Advertisements are fundamentally polysemous, which means that they have the potential to be read in more than one way. While advertisers attempt to convey specific meaning to control brand image and encourage sales, they cannot determine how viewers interpret messages or predict whether or not they will be successful. While De Beers successfully instantiated the tradition of the diamond engagement ring for women, the jewelry industry generally has failed to get men to wear them as well. Historian Vicki Howard (2003) describes how the jewelry industry's 1920s advertising campaigns for men's engagement rings were unable to dislodge the femininity associated with the jewelry: men propose and women get engaged, not the other way around. However, they were able to encourage men to wear wedding rings in the 1940s and postwar period, in part by using them as a symbol to connect soldiers to their stateside brides and to "allay cultural anxieties over homosexuality" in the McCarthy era (p. 850). Advertising can be powerful to persuade, but especially when finding a synergy with other elements of the culture already in play.

Gender, Advertising, and Popular Culture

Though advertising's raison d'être is persuasion, it is much more than this propaganda model implies. Advertising, as Raymond Williams (1962/2009) famously instructed, is a "magic system" that finances our news, television, radio, and more. As such it is deeply intertwined with culture, of which gender is a core component. It is magic in that it imparts a great deal of meaning and values to material goods and services that purport to offer a satisfying life to "consumers," an objectionable term for Williams who sees people as so much more than that term implies. A white dress is not just something a woman wears when she gets married, but something that transforms her into a princess or a celebrity. A motorcycle turns workers into iconoclasts and "real men," while a pair of sunglasses, jeans, or a leather jacket allows the school nerd to be the stud. While these promises are certainly enticing, for Williams the magic of advertising "obscures the real sources of general satisfaction" in a society, "because their discovery would involve radical change in the whole common way of life" (p. 734). The fleeting satisfaction connected to the latest handbag or cell phone stands in for control of the means of production in society and one's work role within it, for creativity, time for important relationships, connections to nature and more.

As part of culture, advertising has also become an object of consumption itself: that more people reportedly watch football's Super Bowl to see the ads than to see the game is a case in point (Nielsen.com, 2010). But probably a more pertinent example, predicted by Frankfurt School social theorists Theodor Adorno and Max Horkheimer in their influential chapter "The Culture Industry: Enlightenment as Mass Deception" (1944), is the collapsing together of advertising and entertainment that can be found in "reality" television shows, such as *Say Yes to the Dress*, where the point of the show is to market wedding dresses and the Kleinfeld Bridal salon to women. Traditionally the purpose of a television program was to draw viewers who would then be sold to advertisers as an audience for their commercials. However, with the advent of technology such as remote controls and digital video recorders, which allow television viewers to bypass commercials, advertisers have resorted to embedding their messages in the content of the shows themselves. Product placement is one strategy long used in film, such as the Aston Martin automobiles and other high-end brands that appear in James Bond films. However, reality television allows the marketer to go beyond product placement by centering the content of the show on the goods themselves. In its early days, MTV mastered this strategy by having a whole channel dedicated to the promotion of music with videos as continuously playing commercials for albums and concerts.

Advertising is a central means of social communication. As such, it tells stories about our wider culture in a popular format, stories that are often gendered in their structure and content (Jhally, 2009; Lears, 1994). For example, advertisements often portray heterosexual women as sexually available and ravenous, such as the model Bar Rafaeli in our opening GoDaddy.com commercial. Advertising messages can gender products as masculine or feminine whether human beings are present or not, such as the 2012 print ads for Toyota's Tundra pick-up truck: "rough and tough like barbed wire and whisky." They can also dictate whether the socially appropriate consumer of a product is a man or a woman. For example, cosmetics are coded feminine and have long been marketed almost exclusively to women (Peiss, 1998). One aspect of advertising frequently studied by feminist researchers is its role in constructing and promoting dominant and controlling images of men and women. This can often relate to stimulating a feeling of lack in the viewer. For example, pervasive images of physically strong men with "six pack" abdominal muscles might make some men feel inadequate enough to purchase protein supplements, gym memberships, or many other personal care products these dominant men presumably use (Blond, 2008).

Historical Context

While the roots of advertising can be traced back thousands of years to barkers and billboards in the oldest markets along trade routes such as the Silk Road, modern advertising through mass media dates to the 19th century and the explosion of industrial capitalism in Europe and North America (Sivulka, 2012). Advertising has been a gendered phenomenon from the beginning of this period in the organization of its workforce, assumptions made about consumers, and the representations used to market products. The following section presents a select history of modern advertising in North America by focusing on three key themes: 1) advertising's role in the construction (and legacy) of the consumer as a White, middle-class woman, 2) the images of ideal men and women used to sell products, and 3) the co-opting of feminism by advertising. These are by no means the only important historical themes, but provide a critical introduction to the contemporary study of gender and advertising.

Advertising Constructs the Consumer

In addition to promoting the sale of products, advertising in the 19th century firmly established the dominant image of the United States as a White consumer nation and promoted White, middle-class women as the ideal consumer. A key vehicle for this promotion was the advertising trade card, popularly played with and shared among girls in a manner akin to boys' stamp collecting. Marilyn Maness Mehaffy (1997) argues that they "helped to situate a middle-class feminine community around the pleasures of playful interaction with the cards and of consuming activities"(p. 139). These trading cards basically validated advertising as a "therapeutic, redemptive epistemology and pursuit" (p. 133) as ideal domesticity became more consumerist.

Not only did White middle-class girls play with the cards, but racialized and racist images populated their content. White, refined ladies and girls in domestic contexts reminiscent of Barbara Welter's (1966) "cult of true womanhood" were juxtaposed with images of physically strong, dirty, animal-like Black women (and children) and sometimes Native American and Irish women as well. These images were so ubiquitous, she contends, that even when Black women were later replaced by such images as French maids, their absence remained present in the firm establishment of White middle-class consumer domesticity that has continued to the present.

This strategy went beyond trading cards to be incorporated in packaging, magazine copy, and even brand identity itself. One of the most recognizable brands of all time, Aunt Jemima Pancake Mix, is a case in point. Early on the R. T. Davis Milling Company used mammy imagery from the Old South to appeal to White women homemakers, encouraging them to feel like they had help in the kitchen at a time when the use of domestic servants was in decline. Though over time the Quaker Oats Company (who bought Aunt Jemima in 1926) changed her appearance by straightening the position of her head, removing her bandana and adding pearls, Aunt Jemima remains a comfort to White women making breakfast and a painful reminder of Black subordination for African Americans (Manring, 1998).

By the 1930s the idea of the White middle-class woman as consumer was firmly established in society and many firms targeted her with advertising. We also know this because when marketers began addressing men, they did so in a way that self-consciously challenged the association of consumption with White feminine domesticity while trying not to emasculate men. A classic, early strategy in this period was employed by Esquire Magazine. Kenon Breazeale (1994) argues that Esquire ran articles describing women as ineffectual housekeepers with bad taste next to advertisements targeting men. Editors communicated that their magazine was not for "effeminate" men by also including "pin-up" style drawings and later photographs of women for the (heterosexual) male gaze. They further used humor in the form of cartoons, including their main figure "Eskey," the sophisticated tuxedo-wearing and yet "dirty old man," to avoid a prurient reputation, which at the time was associated with the working class, and not their middle- and upper-class target market.

Not surprisingly, the women shown as beautiful pin-ups were disproportionately young, White (frequently blond), and thin with long legs, small backsides, and large breasts. Cartoon imagery featured both White women as sexual objects and gold diggers, and Black women as either promiscuous or large and simian. Hugh Heffner, a copywriter at Esquire in the 1940s and early 1950s, took this marketing strategy to the next level in Playboy Magazine; launched in 1953 it continues today, on albeit shaky ground (with poor sales and the widespread availability of free pornography on the Internet), still featuring beautiful, sexually provocative women, cartoons, and also "serious" interviews and articles to market products to discerning heterosexual men. Currently, Esquire.com maintains a "Women We Love" page on their website, complete with half-naked celebrities framed by advertising for Gillette razors.

Gendered messages that were racist continued to populate advertising even after marketers began targeting women of color. For example, Robert E. Weems Jr. (2000) documents how in the first half of the 20th century advertisers began marketing products in newspapers directly to Black women. However, advertising messages implied that the goal of Black female consumption was to approximate White femininity. Advertisers for hair and skin care products were especially notorious for trying to convince Black women that they could become more beautiful by looking more White: straightening their hair, lightening their skin, and thinning their lips. Black business owners such as the legendary Madam C. J. Walker countered these strategies by appealing to such things as healthy hair and not White beauty norms, while marketing their own products. Today women of color are still infrequently used as models in U.S. advertising, with women of Asian, Latino, Native American, or Middle Eastern descent virtually nonexistent. One niche, wedding advertising, not only overwhelmingly features White women in its content, but disproportionately uses blond women as well (Ingraham 1999). When African American models are used, they often are light-skinned with straightened hair.

Ideal Women and Men of Advertising

At this point, you might already see that in the process of constructing the ideal consumer as a White middle-class woman, modern advertisers also went one step further by promoting a particular type of White middle-class woman as the "ideal woman." Like the pin-up models of *Esquire Magazine*, she was and is White, often blond, large breasted, and generally thin. One fallacy that has circulated in popular culture recently is that women portrayed in the 1950s were much larger than they are today. One urban legend in particular is that Marilyn Monroe, often featured in 1950s advertising, wore a size 12 or 14 compared to the size 2 or 4 of supermodels today. Auctions of Monroe's wardrobe confirm that she was about a contemporary size two with a 22-inch waist (Postrel 2011). Clothing of the 1950s did emphasize a smaller waist, relative to the bust, which women actually had at that time because they were not as athletic. While women portrayed today are generally taller, more toned, and, in fashion magazines, emaciated, (attributes further exaggerated with airbrushing, Photoshop and other new technology), the women of 1950s advertising were also thin, a consistent theme over the course of the 20th and into the 21st century.

Women in North American advertising uphold and reinforce normative conceptions of beauty in part because they continue a practice of portraying women as an object of the (heterosexual) male gaze that predates modern advertising. For example, Abigail Soloman-Godeau (1996) describes the nudes made by early 19th- century French lithographers as constructing femininity as "to-be-looked-at-ness"(p. 128), a concept developed by Luce Irigaray and also Laura Mulvey (1975). John Berger (1972) simply, famously states that in representations throughout Western art and advertising "men act and women appear" (p. 47). The purpose of a woman in a painting or photograph is to be seen, either by a man in the image, the viewer, or both, such as in this Calvin Klein advertisement from 2012.

When reflecting on the women who are portrayed in advertising and the normative beauty they display, some contemporary researchers and activists ask whether or not images of women in advertising mirror real women in the flesh. However, what the above reflection suggests is that a deeper problem than "images of women" vs. real women might rather be the politics of representing women *as an image*. This theme will be revisited a bit later in the chapter when examining a recent advertising campaign that responds to feminist criticism by directly addressing how the media constructs women.

What about advertising's ideal man? Is there one? Over the course of the 20th century not only did advertisers target men more, but they also featured men more in their campaigns, especially for high cost items such as automobiles and for men's clothing. *Esquire* was not the only company who faced the conundrum of marketing goods to men in a heteronormative society without emasculating them. In 1924 Philip Morris's Marlboro cigarettes were first introduced to the market as a cigarette for women and in 1927 they became the first company to show a woman smoking a cigarette in a national pictorial advertising campaign. The cigarette regularly had a small portion of market share with sales becoming more stagnant in the immediate postwar period. Philip Morris learned through market research that nearly twice as many men smoked cigarettes as women and that the Marlboro brand was seen by men as "sissy" or effeminate (Brown, 2008). This image was especially problematic as fears about the link between tobacco and cancer grew. The company responded in the 1950s with a major rebranding effort led by Cecil & Presbrey and then Leo Burnett, a company usually affiliated with cartoon character images, such as their Tony the Tiger for Frosted Flakes Cereal. According to Elspeth H. Brown (2008), these advertisers sought an image of heterosexual, butch masculinity in some type of nonconformist, outsider figure. After a long search and several missteps they found Darrell Winfield on a Wyoming Ranch to become one of the most iconic figures in advertising history: the Marlboro Man. From "Marlboro Country" out West, he was an authentic American cowboy: rough, durable and certainly not a sissy who was afraid of getting cancer. To avoid him being in the feminine position of being looked at for viewing pleasure, they made him active (riding horses, roping cattle, and smoking) and also chose him for his weathered face, unlike a Hollywood "pretty boy" type.

While the Marlboro Man is probably the most iconic male figure in advertising history, the campaign is not the only or even the first to rely on outsider masculinity. For example, Gardner Nelson also used this concept in the form of the frontier gunfighter for its 1950s Jack Daniel's campaign that replaced, like Marlboro, a failing strategy of associating the product with urban sophistication (Holt, 2006). What these figures had in common in addition to outsider/butch masculinity was "race." While Black and Hispanic men certainly were cowboys in American history, they apparently did not live in Marlboro (or Jack Daniel's) Country. White, independent, masculine, and even physically dominant men are the ideal men put forth by 20th-century advertising. However, this expanded to include Black men toward the end of the century and into the 21st, especially with the use of professional athletes, a topic that will be taken up again a bit a later in the chapter.

Commodity "Feminism:"
Advertising Co-opts the Women's Movement

A history of gender and advertising would not be complete without addressing how advertisers have co-opted feminist messages to sell products to women. Dubbed by feminist researchers as "commodity feminism" (Dworkin and Wachs, 2009), "new consumer feminism" (Rosen, 2000), "narcissism as liberation" (Douglas, 1995), and even "enlightened sexism" (Douglas, 2010), advertisers have tied notions of women's empowerment to the use of products for self-improvement or celebration. This trend has not all been problematic. Surely some advertising shaped or inspired by ideas from the first and second waves of the women's movement has had a positive impact on society. For example, Nike's "If You Let Me Play" campaign in the 1990s took on sexism and discrimination directly by listing the benefits to girls and women of playing sports, such as having lower rates of breast cancer, depression, and unwanted pregnancies, and being more likely to leave an abusive partner (Holt and Cameron, 2012). However, many advertisers used feminist messages in a superficial manner or with distorted meaning. One might argue that simply using feminism for profit is a problem regardless of the message.

The most famous of these advertising campaigns, "You've Come A Long Way, Baby" for Phillip Morris' Virginia Slims, debuted in 1968 and ostensibly celebrated women's achievement as the second wave of the women's movement took off. Of course the sincerity of that support should be questioned when it is attached to a desire for women to smoke a carcinogen. A more recent version of this theme can be found in Nike's "Voices" commercial, which celebrated the 40th anniversary of Title IX, a portion of the Education Amendments Act of 1972, now called the Patsy Mink Equal Opportunity in Education Act, that calls for gender equality in educational programs funded by the federal government. (While it applies to all aspects of education, Title IX is usually associated with calls for equal funding and opportunity for girls and women in sports.) Nike's celebration shows accomplished, path-breaking athletes, such as marathon runner Joan Benoit Samuelson and basketball player Lisa Leslie, describe what it was like to be an athlete at the beginning of the Title IX era. They employ the effective strategy of cutting between the athletes and young girls (White and of color, dressed as boxers, football players, swimmers, etc.) who appear to be talking with an accomplished athlete's voice, reminding us of their experiences as girls and making the connection to the legacy these athletes leave for the next generation. Benoit Samuelson describes a male runner spitting on her and pushing her out of the way, but that she persevered and still, at 55 years old, runs almost 70 miles a week.

This campaign is quite moving for its celebration of women *as athletes* (and not of women interested in fitness just for the sake of having an attractive body). However, its focus is on the individual athlete with drive when it could focus on teamwork in relation to the collective effort it took to get Title IX passed. Three-time WNBA MVP and four-time Olympic gold medal winner Lisa Leslie states, "Somebody has to be the best. Why not me?" Admittedly this is a small point when compared with GoDaddy commercials which make jokes out of treating women as sex objects. More importantly, in this campaign Nike continues a tradition of presenting itself as a company who cares about women's empowerment, and profits from that association, all the while having their shoes and other athletic gear made by women in the global south for very little money and often in poor conditions (Enloe, 2004).

The focus on individuality in Nike relates to other advertising that draws on women's independence. In another (early) campaign Virginia Slims drew sport and self-reliance together to, again, sell cigarettes, of all things:

"When he offers you a low tar cigarette, tell him you've got one of your own." While the model is dressed as a soccer referee, she is posed more like a traditional fashion model: sitting down, touching her head lightly while smiling, and looking away from the camera, a position that will be discussed in-depth in the next section. The reference to sport obviously is disingenuous. In 2003 De Beers also used the theme of independence to raise its sales of diamonds. Its "women of the world, raise your right hand" campaign paradoxically evoked individuality and self-reliance by claiming that while the "left

65

hand" (where the engagement and wedding ring is worn) is for your relationships, the "right hand" is for yourself. Freedom is another theme from the women's movement that has been used to sell many types of goods, ironically even constricting foundation garments (such as girdles) since the 1960s (Burns-Ardolino, 2007).

Other campaigns transformed feminist demands for social empowerment into self-improvement projects that used the product for sale. L'Oreal hair color notably embraced this theme in 1973 with "Because I'm Worth It," a slogan still at the core of their brand identity. Scores of advertisers have adopted this strategy, to the point that some researchers argue that the meaning of feminism for some now refers solely to the cultivation of the self and to the search for "self-esteem" rather than social justice and social change (Dworkin and Wachs, 2009).

Representations of Femininity and Masculinity

By now I hope it is clear that through most of the 20th century specific types of White people were represented in U.S. advertising as society's ideal men and women, and that rugged masculinity and feminine domesticity were key themes. That this advertising tends to show men as active and women as beautiful objects is significant, as well. The following section delves into representations of femininity and masculinity in advertising in greater detail, first from a semiotic perspective and then by looking at the activity portrayed. The term semiotic refers to the study of signs and so we will first focus on the construction of advertising images. In the second section, the focus will be on what the individuals depicted are doing, especially where women are given an activity other than being nice to view.

Structuring Gendered Images

In the history of the study of gender and advertising, Erving Goffman's seminal *Gender Advertisements* (1976) stands out. Goffman offers a thought experiment for the analysis of gender in commercial imagery. He chose images that seemed unremarkable in their presentation of men and women and asked how these images would be interpreted should the position of the individuals portrayed be reversed. In doing so Goffman identified multiple themes in the sexist representation of women. One such theme is "relative size," where men take up more space. This could simply be with the size of their body or with posture. For example, compare the classic fashion model stance of a woman hunched forward with rounded shoulders and hand on hips while men stand up straight with wide shoulders and puffed chests. The "feminine touch" is another theme, where women use their hands to trace or hold something lightly rather than employ a man's firm, utilitarian grip. The "ritualization of subordination," where women lower themselves physically in some form of prostration or display of weakness is also important. A fourth theme, "licensed withdrawal," where women are rendered as psychologically removed from the situations shown, was also identified in Goffman's work. This contrasts with the way men in advertising look directly into the camera or at another person in the image, rather than off into the distance.

Recall the image of the woman soccer referee from the Virginia Slims advertisement. She is sitting on the ground with her legs extended. Since she is a referee, why is she not at least standing up watching the game or discussing it afterward, where she still could conceivably have a cigarette? This image is a good example of the "ritualization of subordination," even in an ad that is, in theory, trying to convey independence. She is also lightly touching her head with Goffman's "feminine touch." Try to imagine a man sitting in the same position, touching his head with the same light touch while smiling and looking off into the distance. How would he look? Attractive? Sexy? Ridiculous? What kind of story or message about women is being conveyed in the Virginia Slims advertisement?

Goffman's discovery of these themes seems not to have had much influence on the production of advertising as more recent researchers have documented their persistence to the present. In his film *Codes of Gender* (2009), the Media Education Foundation producer and director and University of Massachusetts Professor Sut Jhally shows image after image from magazines and various advertising campaigns constructed with the same themes Goffman identified. Feminist media activist Jean Kilbourne repeatedly updated her research for her highly acclaimed *Killing Us Softly* (2010, 1999, 1987, 1979) films to see if the dominant sexist themes she identified in advertising were still relevant over time. Unfortunately, after reviewing thousands of images, they were and still are. In addition to Goffmanian themes, Kilbourne focuses on several others. These include attention to the flawless beauty that women are supposed to attain, even though they will never be able to live up to the digitally altered images of professional models. Other themes include: 1) the silencing of women, shown with hands held over their mouths, sewn shut, etc.; 2) infantilizing women by portraying them dressed as little girls, sucking on lollipops, having pig tails in their hair or wearing school girl uniforms; 3) portraying women of color, especially Black women, as animals in the jungle or otherwise not fully human; 4) women as sexually available and insatiable; and 5) having violence done to them and often asking for it. Advertisements are not understood as causing violence against women, but as creating a climate where violence is acceptable through its normalization. This image from a Dolce and Gabbana campaign where a woman is held to the ground reminiscent of a gang rape is a case in point.

Doing Gender

During Superbowl XLVII in February 2013 a commercial ran for Dodge Ram Trucks that brought together many themes in the collective representation of masculinity. Conservative radio host Paul Harvey's well-known vignette, "So God Made a Farmer," played as a voiceover with images of farmers and farm life, some black and white, running in montage fashion. In addition to images of rugged masculinity (tending to farm animals, for example), they drew on themes of breadwinning, family, church, and hard work, in sum, the Protestant work ethic at the core of the American Dream. One difference from previous renderings of the theme of rugged masculinity is that this commercial included one White woman and one Black man in the montage of farmers, presumably tiny nods to critics of advertising and perhaps the disproportionately high numbers of women currently becoming organic farmers and the long history of African Americans in agricultural work under slavery and the share-cropping system.

Men are also commonly represented in advertising as breadwinners. This role is often signified by men who come home with their briefcases to a meal prepared by their wife. Men and women are often juxtaposed in their relations with each other, almost exclusively as heterosexual. This is especially apparent in beer commercials. Sometimes men are portrayed as sexy "ladies' men," such as Dos Equis' "most interesting man in the world." Though humorous, he is still tall, dark, and handsome in his masculinity, and more importantly, surrounded by women. On the other side of that coin are men portrayed as losers who attractive women would not dream of dating, much like Walter in our opening GoDaddy commercial. They either have harpies for girlfriends/wives or cannot get the beautiful women they want because the women are superficial, "stuck up bitches." These commercials are both a subtle part of the backlash against feminism and a powerful way of encouraging men to drink with their buddies. No matter how much of a loser you are, you always have Budweiser and your friends (Messner and Montez de Oca, 2005).

One of the most important ways of representing men and masculinity in advertising is as athletes, including the use of professional athletes as spokesmen. This practice opened the door for African American men to be represented in greater numbers. In the early 20th century they appeared much like Aunt Jemima as racist stereotypes from the Old South, such as Rastus for Cream of Wheat Cereal and Uncle Ben for Uncle Ben's Rice. Following the social movements of the 1960s their roles expanded and they appeared in ads for everything from cigarettes to hair care products. Pro football players "Mean" Joe Green for Coca Cola and O.J. Simpson for Hertz Rental Cars are classic examples from the 1970s. Nike brought Michael Jordan on board in the 1980s, but it was not until they developed the theme of "combative solo willpower" in the American ghetto that Nike sales really took off (Holt and Cameron, 2012). According to Douglas Holt and Douglas Cameron (2012), Nike rebranded middle-class-raised Jordan through the use of video with Spike Lee's Mars Blackmon character to associate him with urban life and cast him as a survivor through hard work and perseverance. Virtually every athletic shoe company since has somehow incorporated the imagery of the outdoor, urban basketball court and the athlete who has succeeded against all odds. One might argue that this treatment reached its apex with Latrell Sprewell's television commercial for And1, which appeared after his controversial choking of Coach P. J. Caresimo in the 1990s. Sprewell is shown seated, having his hair put into cornrows, while Jimmy Hendrix's guitar version of the Star Spangled Banner plays in the background. He states, "I've made mistakes, but I don't let 'em keep me down. People say I am what's wrong with sports. I say I'm a three time NBA All-Star. People say I'm America's worst nightmare." And then looking directly into the camera: "I say I'm the American Dream." Seen through the lens of the history of advertising, African American men from the ghetto are yet another form of outsider masculinity, this time in a survival of the fittest contest of athletic achievement.

What do the women of advertising do in addition to being harpies or beautiful, unavailable bitches? Appearing as brides is one dominant theme. Women in wedding gowns sell not just wedding dresses and flowers, but a wide range of other products including deodorant, cell phones, diarrhea medication, and much more. Domesticity remains a common theme. While White women are still prominent, they are no longer shown depending on the labor of servants of color. Domesticity is represented by women of many ethnic backgrounds with White women cleaning toilets and sweeping floors themselves. The food industry is particularly notorious for using a traditional gendered division of labor in its advertising. Despite evidence that growing numbers of men cook, food advertisers generally ignore that activity and portray food preparation as almost exclusively a female domain. Expressing her love for her family, caring for their health and her own health and beauty, and taking care of her children were and are further activities for women in food advertising. Ads portray men as eating, waiting to be fed, or as entitled to criticize their wives' cooking if they are not pleased (Parkin, 2006).

"Superwoman" themes are used now as well. Attractive women with careers, husbands, children, and a social life show how they "have it all" using modern products. One recent example of the superwoman is Kelly Ripa's commercial for Electrolux Appliances. Shown leaving her successful talk show (*Regis and Kelly* at the time, now *Kelly and Michael*) and running home with groceries, she manages to cook for a successful dinner party and her child's sleepover, be a great hostess and put her kids to sleep safely, all because the convenience of these appliances, such as a stove that boils water rapidly, help her to save time.

Ripa's Electrolux commercial is also a subtype of a more general position for women in advertising: the spokesperson/model. These are especially coveted positions for celebrity women given that they can come with a hefty paycheck. Some of these campaigns require the models to perform, such as Britney Spears or Beyoncé singing and dancing for Pepsi. But many others simply show the women using the product, such as Sophia Vergara for Diet Pepsi, Ellen DeGeneres for Cover Girl, Sanaa Lathan for Pantene Pro-V, Aishwarya Rai and Diane Keaton for L'Oreal, Jennifer Aniston for Smart Water and Aveeno, Brook Shields for La-Z-Boy Furniture and Foster Grant sunglasses, Jennifer Lopez for Fiat automobiles, and Martha Raye for Polident denture cleaner.

We already have established that above all else, women are to appear beautiful in advertising. A related theme is that many campaigns showcase the "technologies of the self," in French social theorist Michel Foucault's (1988) terminology, used in order to *become* beautiful. They bathe; apply makeup, lotion and perfume; color and style hair; remove unwanted hair through plucking, waxing and applying depilatories such as Nair; and increasingly have cosmetic procedures such as Botox injections and surgery. Evidence suggests that advertising and popular culture play a central role in the normalization of cosmetic surgery in recent years (Brooks, 2006).

While women are now portrayed as athletes, business women, and in other roles such as a farmer in the Dodge Ram Truck campaign discussed earlier, the dominant images of women in advertising involve domesticity and beauty, as they have for decades. However, that dominance has drawn the criticism of feminist media activists, such as Sut Jhally and Jean Kilbourne, as well as many online bloggers. This negative attention has not gone unnoticed by advertisers. One company in particular has turned this criticism into an advantage.

Advertising Responds to Its Critics

In 2004 Unilever launched a campaign in response to critics who accused advertising of creating unrealistic beauty norms for and exploiting the insecurity in women that it itself had created: the Dove Campaign for Real Beauty. This Ogilvy and Mather designed campaign ostensibly responded to research that found that very few women considered themselves to be beautiful (2%); their goal was to increase those numbers. The first phase displayed a group of women in white bras and panties.

Dove's website describes it as follows:

The Campaign for Real Beauty launched in September 2004 with a much talked-about ad campaign featuring real women whose appearances are outside the stereotypical norms of beauty. The ads asked viewers to judge the women's looks (oversized or outstanding? and wrinkled or wonderful?), and invited them to cast their votes at campaignforrealbeauty.com. (http://www.dove.us/social-mission/campaign-for-real-beauty. aspx)

While these women did not look like the supermodels of fashion magazines, they certainly were not overweight or conventionally unattractive. Later phases focused on six of these women in more detail and then expanded in 2007 with "Beauty Comes of Age" featuring women with gray hair, wrinkles, and/or a bit more flesh. The campaign also contains videos called "Onslaught" and "Evolution" that critique the deluge of media messages women face and expose the technical, unrealistic construction of media images of women respectively. It also promotes Dove's "Self-esteem Fund," which sponsors programs for girls. As of this writing Dove's latest commercial, "Real Beauty Sketches" shows an FBI sketch artist who, without seeing them, draws women's self-descriptions. Then later other women describe the first women to the artist who draws a second portrait. The drama of the commercial comes together when participants face the two images side by side. With just a few examples they relate that most of the women described themselves as less attractive than as seen by others. Women state, sometimes with emotion, that they should be less self-critical and appreciate their own natural beauty more, in part to free up time for more important experiences. The commercial ends: "You are more beautiful than you think." Then the Dove corporate logo appears. There is no mention of a specific product.

By all accounts the campaign was tremendously successful. Millions of women flocked to the Dove website to view and discuss the images and videos, as well as respond to surveys. Sales increased dramatically during the initial phases of the campaign and moderately thereafter, expanding market share for Unilever and establishing brand identity (Spitznagel, 2013).

Feminist media critics responded with mixed appraisals. Some applauded Unilever for sparking a national dialogue among women about beauty, body image, self-esteem, aging, and the role of consumer products in these processes. Women in Media and News's (WIMN) Jennifer Pozner (2005) lauded the campaign for expanding available images of women in the media and exposing some negative, male attitudes toward women's bodies expressed in reaction to them. She and other critics such as Salon.com's Rebecca Traister also criticized the campaign for then hypocritically using those images to sell skin firming cream for treating cellulite (2005). Further criticism came through the revelation that technical touch ups had been done on the images, even if only to deal with color and lighting issues (Neff, 2008) as well as from those who argued that the images still included a narrow range of acceptable appearances, leaving out, for example, women with disabilities (Heiss, 2011).

In their attempt to grapple with women's criticism of mass media images, Ogilvy and Mather employed tactics of self-criticism and appeals to authenticity that have been used by advertisers since the 1960s. The best, if not the first, example can be found in the now iconic Doyle, Dane and Bernbach (DDB) "Think Small" campaign for the Volkswagen Beetle. Minimalist black and white images with additional slogans that included "Lemon" and "Will We Ever Kill The Beetle?" challenged the dominant advertising from 1950s' Detroit auto industry that relied on planned obsolescence to sell cars. (Planned obsolescence means that the automakers intentionally manufactured cars in such a way that they would need to be replaced frequently.) More importantly, this campaign somehow managed to erase the association of the vehicle with the Nazi party that produced it and connect it to the anti-consumerist ethos of 1960s free-love, hippy life. DDB used an analogous strategy in yet another famous campaign, this time for Avis rental cars, proudly stating that since Avis was only "number two" in the industry, they would try harder and serve their customers better. In sum, advertisers directly appealed to consumers' resistance to manipulation by criticizing advertising in advertising's own copy and presenting the Beetle and Avis as *authentically real*. Thus, while the Dove campaign appeared revolutionary to some by addressing normative media constructions of women, their tactics were tried and true. Further, though the images of women are different than the standard in other advertising campaigns, one might ask if the Dove Campaign for Real Beauty reinforces the notion of women as image above all else.

Conclusion

Modern advertising has always been a gendered phenomenon and it is highly unlikely that this characteristic will change anytime soon. As a social communication system that shares cultural values, assigns meaning to material goods, entertains, educates, and persuades us to purchase products and services, advertising shapes and is shaped by gender relations in society, including those that are sexist, racist and homophobic. One would like to argue that media literacy and feminist critique are opportunities for progressive social change. (There is some measure of hope to be found in such figures as "Flo" for Progressive Insurance, a quirky, funny spokeswoman who, while generally attractive, is not featured as a beautiful object for the male gaze.) However, commercial messages such as the Dove Real Beauty Campaign show that this critique can simply be used as inspiration for the next generation of advertising. As Douglas Holt (2002) effectively argued (in relation to Ad Busters and other anti-branding movements) more than a decade ago, "What has been termed 'consumer resistance' is actually a form of market-sanctioned cultural experimentation through which the market rejuvenates itself"(p. 89). The next logical step of activism then, Holt presumes, will be for consumers to want to see how companies treat people when they are not consumers and demand that they "shoulder civic responsibility"(p. 89). Feminists and others who care about gender in advertising will have to decide what this means for them. Will they demand, for example, that Dove stop treating women as an image, not by showing authentically "real women," but by ending their sale of cellulite firming cream altogether? Will Nike have to pay the women who make their shoes a livable wage? Will Madison Avenue need to hire more women of color behind the camera, rather than as Aunt Jemima? As students of gender and advertising, what will you ask of the companies who produce your goods and services? What contributions will you make?

Questions for Class Discussion

1. Do you have a favorite advertisement? Why did it catch your attention and how does it make you feel? Discuss the ad, the product being sold, the people in the ad, and how they appear.
2. What is the difference between comparing images of women in advertising to real women and thinking about the concept of women *as an image*? Explain.
3. Food industry advertising often portrays women cooking for their

families even though men are becoming more involved in food preparation. Why do you think that is?

4. Select an advertisement featuring a man or woman. Now imagine that individual to be the "opposite" gender. How does the image change, if at all? What do you notice? Does it matter what their "race" and/or ethnicity is?

5. Is there such a thing as feminist advertising? Is the Dove campaign an example of feminist advertising? Why or why not?

References

Blond, A. (2008). Impacts of exposure to images of ideal bodies on male body dissatisfaction: A review. *Body Image, 5*(3).

Breazeale, K. (1994). In spite of women. *Signs: Women in Culture and Society, 20*(1), 1–22.

Brooks, A. (2006). Under the knife and proud of it: An analysis of the normalization of cosmetic surgery. In S. Pfohl, A. Van Wagenen, P. Arend, A. Brooks, & D. Leckenby (Eds.), *Culture, power, history: Studies in critical sociology* (pp. 23–58). Leiden, The Netherlands and Boston, MA: Brill.

Brown, E. H. (2008). Marlboro men: Outsider masculinities and commercial modeling in postwar America. In R. L. Blaszczyk (Ed.), *Producing fashion: Commerce, culture and consumers* (pp. 187–206). Philadelphia: University of Philadelphia Press.

Burns-Ardolino, W. (2007). *Jiggle: (Re)shaping American women.* Lanham, MD: Lexington Books.

Douglas, S. J. (2010). *The rise of enlightened sexism: How pop culture took us from girl power to girls gone wild.* New York, NY: St. Martin's Griffin.

Dworkin, S. L., & Wachs, F. L. (2009). *Body panic: Gender, health, and the selling of fitness.* New York, NY: New York University Press.

Enloe, C. (2004). *The curious feminist: Searching for women in a new age of empire.* Berkeley, CA: University of California Press.

Foucault, M. (1988). Technologies of the self. In M. H. Luther, H. Gutman, & P. H. Hutton (Eds.), *Technologies of the self: A seminar with Michel Foucault* (pp. 16–49). Amherst, MA: The University of Massachusetts Press.

Friedan, B. (1963). *The feminine mystique*. New York, NY: Dell Publishing Co.

Goffman, E. (1976). *Gender advertisements*. New York, NY: Harper & Row.

Heiss, S. N. (2011). Locating the bodies of women and disability in definitions of beauty: An analysis of Dove's campaign for real beauty. *Disability Studies Quarterly, 31*(1).

Holt, D. (2002). Why do brands cause trouble? A dialectical theory of consumer culture and branding. *The Journal of Consumer Research, 29*(1), 70–90.

Holt, D. (2006). Jack Daniel's America: Iconic brands as ideological parasites and proselytizers. *Journal of Consumer Culture, 6*(3), 355–377.

Holt, D., & Cameron, D. (2012). *Cultural strategy: Using innovative ideologies to build breakthrough brands*. Oxford, UK: Oxford University Press.

Howard, V. (2003). A 'real man's ring': Gender and the invention of tradition. *Journal of Social History, 36*(4), 837–856.

Jhally, S. (Director). (2009). *The codes of gender: Identity and performance in popular culture*. US: Media Education Foundation.

Johnston, J., & Taylor, J. (2008). Feminist consumerism and fat activists: A comparative study of grassroots activism and the Dove Real Beauty Campaign. *Signs: Journal of Women in Culture and Society, 33*(4), 941–966.

Kilbourne, J. (1999). *Deadly persuasion: Why women and girls must fight the addictive power of advertising*. New York, NY: The Free Press.

Kilbourne, J. (Creator). (1979). *Killing us softly*. US: Cambridge Documentary Films.

Kilbourne, J. (Creator). (1987). *Still killing us softly: Advertising's image of women*. US: Cambridge Documentary Films.

Kilbourne, J. (Creator). (1999). *Killing us softly 3*. US: Media Education Foundation.

Kilbourne, J. (Creator). (2010). *Killing us softly 4: Advertising's image of women*. US: Media Education Foundation.

Lears, J. (1994). *Fables of abundance: A cultural history of advertising in America*. New York, NY: BasicBooks.

Little, A. (2013, February 4). *Top five sexist super bowl ads*. Retrieved from February 4, 2013, from http://msmagazine.com/blog/2013/02/04/top-five-sexist-super-bowl-ads-2013/

Manring, M. M. (1998). *Slave in a box: The strange career of Aunt Jemima*. Charlottesville, VA: University of Virginia Press.

Mehaffy. M. M. (1997). Advertising race/racing advertising: The feminine consumer (-nation), 1876-1900. *Signs: Journal of Women in Culture and Society, 23*(1), 131–174.

Messner, M. A., & Montez de Oca, J. (2005). The male consumer as loser: Beer and liquor ads in mega sports media events. *Signs: Journal of Women in Culture and Society, 30*(3), 1879–1909.

Mulvey, L. (1975). Visual pleasure and narrative cinema. *Screen, 16*(3), 381–389.

Nielsen.com. (2010, January 20). *Survey most Super Bowl viewers tune in for the commercials*. Retrieved from http://www.nielsen.com/us/en/newswire/2010/survey-most-super-bowl-viewers-tune-in-for-the-commercials.html

Neff, J. (2008, May 7). Dove's Real Beauty pics could be big phonies. *Advertising Age*. Retrieved August 6, 2013, from http://adage.com/article/news/dove-s-real-beauty-pics-big-phonies/126914/

Parkin, K. J. (2006). *Food is love: Advertising and gender roles in modern America*. Philadelphia, PA: University of Pennsylvania Press.

Peiss, K. (1998). *Hope in a jar: The making of America's beauty culture*. New York, NY: Henry Holt and Company.

Postrel, V. (2011, June 24). Hollywood auction ends myth of zaftig Marilyn. *Bloomberg.com*. Retrieved from http://www.bloomberg.com/news/2011-06-24/hollywood-auction-ends-myth-of-zaftig-marilyn-virginia-postrel.html

Rosen, R. (2000). *The world split open: How the modern women's movement changed America*. New York, NY: Viking.

Scanlon, J. (1995). *Inarticulate longings: The ladies' home journal, gender, and the promises of consumer culture*. New York, NY and London, UK: Routledge.

Scanlon, J. (Ed.). (2000). *The gender and consumer culture reader*. New York, NY: New York University Press.

Sivulka, J. (2012). *Soap, sex and cigarettes: A cultural history of American advertising* (2nd ed.). Boston, MA: Wadsworth.

Spitznagel, E. (2013). How those Dove 'real beauty sketch' ads went viral. *Bloomberg BusinessWeek*, Retrieved from http://www.businessweek.com/articles/2013-04-26/how-those-dove-real-beauty-sketch-ads-went-viral

Soloman-Godeau, A. (1996). The other side of Venus: The visual economy of feminine display. In V. de Grazia with E. Furlough (Eds.), *The sex of things: Gender and consumption in historical perspective* (pp. 113–150). Berkeley, CA: University of California Press.

Weems, R. E. Jr. (2000). Consumerism and the construction of Black female identity in twentieth-century America. In J. Scanlon (Ed.), *The gender and consumer culture reader* (pp. 166–178). New York, NY: New York University Press.

Welter, B. (1966). The cult of true womanhood: 1820–1860. *American Quarterly*, *18*(2), 151–174.

Williams, R. (2009). Advertising: The magic system. In S. Thornham, C. Bassett, & P. Marris (Eds.), *Media studies: A reader* (pp. 730–735). New York, NY: New York University Press. (Original work published 1962).

Chapter 4
From Lady Gaga to Consciousness Rap:
The Impact of Music on Gender and Social Activism
Adrienne Trier-Bieniek & Amanda Pullum

In 2011 Lady Gaga created the Born This Way Foundation with the mission of "empowering youth, inspiring bravery." Named after her hit song, which encourages people to embrace themselves, the Born This Way Foundation quickly amassed followers, a strong position on Facebook, and became a centerpiece of Lady Gaga's 2012-2013 world tour. While some may argue that celebrity intentions are less than altruistic when they create or support a cause, Lady Gaga's perspective on creating the Born This Way Foundation seemed to be the outcome of academic research done by professionals, her own experiences with fans, and a national outpouring of support for lesbian, gay, bisexual, and transgender youth who face bullying and taunting based on their sexual orientation or gender identity. While some may contend that the foundation is simply another feather in the cap of a celebrity, many signs point toward a feminist reaction to watching social inequality unfold and wanting to follow suit with the feminists who have come before her. The foundation is only one part of Lady Gaga's effort; the other part is the message of inclusivity and tolerance in the music that inspired the foundation. Lady Gaga is using her music and celebrity to address social inequality via intersections of gender, class, and sexuality. She is building her music and persona around a blend of consciousness-raising and social action.

Lady Gaga's efforts serve as the perfect backdrop for this chapter. In the pages that follow we focus on gender through the lens of music, particularly when music is used as a catalyst for feminist activism. To do so, we examine the songs and impact of three artists. We begin with Ani DiFranco and her song "Which Side Are You On?" the lyrics of which combine feminist consciousness-raising with folk music. We then address Lupe Fiasco and present his song "Bitch Bad" as an example of how a song about gender stereotypes sparks conversation

A. Trier-Bieniek et al., (Eds.), Gender & Pop Culture, 81–102.

about feminist activism. Finally we look at Beyoncé's song "Run the World" as a celebration of feminist activism. Each is an example of how the third wave of feminism created mantras for new generations of feminist activists. First we offer the groundwork for the ways gender and music are connected.

Foundations of Gender and Music

Pop music has always created and portrayed gender roles. In general, men are presented as hyper-masculine, performing songs that make the girls in the audience scream, while holding their guitars at pelvic-height, an obvious ode to their masculinity. Female musicians are usually expected to be attractive, per the cultural standard, above all else. Further, female fans of music are usually pegged as the "teeny bop" crowd, girls and women who are infatuated with male performers. This dichotomy was first addressed in Frith and McRobbie's 1978 study which differentiated between "cock rock" and "teeny bop." The authors discussed male musicians as performing masculinity, while female fans are consumers of those performances. They note, "the male musician is typically portrayed as aggressive, dominating, boastful, and constantly seek[ing] to remind the audience of their prowess, their control. Their stance is obvious in live shows; male bodies on display, plunging shirts and tight trousers, a visual emphasis on chest hair and genitals (p. 25)." Further, as was noted in her book *Sing Us a Song, Piano Woman: Female Fans and the Music of Tori Amos* (2013), Trier-Bieniek addressed the ways that Frith and McRobbie's observations can be channeled into the 21st century. She contends that artists like Justin Bieber, Usher, and Chris Brown each present a sort of uber masculinity on stage and, while the visual elements of masculinity are present (i.e. crotch grabbing) there is an added element of "swagger" which is customary for male performers to use as an indication of their dominance.

Performers displaying their gender has roots in gender theory such as West and Zimmerman's (1987) concept of "doing gender." West and Zimmerman asserted that gender is something that is not just taught; it is something that people perform in their everyday lives. Additionally, as Butler's well-known 1999 book *Gender Trouble* explained, gender is an identity which is created by culturally acceptable acts such as dress, physical appearance, etc. Thus, for our purposes, looking at gender via the lens of music serves to illustrate the society's expectations of people based on their gender, or to illustrate what a culture's expectations are for each gender.

In her 2009 book *Gender in the Music Industry* Marion Leonard combines discussion of gender and music with the music industry's and rock journalists' reproduction of gender stereotypes. The music industry, she argues, is still constructed by men who dominate the position of music executive, music journalist, fan, academic, and listener. "The concern is to uncover how this gendering of rock is articulated, with particular attention to how a masculinist tradition is established, reproduced and maintained..." (p. 23). She goes on to give the example of phrases like "women in rock" or "the year of the woman in music" as problematic. "Rather than simply pointing to the activity of female musicians within a particular music genre, the phrase usually works to peculiarise the presence of women rock performers" (p. 32). Indeed, the presence of women in music is often addressed as an anomaly, a rare gem which can only hold the culture's focus for a moment.

Press coverage also impacts the image of men and women in music. As Feigenbaum (2005) notes, many rock journalists have made attempts to examine the place of women in music. Lucy O'Brien is notable because of her double-book-biopic of women in music, *She Bop* and *She Bop 2*. In both books O'Brien chronicles the history and trends of female musicians, looking at everyone from Memphis Minnie (1920s and 1930s soul and rock musician), Sister Rosetta Tharpe (popular in the 1930s and 1940s for her mixture of rock and gospel music) to Wanda Jackson, Dolly Parton, Carley Simon, the Riot Grrls, Alanis Morissette, Tori Amos, and Ani DiFranco to name a few. There have also been biographies written by journalists about female performers such as *Tori Amos: Piece by Piece* which was co-authored between Amos and rock journalist Ann Powers. Yet, as Feigenbaum notes, these types of books are written to combat the sexism published in commercial news media, particularly with the ways female musicians are presented. As she writes,

Adjectival gender markers and gender binaries also work to support an authentic/inauthentic dichotomy that devalues women. This type of distinction often precedes a non-gender specific noun such as, 'the girl rocker' or 'the chick singer.' These markings are usually employed only when women are being referred to. One does not often come across 'the male rocker', just 'the rocker.' (p. 40)

Examples like this coupled with the work of Frith, McRobbie, and Leonard, provide some context for the following discussion of how gender and music converge. In this chapter we take the issues raised and apply them to the ways that feminist music has been used as a consciousness-raising tool in the spirit of feminist activism.

Gender and Social Movements: A short history

The American women's movement can be traced back to the late 19th century, with the rise of the women's suffrage movement and the Seneca Falls Convention of 1848 (Pedriana, 2004). At that time, many Americans espoused a belief in "separate spheres," the idea that the public sphere (including politics) should be the domain of men, and the home should be the domain of women. Suffragists boldly challenged this concept of sex roles, giving public speeches and marching in suffrage parades that drew up to 20,000 participants (McCammon, 2003). While American women gained the right to vote in 1920, it took another 60 years for women's electoral turnout to equal men's (Paxton et al., 2007). Following World War II, Americans' increased social and cultural emphasis on "traditional" sex roles made it even more difficult for the women's movement to effect social change. However, during this period of decreased political and cultural opportunities, the women's movement was sustained by a small core group of committed activists. These activists created a strong community that held members together until conditions were better for mobilization.

This community was the foundation for the women's movement of the 1960s, which is commonly called the second wave of feminism. In 1966 the National Organization for Women (NOW) was founded by noted feminists such as Betty Friedan (author of *The Feminist Mystique*) and Pauli Murphy (the first African American female

Episcopal priest). NOW grew quickly, and by the early 1970s, there were chapters in several large U.S. cities (Reger & Staggenborg, 2006). This re-awakening of the women's movement occurred in the context of widespread activism in the United States, including the Civil Rights and the anti-Vietnam War movements.

A major outcome of feminist activism in the 1970s was the concept of "consciousness-raising." By consciousness-raising we mean specifically work done to draw people's attention to a social problem, increase their understanding of it including how it personally impacts them, and hopefully motivate them to help solve the problem (although almost all social movements try to do this, it was the feminist movement that pioneered this concept). Feminists in the 1970s called for women to meet and talk about their experiences in order to understand the challenges and oppression they all faced, and to work together to address these problems (Sowards & Renegar, 2004). In addition to discussion, activists can also raise consciousness through public protest (Valocchi, 2009). And here is our connection to music. Music became an important tool for sharing feminist consciousness-raising messages with a broad audience.

Gender, Movements and Music

Music has played a central role in mobilization, framing, and collective identity formation in many social movements. Oppressed populations, such as enslaved Africans in the American south, have long used music as a tool for coded communication, morale boosting, and solidarity-building. This tradition continues today, as examples of songs about racial inequality and Black oppression can be found in Black gospel music, R&B, rap, hip-hop and many other genres. Music can be used to make an emotional appeal to potential supporters, and to spread this call across wide distances (Pratt, 1990).

In addition, music helps movements shape and change the cultural contexts in which they work. Goodwin et al. (1999) argue that musical traditions which challenge dominant beliefs and practices, such as folk or hip-hop, should themselves be studied by scholars of social movements. In short, music is both a crucial component of many social movements and a vehicle for social change in itself.

Although the term "protest songs" might conjure up images of historical progressive movements like the labor, Civil Rights, and anti-Vietnam War movements, other movements across the political spectrum have used music to communicate their messages and attract crowds to concerts, where listeners might be persuaded to join in the movement's efforts (Blee & Creasap, 2010). Of course, music can be used to spread messages of hate and division just as well as messages of progress and tolerance. White supremacists and neo-Nazis have recorded clearly racist music, though few studies of the use of music in these groups exist (Weissman, 2010).

Concerts can provide activists with renewed dedication to the effort, give new activists a fun way to connect with the movement, and offer sympathizers a low-risk way to get involved (Futrell et al., 2006). These events can also provide fundraising opportunities for social movement organizations, bringing in much-needed resources while spreading the message. Staggenborg (1998) points out that organizations may choose to hold concerts in strategic locations that potential sympathizers already frequent. However, concerts are understudied aspects of social movements, because many researchers do not count them as "protest activities," preferring to think of consciousness-raising as occurring in traditional street protests.

In the late 19th and early 20th century US, much of the music that was explicitly used as a tool for social change, rather than just social commentary, was connected to the labor movement. The IWW (Industrial Workers of the World, or "Wobblies") is perhaps the first American labor organization to use music as a primary organizing tool. They began using music in 1908 in order to be heard in the busy streets, and their songs—which both attracted an audience and communicated the union's political messages—were so popular that the IWW published and sold its own songbook. *Solidarity Forever*, a widely known IWW song, was re-written by women in the 1970s; they added verses asserting that union women will fight for women's rights.

As music has grown and changed, political dissent continues to be a focus. As O'Brien writes, "from the angry blues singers of the 1940s to Communist folkies in the 1950s and various vast Stadium Aid spectacles of the 1980s, performers have used the medium of rock as a mass vehicle for protest"(O'Brien, 2002, p. 383). Additionally women's voices in protest songs can be traced back to the 1920s and 1930s with women like Mollie Jackson, who sang at union meetings and picket lines, and Memphis Minnie, whose song "When the Levees Brake" was written as a reaction to the 1929 upheaval following the Mississippi floods. The 1960s brought the trifecta of Carol King, Carley Simon, and Joni Mitchell. Each had multiple songs to their credit that spoke to the liberation of women and the second wave of feminism. In the 1980s, Queen Latifah's songs chronicled the place of women of color in social movements. Tracy Chapman came onto the music scene in 1988 when she played for Nelson Mandela's birthday concert and made race and gender the focal points of her songwriting with songs like "Born to Fight," the video of which showed various civil rights leaders.

The 1990s gave way to women like Tori Amos whose song "Me and a Gun," which chronicled Amos's rape by a fan after a concert, paved the way for Amos to begin RAINN, (the Rape, Abuse and Incest National Network). The 1990s also brought singer/songwriter Ani DiFranco, whose work we address further later in this chapter. Additionally, movements like the Riot Grrrls, which centered on bands that emphasized feminist consciousness-raising, demonstrated that many women were less interested in watching male band members perform and more interested in starting their own band.

"Protest songs" are not always classic, and sometimes tired, old tunes. Modern pop and rock music have been influenced by the protest songs of the past, and many artists incorporate commentary on social problems within their lyrics, as you will read later in this chapter. In the 2000s, music as activism has morphed into consciousness-raising lyrics rather than protest tools like the IWW's songbook. Additionally, because of this shift to consciousness-raising, many musicians are generally received by a following of people who want to listen to music that makes them more aware of social issues.

As we will demonstrate in this chapter, sometimes consciousness-raising leads to a direct monetary contribution to social movements, as with Lady Gaga and the Born this Way Foundation or Beyoncé's Chime for Change foundation. Other times the result is an artistic contribution (via a manifesto, creation of an anthem, etc.) to the women's movement. Most of the time feminist music does what music has always done for social movements: it educates listeners about women's struggles and motivates them to create social change.

Case Studies

Ani DiFranco- Which Side Are You On?

We begin with Ani DiFranco because, of all the people we are going to discuss, DiFranco is the most outspokenly feminist. Ani DiFranco's music addresses politics, feminism, and the women's movement and is often cited as one of the foundations for exploring gender and music in contemporary society.

Background

Since 1989, DiFranco has been writing and performing songs that address the impact of patriarchy on society as well as declaring a feminist agenda. Not willing to compromise her art for a contract with a major record company, DiFranco chose to write and produce her music through her own label Righteous Babe Records. DiFranco's musical style mixes poetry with rock, often categorized as "folk rock." Her lyrics draw from the folk tradition, with inspiration found in union songs and protest songs, as well as a feminist political commentary on everything from consumerism to sexuality (DiFranco identifies as bisexual). Her mission as a musician is to illustrate a challenge to patriarchy. DiFranco has become known for songs which both make the listener think while also promoting feminist activism. "Whether they describe a failing romance or the faults of national policy on gun control, her lyrics typically contain intersections of the personal and the political..." (Garrett, 2008, p. 383). This combination is a textbook example of consciousness-raising in music.

DiFranco's lyrics and storytelling exemplify feminist standpoint theory. The purpose of feminist standpoint theory is to place the stories and experiences of women at the center of research. This translates to DiFranco's work because her songs chronicle the experiences of women and, while she may not be conducting formal research, she is declaring that women should be able to talk about their own lives and knowledge using their own language and in their own way. DiFranco's most notable songs include "Not a Pretty Girl," where she describes her goals in life to be about more than being perceived as pretty and declares that she is not a damsel in distress who needs to be rescued. "32 Flavors" has lyrics which reference the ways a woman's appearance is scrutinized by just about everyone, including other women. Many of her songs reference the lack of respect for feminists, and the idea that feminism should be a common mindset for most people, particularly women. In "Grand Canyon" she expresses this, saying that all men and women should call themselves feminist out of respect for the people who fought for women's rights. In the song "Alla This" DiFranco illustrates her feminist activism as something she will continue to do, that she will not stay silent and buy into any cooperate ideas about what women should be like. The title of the spoken word piece "Self-Evident" is taken from the opening line of the U.S. Declaration of Independence. DiFranco wrote the piece in the days following September 11th as a means to challenge the Bush administration's call for war as well as the contested 2000 election. The piece stands as an exemplar of DiFranco's ability to fuse feminism with political commentary and mix both with folk music.

Which Side Are You On?

With the preceding in mind, we discuss her song "Which Side Are You On?," the title track of her 2012 album. The origins of the song lie in a 1931 labor song written by Florence Reece and made popular by Pete Seeger. (Seeger, who was 92 at the time, recorded banjo riffs for DiFranco's version of the song.) Reece was the wife of Sam Reece, a labor organizer in Kentucky and the song was written as an anthem for workers, something they could rally around in support of their union. Among other things, the song encouraged workers to organize because the bourgeoisie (their bosses) were not going to look out for their best interests. DiFranco took the main themes of the song, including the references to people as the "good workers," kept the original chorus, and transformed "Which Side Are You On?" into a 21st-century call for social change. DiFranco's adjusted lyrics address the 2008 housing crisis, the ways election fraud was corrected with the election of President Barack Obama, the impact of Reagonomics, and the responsibility of feminists to fight for consciousness-raising. Additionally, DiFranco recruited two youth music education programs, The Riverstown Kids and The Roots of Music Marching Crusaders, to sing and play backing instruments on the song, both groups focus on helping "at-risk" youth get into music.

In his review of the album and song, *Consequence of Sound* writer Paul De Revere said, "DiFranco's adaptation of a Pete Seeger song 'Which Side Are You On?' throws fire. DiFranco retools the tune from labor protest song to a broader inventory of the surging leftist politics of today, evoking the cause, or at least the spirit, of the Occupy movement... No one can ever fault DiFranco for her apathy or lack of passion" (De Revere, 2012). When reviewing the album for *The Independent*, Andy Gill noted that "[i]t's no surprise to find her covering that most direct and confrontational of protest anthems... the presence of 92-year-old Pete Seeger's banjo alongside the brass of youthful New Orleans marching-band musicians make an explicit point about the perennial persistence of certain political issues" (Gill, 2012). Further, when being interviewed by the *Windy City Media Group*, DiFranco said the following about the song,

> I feel a little bit frustrated, politically desperate. After having written hundreds of songs over decades, I think "Now what? How far can I go with this? "I guess I've been pushing my own boundaries of politics and art. Seeing what people have the ears to listen to. How big is my mouth? What I can get out of it successfully? (Windy City Music Group, 2011 para 6)

When considering the connections between gender, music and consciousness-raising DiFranco is probably the easiest artist to analyze. With "Which Side Are You On" DiFranco is inserting a feminist consciousness into the song, drawing on its roots as an organizing anthem to create a 21st-century call for activism. As we mentioned earlier, consciousness-raising is used to draw people's attention to a social problem. With this song, DiFranco does just that while also challenging what is expected of women in music. DiFranco's challenge is more than telling the listener what she or he should be aware of; she is also addressing how society's perception of gender impacts its culture and social environment. "Which Side Are You On?" becomes a call for activism that challenges patriarchal culture. When she sings about feminism being akin to raising consciousness and connects this with bringing an end to war and violence, DiFranco is also addressing gender socialization. If we consider how we "do" our gender, as West and Zimmerman noted, we also must consider how our gender socialization impacts every aspect of our lives, including the political decisions we make. As Garrett writes, "By interweaving more flexible notions about gender and sexuality with the activist impulse of earlier feminist movements, DiFranco's lyrics, public remarks, and off-stage activities can be understood as products of third-wave feminism" (2008, p. 383).

Lupe Fiasco- "Bitch Bad"

With "Bitch Bad" we address Lupe Fiasco's deconstruction of the word "bitch" in hip-hop, framing it as a consciousness-raising tool and the spark which ignited many Internet and social networking discussions about feminist activism and rap music.

Background

Lupe Fiasco, born Wasalu Muhammad Jaco in 1982, was raised in Chicago's west side. During childhood he was surrounded with music provided by his family, his father was an African drummer and member of the Black Panther Party. Fiasco was influenced early on by a combination of a love of education, books, and jazz. By middle school Fiasco was writing rap lyrics and by high school he was making records in his father's basement via secondhand mixing boards and record players. When he was 19 he briefly dabbled in "gangsta rap" but eventually left the genre because it did not feel true to his ideals. After being given the work of The Watts Prophets, a hip-hop group born from the Civil Rights movement of the 1960s who fused music with spoken word performance, Fiasco found a niche. Their influence led Fiasco to briefly be mentioned on MTV, an eventual deal with Atlantic Records, and a mentorship from fellow rapper (and one of Fiasco's inspirations) Jay-Z. Along with rappers like Common and Mos Def, Lupe Fiasco is known for what is being called the "conscious hip-hop movement," or a turn in hip-hop toward using rap to raise consciousness.

Bitch Bad

It is with this background in mind that we look at the song "Bitch Bad" which is from Fiasco's 2012 album *Food & Liquor II: The Great American Rap Album pt. 1*. In the vein of conscious hip-hop, "Bitch Bad" was written as a way to discuss the use of the word "bitch" by women, about women. By exploring the word "bitch," Fiasco taps into the sociological theory of symbolic interaction, a concept that asserts that people get meaning from things like music based on what meaning it has for them (e.g. Blumer 1969, Goffman 1954). To put it another way, people will connect with songs that they can connect to or derive meaning from. Additionally, the term "bitch," for example, can carry different meanings in different contexts and for different listeners. Essentially, Fiasco is asserting that the word "bitch" has two meanings, either empowerment or degradation. When asked about the inspiration behind the song, Fiasco said,

> The idea is the role model for today for youth and the personification of this imagery. I wrote the record because I have little sisters and I walked into the room and they were looking at Korean J-Pop. And I was thinking "Ok, I am glad they are seeing this..."" But I was thinking "What are the three little girls in the next house listening to?" (HOT97NY, 2012)

The lyrics of "Bitch Bad" begin by talking about a little boy riding in the car with his mother. The boy hears the mother singing along to a song, referring to herself as a "bad bitch." Not realizing that the term could be disrespectful and because the boy respects his mother, he sees a "bitch" as a strong woman, like his mother. This leads into the chorus of the song which attributes the term "bitch" to something that is bad, "woman" to something that is good and "lady" as a preferable term for a woman. However, as the song continues, Fiasco paints a portrait of another child, this time a group of girls who are aged nine through twelve. He describes them as sitting around watching videos on the Internet by themselves and notes that, with kids, having their parents' permission to access information on the Internet is often moot because they have learned how to get around parental controls. They see their favorite singer start talking about "bad bitches," but being young girls they are most affected by the girls dancing in the video, the imagery as connected to the lyrics. These women, dressed in high heels, curvy and undoubtedly considered sexy, are the personification of what the girls think a "bad bitch" is. As Fiasco is careful to point out, the girls don't see an actress who is paid to portray an image, they see an example of what a woman should look and act like. This is consistent with West and Zimmerman's conclusion that people "do gender" by performing what they think their gender should be. Further, the image presents a heterosexual, masculine ideal of beauty. Fiasco goes on to say that one day the boy and girl he described will meet and he will see her as distasteful and she will see herself as an illusion.

The images that Fiasco is presenting via the song's lyrics and video are not new news to most people who research hip-hop. As Rebollo-Gil and Moras write,

> Many of us abhor the misogyny in the music and videos; the unabashed glorification of crime and the unrelenting objectification of black women. Yet a good number of us cannot help but purchase the albums and focus instead on the lyrical dexterity of the artists or on the potential for social and political critique present in the music… HipHop as a cultural and economic powerhouse invites a critical eye. It deserves our scrutiny. (2012, p. 118)

Rebollo-Gil and Moras analyzed the presence of women of color and hip-hop, noting that women are often presented as oversexed, animalistic, and overtly erotic. The result of these images is the loss of a self-defined sexuality for women of color. This is particularly pervasive in hip-hop because it is a means to define women as objects, things that need to be controlled by men.

> The fact is that much of black male rappers' energy is spent trying to either keep women quiet or getting them to shut up. The rest is spent trying to get them into bed or in cases even condoning or bragging about sexual assault/rape which ultimately has the same silencing effect. (2012, p. 126)

This model seems to be what Fiasco is trying to combat with "Bitch Bad" in particular and with consciousness-raising rap. He draws the listener's attention to the problem of women's sexuality being defined

93

by male artists, often in negative ways, making it difficult for women to form their own authentic self-images. Through his music, Fiasco attempts to flesh out this problem, using words like "bitch" as a catalyst for discussion.

Internet discussion of "Bitch Bad" has sparked a lot of outrage and strong opinions, most notably after the music magazine *Spin* posted a scathing review of the song, marking Fiasco as "mansplaining" and declaring the song a poor, unthoughtful example of someone trying to use hip-hop to raise consciousness. The author's main contention was that the word "bitch" had a gendered connotation and therefore should be defined only by women.

However, comments on the *Spin* article indicated shock and disbelief that Fiasco's song was being considered a light-weight addition to discussions of sexism in rap music. What may be even more poignant, though, was the gender study and feminist terminology that accompanied the criticism. The writers were not your run-of-the-mill commentators for blog sites who took pride in ignorant, racist, or sexist terms. Rather, many presented thought-out arguments and referenced the work of feminist theorists like bell hooks and Patricia Hill Collins, particularly their theoretical assertions that women of color will almost always be caught in "double jeopardy" because they have interlocking racial and gender oppression to overcome. Comments included statements like "Your privilege is disgusting", "Go read some bell hooks." One person even wrote that he is taking a course in feminist theory and wanted to thank the author for giving him an example of how music critics scapegoat any real conversations about sexism in their reviews of rap music.

The magazine *The Atlantic* published a similar review of "Bitch Bad." However, Mychal Denel Smith, the author of the piece noted that,

> And so imperfect as it may be, "Bitch Bad" is a needed piece in the on-going dialogue surrounding gender politics. It's a misguided step, and one that shows us just how far we haven't gotten, but there are valuable takeaways. Chief among those is that the answer to the misogyny in hip-hop and in the broader culture in general isn't to replace it with a nice-guy-misogyny

that's equally as limiting in its definition of women. For now, though, it'll have to do. (Smith, 2012)

The scrutiny that Smith's review received was similar to what happened at *Spin*. However, it brought about a different conversation about which rappers should be looked to for feminist consciousness-raising. One commenter noted that if Fiasco is going to be taken to task for his use of the word "bitch" then the same standard should be applied to Rick Ross, Nicki Minaj, L'Wayne, Drake etc. The response was a handful of people saying that Fiasco's discussions of feminism and women in music are different because his goal is to raise consciousness. Not many people are looking to Rick Ross for this. Further, the commentators were, again, versed in feminist theory, particularly Black feminist theory (which is attributed to Patricia Hill Collins 1990 book *Black Feminist Thought*). These people mentioned that Fiasco is challenging women, particularly Black M.C.'s, to define feminism in hip-hop citing that feminism and feminist consciousness-raising has yet to have a clear agenda with rap and hip-hop.

Consciousness-raising in rap music has the potential to help legions of people develop a feminist consciousness and we think that was one of Fiasco's goals when he wrote the song. But, inspiring people toward feminist activism often begins with a conversation about what feminist activism is. By beginning with the word "bitch," Fiasco is trying to dialogue not just about how men treat women or present women in pop culture, but also how women treat each other and present themselves in pop culture. When feminist consciousness-raising in pop music is done well, it sparks a debate that is equal parts intellectual and utilitarian.

Beyoncé —"Run the World (Girls)"

In Beyoncé's "Run the World (Girls)," we turn our attention to a song celebrating and encouraging strength, accompanied by a music video that calls into question the role of women's sexuality in empowerment. Rather than focusing on raising public consciousness about women's struggles, "Run the World (Girls)" celebrates some of the achievements of the women's movement.

Background

Beyoncé Giselle Knowles-Carter started her musical career when she was only 8 years old, as part of an all-girl group that would eventually become known as Destiny's Child. Extremely successful throughout the 1990s and early 2000s, in 2006 Destiny's Child was named by Billboard magazine one of the most popular female groups of all time. The group became famous for songs like "Independent Women," which praised women's financial independence and urged female listeners to depend only on themselves. The theme of not needing anyone to support you quickly became a cornerstone of the trio's music.

After Destiny's Child broke up in 2006, Beyoncé focused on a solo musical career. She quickly became known for lyrics that were viewed as promoting women's empowerment in their personal lives and romantic relationships. In a pair of songs released in 2008, "Single Ladies (Put a Ring on It)" and "If I Were a Boy," Beyoncé encouraged men to commit to marry their long-term girlfriends, and criticized the double standard that allows men to care little about their appearance, hook up with little fear of repercussion, and take their female partners for granted.

Run the World (Girls)

"Run the World (Girls)" was released in April 2011 from Beyoncé's album *4*. Continuing in the vein of earlier songs like "Independent Women." Beyoncé's "Run the World" celebrates the increasing number of female college graduates who are taking over the world, and working mothers whom she portrays as strong women who can give birth and also be successful in business. She praises men who love and support educated, independent women.

In the video for "Run the World," Beyoncé rides on horseback into a depressing, post-apocalyptic world that resembles a scene from the movie *Mad Max*. A large, racially diverse crowd of women assembles behind her, wearing the only bright colors in this bleak, dusty scene, while she is flanked by a pair of male dancers. As they are approached by a seemingly aggressive group of men, Beyoncé states that the girls are in charge. The men appear confused and surprised as Beyoncé drapes her arms around them while pickpocketing one of the men. Later, the women (in bright, flowing dresses) and the men (in riot gear, complete with shields) charge toward one another, but the men stop and watch in amazement as Beyoncé informs them that she can build countries through dialogue and love—not, we can assume, through violence. At the end, Beyoncé rips a badge off the vest of one of the men and places it on her own chest as all the women salute.

While the messages in "Independent Women" and "Single Ladies" encourage women to be financially independent and to demand support and respect from their partners, these messages are also highly heteronormative—that is, they discuss only heterosexual relationships, and emphasize women's empowerment while still within traditional gender roles. In "Single Ladies," men are cautioned that they should propose before their long-term female partners find another man who will. In "Independent Women," the lyrics describe a woman who bought her own house and car, but most of the things she has bought for herself such as shoes, clothes, jewelry, and diamonds are stereotypically feminine.

In "Run the World," Beyoncé tries to move beyond this focus on traditional, stereotyped gender roles. She emphasizes women's power, strength, and intelligence, and reminds girls that they can indeed "run the world." But the highly sexualized dance moves and outfits in the video—including Beyoncé crawling between a man's legs, women on all fours while thrusting their bottoms rhythmically into the air, and backup dancers dressed in bras and skirts or corsets and fishnet stockings, all while men stare at them in awe—suggest that the male gaze upon women's sexuality is the reason for women's power.

Unlike "Bitch Bad," which challenges misogynistic words and actions in pop culture, or "Born This Way," which celebrates love and acceptance regardless of sexual orientation, gender identity, race, or other differences, "Run the World" presents a message that is simultaneously encouraging and largely noncontroversial. Some reviews of "Run the World" note that the song is one of Beyoncé's "most empowering and authentic" and proclaim that "Beyoncé is a role model for women all around the globe" (MTV UK, 2013), but others, such as a blog post from *Ms. Magazine* about the "Run the World" video, take a more critical approach calling the video "clichéd" and a "sexual spectacle." Additionally, some have taken issue with Beyoncé declaring herself a modern-day feminist. Reflecting the divisions and disagreement within the modern feminist movement, she has been criticized for actions that some observers view as counter to feminist goals (Cubarrubia, 2013). Beyoncé argues through her words and music that being a feminist does not mean that women cannot want marriage, children, or traditionally "feminine" things; her vision of feminism seems to focus on empowering women to go to school, have a career, and be able to support themselves financially.

This is not to say that "Run the World" does not make important contributions to the women's movement; in fact, it helps in raising consciousness of both women's achievements so far and the struggles that still exist. In 2013, Beyoncé became a founding member of the "Chime for Change" organization which is "[a] community of people working to promote Education, Health and Justice for every girl, every woman, everywhere" (Chimeforchange.org). Essentially, Chime for Change serves as a massive fundraising project where organizations and non-profits can post their need for donations and people can search a website to help fund different projects. Education is a key component of Chime for Change, particularly because, as of 2013, there are 57 million children in the world who do not get to go to school at all, and many more who learn in unsafe or otherwise poor environments (A World At School, 2013). Most of those children are girls. In some parts of the world, it is very dangerous for girls to go to school; Malala Yousafzai became an activist for compulsory free education for all children after she was shot in the head by the Taliban in her home country of Pakistan as retaliation for her work toward girls' rights, including their right to an education. In the United States, about 3% of girls dropped out of high school in the 2009-2010 school year (Stillwell & Sable, 2013).

Beyoncé's music teaches a message of empowerment but, unlike Ani DiFranco, that empowerment occurs largely within existing gender norms. Despite this criticism, however, the song's message serves as a rallying call, encouraging women to continue the fight for access to education and for social, cultural, and political empowerment.

Conclusions

Almost all social movements say that at least one of their goals is to educate the public about some problem in society, and to encourage people to take action to solve the problem. These movements are engaging in consciousness-raising and often they use music to accomplish this. In many ways, this was what Lady Gaga is attempting to create with the Born this Way Foundation by making things like counseling and support services available alongside educational and fundraising opportunities. Consciousness-raising music may be endorsed by social movement organizations (like "Solidarity Forever," which was written for the IWW) or it may be created by others who support the movement (like the pop songs we have discussed). Either way, these songs ask everyone who hears them to think more deeply about social issues like workers' rights or women's rights. The feminist movement has a long history of using music to inspire, to teach, and to celebrate women's victories. Songs like "Which Side Are You On?" situate the feminist movement within a larger framework of social justice activism, while "Bitch Bad" uses intentionally controversial language to encourage listeners to think about how women are portrayed in popular culture, and "Run the World" celebrates women's achievements and the power they have earned.

Questions for Class Discussion

1. In "Bitch Bad, " Lupe Fiasco argues that a term frequently used in a demeaning way toward women can instead become empowering. Do you think that this shift in our language is possible? Is Fiasco's redefining of the word "bitch" a good solution to the problem of sexism in rap music?
2. Think of a song you have heard recently, or a video you have watched, that portrayed women in a positive way. How did it make you feel? What specific messages did the song send about women?
3. Ani DiFranco's "Which Side Are You On?" discusses many issues, not just sexism. Either by reviewing this chapter or listening to the song, list the issues she mentions in her lyrics. How are these issues related to gender? What other examples of social inequality do they provide?
4. Think of some examples of feminists in music, television, movies, or other media. What makes these people/characters feminist? How does feminism connect with pop culture?

5. As we have discussed, music can be a very powerful tool for a social movement. Taking another perspective, brainstorm a list of possible obstacles or drawbacks to music that is used to raise consciousness. How might social movements overcome these problems?

References

A World At School. (2013, July 12). *About us and our mission.* Retrieved July 12, 2013, from aworldatschool.org: http://www.aworldatschool.org/pages/about-us

Bertrand, M., & Hallock, K. F. (2001). The Gender Gap in Top Corporate Jobs. *Industrial and Labor Relations Review, 55*(1), 3–21.

Blee, K. M., & Creasap, K. A. (2010). Conservative and right-wing movements. *Annual Review of Sociology, 36*(1), 269–286.

Brissenden, P. F. (1919). *The IWW: A Study of American Syndicalism.*

Butler, J. (1999). *Gender trouble.* New York, NY: Routledge.

Collins, P. H. (2000). *Black feminist thought: Knowledge, consciousness, and the politics of empowerment* (2nd ed.). New York, NY: Routledge.

Cubarrubia, R. J. (2013, April 3). *Beyoncé calls herself a modern-day feminist.* Retrieved July 11, 2013, from rollingstone.com: http://www.rollingstone.com/music/news/beyonce-calls-herself-a-modern-day-feminist-20130403

Earl, J., Martin, A., McCarthy, J. D., & Soule, S. A. (2004). The use of newspaper data in the study of collective action. *Annual Review of Sociology, 30*(1), 65–80.

Feigenbaum, A. (2005). 'Some guy designed this room I'm standing in': Marking gender in press coverage of Ani DiFranco. *Popular Music, 24*(1), 37–56.

Frith, S., & McRobbie, A. (1978). Rock and sexuality. *Screen education.*

Futrell, R., Simi, P., & Gottschalk, S. (2006). Understanding music in movements: The white power music scene. *The Sociological Quarterly, 47*(2), 275–304.

Goodwin, J., Jasper, J. M., & Khattra, J. (1999). Caught in a winding, snarling vine: The structural bias of political process theory. *Sociological Forum, 14*(1), 27–54.

Huffington, C. (2013, February 2). *Top job for women is secretary – The same today as it was in 1950.* Retrieved May 24, 2013, from The Huffington Post: http://www.huffingtonpost.com/2013/02/01 /top-job-for-women-secretary-same-as-1950_n_2599560.html

Leonard, M. (2007). *Gender in the music industry.* London, UK: Ashgate Publishing, Ltd.

McCammon, H. J. (2003). Out of the parlors and into the streets: The changing tactical repertoire of the US women's suffrage movements. *Social Forces, 81,* 787–818.

MTV UK. (2013, June 2). *Beyoncé calls for girls to run the world at sound of change.* Retrieved July 12, 2013, from mtv.co.uk: http://www. mtv.co.uk/news/beyonce/383283-beyonce-calls-for-girls-to-run -the-world-at-sound-of-change-review

O'Brien, L. (2002). *She bop II.* New York, NY: Continuum Intl Pub Group.

Paxton, P., Kunovich, S., & Hughes, M. M. (2007). Gender in politics. *Annual Review of Sociology, 33*(1), 263–284.

Pedriana, N. (2004). Help wanted NOW: Legal resources, the women's movement, and the battle over sex-segregated job advertisements. *Social Problems, 51*(2), 182–201.

Pratt, R. (1990). *Rhythm and resistance: Explorations in the political uses of popular music.* New York, NY: Praeger.

Reger, J., & Staggenborg, S. (2006). Patterns of mobilization in local movement organizations: Leadership and strategy in four national organization for women chapters. *Sociological Perspectives, 49*(3), 297–323.

Sowards, S. K., & Renegar, V. R. (2004). The rhetorical functions of consciousness–raising in third wave feminism. *Communication Studies, 55*(4), 535–552.

Stillwell, R., & Sable, J. (2013, July 12). Public school graduates and dropouts from the common core of data: School year 2009–2010. Retrieved July 12, 2013, from U.S. Department of Education: http: //nces.ed.gov/pubs2013/2013309rev.pdf

Trier-Bieniek, A. (2013). *Sing us a song, piano woman: Female fans and the music of Tori Amos.* Lanham, MD: Scarecrow Press.

Valocchi, S. (2009). The importance of being we: Collective identity and the mobilizing work of progressive activists in Hartford, Connecticut. *Mobilization: An International Quarterly*, *14*(1), 65–84.

Weissman, D. (2010). *Talkin' 'bout a revolution*. New York, NY: Backbeat Books.

Welter, B. (1966). The cult of true womanhood: 1820–1860. *American Quarterly*, *18*(2), 151–174.

West, C., & Zimmerman, D. H. (1987). Doing gender. *Gender and Society*, *1*(2), 125–151.

Chapter 5
"As Seen on TV": Gender, Television, and Popular Culture
Jenn Brandt

Are you tired of long, boring discussions on the social construction of gender? Are you fed up with assignments that make no sense? Some days you feel like you will never get through your reading before class begins. Introducing "As Seen on TV: Gender, Television, and Popular Culture," the revolutionary new chapter that makes reading about TV almost as fun as watching it. The secret is a mix of historical context and contemporary examples that making learning about gender performativity a blast. You will be amazed at television's role in shaping attitudes about masculinity and femininity. Best of all, you will be learning information that is not only relevant to your coursework, but that you can also share with your family and friends. Here is how it works: read the following chapter, making sure to note relevant terms, trends, and theories. Then, using your very own patented critical thinking skills, reflect on the given examples, make connections to your experiences, and engage in media literacy for hours of enjoyment. Easy! *But wait, there's more!* Read now, and at the end of the chapter you will find handy questions for discussion and further suggestions for reading – absolutely free!

The "Golden Age of Television"

In the same way that "As Seen on TV" products can now be purchased online and in stores, TV viewership has crossed platforms and is no longer solely relegated to "traditional" television sets. While the average American spends over hours a day watching live television, increasingly people's viewing habits are adjusting to include watching *time-shifted programming* (such as DVR recordings) and *streaming programming*, whether on traditional television sets, tablets, or mobile devices. This shift in viewing habits reflects not only technological advances, but also the persistence of television viewing in popular culture.

A. Trier-Bieniek et al., (Eds.), Gender & Pop Culture, 103–120.

Early prototypes of what would become commercial television date back to the turn of the 20th century, with England's BBC beginning limited broadcast service in 1932. Although experimental broadcasting occurred in the United States in the early 1930s, it was not until the 1939 New York's World's Fair that Americans really got a taste of the medium that would come to transform the landscape of popular culture in the latter half of the 20th century. World War II delayed widespread manufacture, but by 1950 some 6,000,000 homes in the United States owned a television set, with that number reaching close to 60,000,000 by 1960. Programming during the early years borrowed from radio shows, with the broadcast networks NBC, CBS, and ABC also looking for new content that would shape the medium. During this period, sometimes referred to as the "Golden Age of Television," families, perhaps joined by neighbors and friends, gathered together around the set as viewing tended to be communal and the content family friendly.

Popular series making the transition from radio to television during the Golden Age include *The Goldbergs* (1949–1956), *The George Burns and Gracie Allen Show* (1950–1958), and *Father Knows Best* (1954–1960). As *The Goldbergs*'s creator, writer, producer, and star, Gertrude Berg was one of the first, and most successful, women in television. The series centered on her character Molly Goldberg, a Jewish-American matriarch living in NY tenement. With a few exceptions, the show mostly avoided serious issues related to the Jewish-American experience, instead focusing on more family-centered topics. The appeal of Molly Goldberg transcended religion and ethnicity, as she dispensed her loving, if at times meddlesome, motherly advice. The character's—and actress's—widespread appeal earned Berg the first Emmy Award for Best Actress in 1951, helping to cement the importance of the archetypal "mother" character in television programming.

Like Berg, Gracie Allen was another woman to successfully transition from radio to television stardom. As part of a duo with her husband, George Burns, Allen helped create the archetype of the lovable, but ditzy wife. Although quite shrewd offscreen, the running gag of the series was Allen's screwball antics played against Burns's "straight man." The pair realized early on that it was Gracie who got the laughs, and the series' humor centered on Allen's skewed logic and the inevitable misunderstandings that would result. Allen's character became the model for many daffy Hollywood wives, from Jessica Simpson's persona on *Newlyweds: Nick and Jessica* to the character of Gloria Delgado-Pritchett (played by Sofia Vergara) on *Modern Family*. Perhaps, though, the most famous TV wife to be influenced by Allen was Lucy Ricardo, played legendarily by Lucille Ball on *I Love Lucy* (1951–1957).

Television series during this time were regulated by the "Code of Practices for Television Broadcasters," and this moral imperative not only helped shape the broadcast content of the era, but also solidify America's perception and ideal of moral citizenship and the "nuclear family." The television code was in effect from 1951 to 1983 and mandated that, "Program materials should enlarge the horizons of the viewer, provide him with wholesome entertainment, afford helpful stimulation, and remind him of the responsibilities which the citizen has toward his society (para 10)." At this time, television was seen as a medium that had the potential to provide educational and cultural advancement in its daily reach into American homes. This meant that television during this era was devoid of the sex, crimes, and profanity that proliferate our screens today, and that clothing and attire was "within the bounds of propriety" and avoided "exposure or such emphasis on anatomical detail as would embarrass or offend home viewers." Children, in particular, were "protected" under the code, with strict prohibitions on violence and crime targeting or promoted to children.

The ideal of the nuclear family was strengthened post-WWII, and placed a premium on the image of the "white picket fence" family: dad as the breadwinner, stay-at-home mom, and two smiling and obedient children. This picturesque version of domesticity was *heteronormative* (the belief that sexual and marital relations are only "normal" when engaged in by two people of the opposite sex) in its upholding of the White, middle-to-upper-middleclass, and heterosexual family as the ideal. Unmarried, divorced, or same-sexed parents were absent from this landscape, as were most African Americans and minorities. While not necessarily an accurate representation of America at the time, television was key in promoting the *image* of domestic bliss. In order for this to be achieved, a very strict *gender binary* was observed. In general, men were seen as figures of authority and reason, with women portrayed as emotional, childish, and submissive by comparison. For example, as a radio broadcast *Father Knows Best?* (1949–1954) questioned the legitimacy of paternal superiority with the father, Jim Anderson, often sarcastic and gruff. In its transition to television, however, the series dropped the question mark—both literally and figuratively—and *Father Knows Best* (1954–1960) became an assertion of this developing medium.

While the television code maintained strong imperatives for moral decency, these, too, played heavily into developing gender constructions. When Lucille Ball's real-life pregnancy was written into *I Love Lucy* in 1952, the series was barred from using the word "pregnant." (One wonders what the authors of the television code would make of such family fare as *16 and Pregnant* and *Teen Mom*.) Yet, no eyebrows were raised when Ricky Ricardo (played by Ball's real-life husband Desi Arnaz) "punished" his wife by taking her over his knee and giving her a good spanking (as seen in the episodes "Lucy Plays Cupid," "The Ricardos Change Apartments," "Ricky's 'Life' Story," and "Ricky Loses His Temper"). In fact, domestic violence—real or threatened— was often seen as the punch line (no pun intended) to television's humor, such as with *I Love Lucy*'s spankings and *The Honeymooners*'s (1955–1956) Ralph Kramden's (in)famous lines to his wife Alice, "One of these days … Pow! Right in the kisser!" and "Bang, zoom … to the moon, Alice!" These depictions are troubling for a number of reasons. At a basic level, they reflect a normalization and acceptance of domestic violence at this time in history. All Kramden had to do was shake his fist and utter "Bang, zoom," and audiences knew he was suggesting that one of these days he was going to hit Alice so hard he'd send her to the moon. The fact that he never follows through on his promise does not make it any less disconcerting. He is still portrayed as the authority and within his right as a man and a husband to "reprimand" his wife as he sees fit. Similarly, although Ricky's spankings are played for laughs, they portray Lucy as a child and perpetuate the stereotypes of male dominance and female subordination. These depictions are made complicated, however, by the fact that Lucy and Alice often have the upper hand in their relationships, continually outsmarting their husbands. While Lucy's antics were forever meeting Ricky's disapproval, America loved Lucy. Though her character never makes it into show business (Lucy's desperate dream), Ball did, and this distinction speaks to the image of womanhood portrayed on television in contrast to the actual aspirations and accomplishments of female audiences.

The complications and tensions surrounding the feminine ideal in comparison to women's actual lives and experiences continued to grow and be more explicitly explored in television of the 1960s and 1970s. Samantha on *Bewitched* (1964–1972) and Jeannie on *I Dream of Jeannie* (1965–1970) provide two good examples of the nervousness surrounding women's growing empowerment. As a witch, *Bewitched*'s Samantha is endowed with a number of supernatural powers. Yet, she is willing to abandon her gifts in order to marry a "mortal" and live the life of a typical suburban housewife. The allure of magic, however, is hard to resist, and most of the episodes' plots revolve around Samantha's attempts to correct the mayhem caused by one of her magic spells. Similarly, *I Dream of Jeannie* revolves around a blonde, midriff-exposing genie (appropriately named Jeannie) and her attempts to please her "Master," Tony. Jeannie is hopelessly in love with Tony and her relentless devotion eventually results in their marriage. In both series, the female protagonists possess formidable powers, yet they choose to diminish and/or exchange their strengths in order to become happy homemakers. Like the Alice Kramdens and Lucy Ricardos before them, these women were constantly challenging gender norms, while enforcing stereotypes at the same time.

Although women enjoyed starring roles in sitcoms (however clichéd in their gender constructions), in 1952, 68% of the characters in prime-time dramas were male with this number increasing to 74% by 1973. Similar to the dramatic genres of film at this time—westerns, medical dramas, "whodunits"—these narratives were masculine in their narrative focus. Since these dramas were most often set in the workplace, women were relegated to the periphery in supporting roles (as victims, secretaries, nurses, and wives), while men were depicted as independent and integral in advancing the narrative plot. This "golden era" then, would become the age that defined many of the gender stereotypes that persist in television today. with men depicted as active agents—brave, stoic, and independent—and women as their dependent counterpoints—supportive, attractive, and ready to serve.

The 1970s: A Decade of Change

The influences of the Civil Rights movement, second wave feminism, and the sexual revolution of the 1960s slowly made their way to television. As the country's sentiments began to mature, so too did television's offerings. Television of the late 1960s and 1970s reflected the changing face of America, with genres defined, as the medium came into its own. By its definition, *genres* are a series of inventions and conventions that are refined over time and respond to audience expectations. Technological innovations not only ushered in the era of the colored television set, but also film and production advances that made the way for expanded news coverage and the refinement and development of genres such as children's television, soap operas, talk shows, and hour-long dramas.

As the Golden Age began to fade, American television was grittier, and matched the political turmoil of the American landscape during the Vietnam era and the Nixon years. One creative mind that dominated television in the 1970s and ignited a large shift in the style and content of programming was Norman Lear. A writer and political activist, Lear was responsible for the production of some of the most popular and memorable programs of the 1970s, including: *All in the Family* (1971–1979), *Maude* (1972–1978), *Sanford and Son* (1972–1978), *Good Times* (1974–1978), *The Jeffersons* (1975–1986), and *One Day at a Time* (1975–1984). Arguing against network censorship and discussing its effect on creativity, Lear (1972) dispelled the myth that Americans only want "escapism, entertainment, and fluff," and proclaimed it was "time to take a new direction in television. There is nothing to lose and everything to gain." Lear's vision entailed using television as a mirror for American society, a tool for exploring and changing not only how we looked at television, but also how we looked at America.

Under Lear's direction, television began tackling issues of race, gender, and class head on, and perhaps no show did this better than *All in the Family*. Set in Queens, NY, the show revolved around working-class husband and wife Archie and Edith Bunker, along with their adult daughter, Gloria, and her husband, Mike. As a bigoted, World War II veteran, Archie was politically at odds with his feminist daughter and his liberal son-in-law. As suggested by the show's opening theme song "Those Were the Days," Archie is reminiscent of a time where "girls were girls and men were men," and had little use for the changing times brought on by the counterculture revolution of the 1960s. Although Lear originally intended for the character to be unlikeable, America fell for the "loveable bigot," and over time Archie came to represent an aging generation of White, patriarchal, and conservative values called into question by the shifting political and social milieu. His appeal was based upon the fact that although his prejudices seemed to know no bounds, they were motivated less by hate and more by fear and confusion of the rapidly evolving social and political climate of America. The clash of values represented by Archie and Mike was reflective of the progression of American beliefs at the time, and Archie's gradual acceptance of those of other races, religions, and ethnicities provided a model of tolerance.

Other Lear sitcoms, such as *The Jeffersons, Sanford and Son*, and *Good Times*, placed a heavy emphasis on race relations, and provided the opportunity for a greater racial diversity of roles to be seen on television. For the first time, African Americans became the stars and focus of prime-time television series, reflecting the progress and gains of the Civil Rights movement. Similarly, *Maude* and *One Day at Time* mirrored the changing role of women in response to *second wave feminism. One Day at a Time* centered on the struggles of a newly divorced mom, Ann Romano, raising her two teenaged daughters, and *Maude* tackled women's rights alongside heavy topics such as alcoholism and mental illness. In perhaps its most famous storyline, the show's protagonist, Maude (played by Bea Arthur), decides to have an abortion after unexpectedly finding herself pregnant at the age of 47. In the two-part episode "Maude's Dilemma," after much soul searching, Maude decides to terminate her pregnancy. The episodes aired in November of 1972, two months before the landmark *Roe v. Wade* decision of January 22, 1973. While a small number of station affiliates chose not to re-run the episode, for the most part "Maude's Dilemma" aired without the controversy or fanfare that one might expect today. The progressive agenda and popularity of Lear's sitcoms mark not only an important time in television history, but serve as an interesting point of comparison to the character types and subject matters of current television programming.

All of this is not to say that television of the 1970s was a model of gender equality. While the types of roles available to women were expanding, quite often in their presentation they relied on sexual— and sexist—stereotypes. Similar to the *male gaze* that Laura Mulvey (1973) argued women are subjected to in film, women on TV were also primarily valued for their "to-be-looked-at-ness." Hence the rise of *jiggle TV* in the late 1970s. As a reaction to the social consciousness that dominated television in the early-to-mid-1970s, jiggle TV emerged as an escapist alternative, with uncomplicated plots and amped-up sex appeal. Characterized by female leads in tight revealing clothing, shows such as *Wonder Woman* (1975–1979), *Charlie's Angels* (1976–1981), and *The Bionic Woman* (1976–1978) appeared to depict women in positions of authority and power. The plots of these series, however, were often sexist, with their female leads taking orders from men and put in situations that focused on accentuating the jiggle of their breasts and buttocks, rather than their skills, resourcefulness, or minds. While contemporary viewers might find these depictions chaste compared to today's standards, they offered the first hint of the increasing sexualization that has become commonplace on television today.

Deregulation and Television of the 1980s and 1990s

The prominence and popularity of jiggle TV demonstrated how obsolete the television code had become by the 1980s. Under the Federal Communications Commission (FCC) a series of deregulation changes in the 1980s changed a number of restrictions related to media guidelines, limiting the control of the U.S. government in broadcast ownership. Guidelines for educational and non-entertainment programming were abolished, as were restrictions limiting the amount of advertising minutes per hour. Along with the remote control, VCR, and a proliferation of cable television networks, the landscape for television changed dramatically in the 1980s. MTV, QVC, and other "specialty" channels increased the number of offerings for American viewers. The growth in viewing options had networks rushing to fill programming hours while attempting to attract and keep viewers.

At the same time, however, this scramble for viewership left network executives less worried about the quality of programming and more preoccupied with the quantity of profits. No longer was television concerned with making good citizens—the goal was to make good consumers. Children's shows such as *He-Man and the Masters of the Universe* (1983–1985), *Transformers* (1984–9874), and *My Little Pony* (1984–1987) became vehicles for manufacturers to sell their goods, and these shows have continued to be recycled as toys, television series, and films for subsequent generations. Adults got a taste of the "high life" through shows such as *Dallas* (1978–1991), *Dynasty* (1981–1989), and *Lifestyles of the Rich and Famous* (1984–1995), which also have been updated and repackaged for contemporary audiences. From shoulder pads to big hair, the excess of the 1980s was magnified in all its glory on television.

"Baby boomers" were coming of age, and television reflected the tensions of the culture clash between the liberal ethics of the 1960s and 1970s, and Reagan-era conservatism. This cultural anxiety was played out on comedies such as *Family Ties* (1982–1989) and dramas such as *Thirtysomething* (1987–1991), and with the added dimension of race (though not explicitly addressed) on *The Cosby Show* (1984–1992). Female characters were more likely to have careers outside of the home (although they were rarely, if ever, seen engaging in their jobs) and men were portrayed with more emotional depth, but in many ways these shows were a return to the "idyllic" family constructions of the 1950s.

By the late 1980s, however, television programming started to move away from the nostalgia of family values and began to anticipate the social liberalization of the 1990s. Blue-collar and non-traditional families with strong female leads were featured on shows such as *Roseanne* (1988–1997) and *Grace Under Fire* (1993–1998), and *Murphy Brown*'s (1988–1998) 1992 out-of-wedlock pregnancy storyline made national news when then-Vice President Dan Quayle criticized the character and show for de-valuing fathers and glamorizing single motherhood. Meanwhile urban comedies such as *Seinfeld* (1989–1998), *Living Single* (1993–1998), and *Friends* (1994–2004) focused on successful, professional adults enjoying non-marital relationships and forming family-like units through their friendships.

111

The 1990s also marked an important milestone in television history when *Ellen* (1994–1998) became the first prime-time network sitcom to feature an openly gay lead actress and character. Played by comedian Ellen DeGeneres, character Ellen Morgan's coming out on April 30, 1997 signaled not only a cultural shift in the acceptance of homosexuality but also paved the way for future shows such as *Will and Grace* (1998–2006), *Queer Eye for the Straight Guy* (2003–2007), and *Modern Family* (2009–).

"As Seen on TV" – Gender and Television Today

Reflecting on the history of television provides the necessary context for understanding its place in popular culture and its continual role in presenting models for the performance of masculinity and femininity. While the average viewer is most likely unaware of the social construction taking place through television programming, its effects are internalized nonetheless. Indeed, a large part of the success and popularity of television is its ability to anticipate and respond to cultural concerns and audience desires, presenting them in a way that briefly satiates public need. The fulfillment is short-lived and illusory, however, which is what keeps viewers tuning back in week after week. In its capacity to shift with public sentiment, television helps to "normalize" emergent trends and lifestyle changes by presenting them alongside traditional and stereotypical representations. This is seen with the increasing prevalence of LGBTQ characters, from "style" shows with their reliance on the "fashionable gay" stereotype, to *Modern Family*, with its two-fathered family that is traditionally structured (Cam is a stay-at-home dad for the first three seasons), yet rarely shown as physically intimate.

Specifically, in regards to gender, television continues to rely on binaries, which posit men and women as complete opposites (think "men are from Mars, women from Venus."). These binaries do very little in the way of providing healthy models of masculinity and femininity, and they are often unrealistic and sexist in their depictions. Susan J. Douglas (2010) has argued that contemporary television operates on the notion of *enlightened sexism*, which is "a response, deliberate or not, to the perceived threat of a new gender regime. It insists that women have made plenty of progress because of feminism—indeed, full equality has allegedly been achieved—so now it's okay, even amusing, to resurrect sexist stereotypes of girls and women" (p. 9). Douglas contends that the gains of the women's movement have become part of the cultural landscape and that enlightened sexism functions as a means to undo the advances of feminism. Franchises such as *Law and Order* and *CSI* are prime examples of this mix of embedded feminism and enlightened sexism. Often using plots "ripped from the headlines," these crime dramas feature strong female investigators, medical examiners, and law enforcement officials alongside their male counterpoints. This professional equality has come at a cost though, as these characters are often single, childless, and/or incapable of managing to successfully "have it all." Further, women are disproportionally portrayed as victims on these dramas, often of sexual crimes. In both cases, these women (and programs) serve as warnings of the supposed "dangers" that women face in society.

Sexist attitudes are not only relegated to dramas; they often tend to be more obvious and prevalent on some of the most popular comedies today. In part, this has to do with an absence of women in leading roles on today's sitcoms. The Center for the Study of Women in Television and Film (2012) reports that while 45% of characters on contemporary dramas are played by women, the number falls to 10% for comedies. Considering that women make up 51% of our population, these numbers seem more than a little off. When you factor in that most of the women seen on television (regardless of the genre) are in their twenties and thirties, it becomes obvious that female *under*representation is a persistent force on television.

It is important to note, though, that television's presentation of sexist stereotypes offers problematic notions of masculinity as well as femininity. The popularity of "retrosexual" characters such as Charlie Harper (played by Charlie Sheen) on *Two and a Half Men* and Barney Stinson (played by Neil Patrick Harris) on *How I Met Your Mother*, speaks to society's acceptance of a model of masculinity that objectifies women and endorses men rejecting adult male responsibility. In its first 10 years, *Two and a Half Men* (2003–) has consistently been a weekly ratings winner, helping CBS dominate prime-time viewer ratings and become the most watched broadcast network in recent years. As

113

suggested by the complexity and subtlety of the program's opening lyrics ("Men, men, men, men, manly men, men, men"), the show is about men, specifically what makes a "manly" man. The premise of the first eight seasons revolves around the hijinks that ensue when Charlie's recently divorced brother, Alan, is forced to move in with Charlie. Joining them is Jake, Alan's adolescent son, who lives with his father and uncle part time. After Sheen's off-screen antics (which, in reality, were not that dissimilar to the behavior of his character) got him fired, the show killed off his character, bringing on Ashton Kutcher (of *That Seventies Show* and *Punked* fame) to play eccentric billionaire Walden Schmidt.

Charlie's influence on his young nephew is a large part of the show's humor. In the first season's episode, "Just Like Buffalo," eight-year-old Jake declares he wants to be a bachelor like his Uncle Charlie when he grows up, reasoning, "as long as I got someone to clean my house and some action on a regular basis, I don't need a wife." Worried about the effect his brother is having on his son, Alan chides Charlie, arguing, "Your sexist, manipulative attitude toward women just got into Jake's head, and he spewed it out in front of his mother's angry women's support group!" Charlie quickly diffuses the situation by asking if it is "a women's support group that's angry, or a support group just for angry women," shooting down his brother's accusation by relying on the stereotype of the "angry feminist."

This scene, and episode, is a prime example of how the series acknowledges—even celebrates—its own sexist attitudes, but presents them in a way that makes it seem okay. If we are all in on the joke, then no one gets hurt, right? Well, not so fast. At the start of the episode, we see that Charlie's behavior has an obvious influence on his nephew, which should remind audiences of how impressionable children (and viewers) can be. Then, as Alan confronts his brother, his own sexist attitudes are revealed when he refers to his ex-wife's "angry women's support group." The conversation shifts the blame—and humor—away from Charlie and onto Judith (Alan's ex-wife) and the stereotype of the "angry woman" (i.e., feminist). When Judith decides that Jake should no longer spend weekends with Alan at Charlie's, Charlie confronts Judith and the support group, ultimately winning the women over with his "charm." The episode's conclusion of the women's group singing and laughing at Charlie's home works to neutralize the show's sexist overtones. In the end, Charlie's mode of thinking wins everyone over, and the women's acceptance of Charlie's sexism gives permission to the audience to feel and do the same.

This pattern repeats itself throughout the series, with the "old hump'em and dump'em" attitude of Charlie serving as the series' dominant model of masculinity. Women, meanwhile, are sexualized, objectified, and/or reduced to caricatures of flawed femininity such as stalkers, ditzes, housekeepers, bad mothers, and alimony-loving ex-wives. Although not quite as egregious as *Two and a Half Men*, CBS's other hit comedy *How I Met Your Mother*, endorses a similar model of masculinity in the character of Barney Stinson. Barney's "Bro Code," with its number one rule "Bro's before ho's," is a running gag of the series, becoming so popular it was released as a book in 2008. Offering wisdoms such as "a Bro never cries" and "a chick has a free pass to slut it up on Halloween," *The Bro Code* relies on similar sexist stereotypes of women and men. Although the other male characters, Ted and Marshall, demonstrate more mature and sensible models of masculinity, their friendship with Barney offers a tacit approval of his behavior. The fact that Barney's sexism is not questioned, and at times is abetted, by the other characters—male and female—becomes another means by which this "bro" masculinity has become naturalized.

Even ensemble comedies such as *The Big Bang Theory*, while not outwardly sexist, still present models of masculinity and femininity that conform to stereotypical binaries, with the geeky brainiacs Sheldon and Leonard played against the beautiful but less intelligent and less successful Penny. When intelligent women are introduced on the series, such as Leslie and Amy, they are depicted as unfashionable and socially awkward. The show reaffirms the notion that a woman's real value lies in her appearance, and that happy relationships, not a successful career, are the ultimate goal for women.

As a pushback against women's strides for equality, perhaps no genre has been more successful or detrimental in its presentation of femininity than reality television. This label, alone, should give us pause and make us wonder how "real" the lifestyles are portrayed on these programs. Even with most people prepared to acknowledge the scripted and fabricated nature of reality television, there is still a willingness on the part of audiences to buy into the artificial reality of programs such as *The Hills*, *Jersey Shore*, and *The Real Housewives* franchise. Although masculinity is certainly distorted by these shows (i.e., *Jersey Shore*'s "GTL"), overwhelming women take the brunt of the abuse served up on reality television. Stereotypes are taken to an extreme level, with men reduced to their libidos and women *literally* judged on their appearance (*Toddlers & Tiara*, *The Swan*, *America's Next Top Model*), placed in "catty" competition with each other (*The Bachelor*, *Charm School*), or encouraged to demonstrate empowerment through consumerism (*What Not to Wear*, *Say Yes to the Dress*). Certainly there are some exceptions (*Project Runway*, *Top Chef*), but there are also plenty of shows whose titles say it all (*The Bad Girls Club*, *Bridezilla*, *Wife Swap*, *Here Comes Honey Boo Boo*).

One of the most successful examples of reality television programming is Bravo TV's franchise *The Real Housewives*. *The Real Housewives of Orange County*, which first premiered in 2006, recently had its 100th episode, and there have been multiple seasons of spin-offs in New York, Atlanta, Miami, Beverly Hills, and New Jersey, as well as a single season in Washington, D.C. At its inception, *The Real Housewives of Orange County* was inspired by the success of television series like Fox's *The O.C.* and ABC's *Desperate Housewives*. In its first season, episodes focused on life within the exclusive Orange County, California gated community of Coto de Caza and was marketed to be the "real" story of housewives and the Orange County experience. Subsequent seasons and locations have moved away from the gated community aspect of the show while still focusing on the lavish lifestyle of the women featured. Although ostensibly about "housewives," the women featured range from having never been married to divorced, alongside women who are happily (and not-so-happily) married. Further, most of the women work to varying degrees outside of the home, and the show rarely, if ever, portrays them in engaging is typical housewife activities (cooking, cleaning, schlepping kids to and from soccer practice).

Therefore, the model of "reality" the show is selling is marked by conspicuous consumption, and although the women are not placed in direct competition with each other, their feuds and obsession with youth and beauty fuel many of the series' "plots." Even as the women display outlandish behavior though, the franchise is fairly conservative in its treatment of gender roles. Orange County housewife Alexis Bellino refers to her husband as her "king," and New Jersey husband Joe Gorga discusses his "duty" to "educate" his wife, Melissa, when she steps out of line. In one of the more disconcerting exchanges on any of the installments, in the episode "Everything Is Coming Up Rosie," Caroline Manzo's son, Christopher (who once declared his desire to start a chain of stripper car washes), explains to his mother and siblings that he does not want daughters because, "If I have a girl, right to the church steps they go. Because from zero to ten, right, I need to make sure to keep the thing alive. From ten to twenty-five, I need to make sure it is not a whore." He then goes on to add that his sister, Lauren, was "fat" in her "whore years," and was, therefore, only a "blow job queen." Rather than being appalled by her children's attitudes toward sex, gender, and physical appearance, Caroline chuckles along with her kids as they laugh about daughter Lauren's weight and young women being either "whores" or "blow job queens." Although presented as a joke, Christopher's repeated sexist comments seem to draw no criticism from his family. Further, given Lauren's openness about her struggles with low self-esteem and body image (and her subsequent decision to undergo lap band surgery in 2011), this seems especially disturbing. The fact that Caroline regards her children's behavior and attitudes as normal is, sadly, one of the truest reflections of reality that the series offers.

Stay Tuned – The Future of Television Programming

Reality television's relationship to "reality" becomes further complicated when one considers the increasing participatory nature of these texts. For instance, each season of *The Real Housewives* ends with a "reunion special," which recaps the season with the housewives and features questions sent in by viewers. Further, in more recent seasons, social media has become an active component of the series with viewers "tweeting" comments via Twitter with the hopes of being featured in the "Social Edition" re-airing of episodes. Viewers, thus, have an active role not only in the reception of these shows, but also hold the women featured responsible for their actions and have the potential to influence future behavior.

The participatory nature of reality television also creates an opportunity for a national dialogue on attitudes toward gender, race, and sexuality. For example, viewers of the Internet live feed of *Big Brother 15* (airing on CBS during the summer of 2013) brought attention to a number of racist and homophobic comments made by more than one of the show's "Houseguests." Media outlets began reporting on the controversy and a petition was started on Change.org for contestant Aaryn Gries to be removed from the house because of her repeated offensive comments. Due in part to the media attention, two of the women were fired from their jobs as a result of their conduct on the show, demonstrating a progressively more vocal resistance to discriminatory behavior.

Reality television is not the only programming to benefit from increased media savvy. In addition to assisting viewer interaction, the Internet and social media also play a large role in television's shift toward *transmedia storytelling*. As evidenced by the success of AMC's *The Walking Dead* (2010–), television programming is not only getting more sophisticated, but is benefitting from the creation of storylines along multiple platforms. Although cable networks were at the forefront of this trend, more and more broadcast networks are using a variety of means to deliver unique and complimentary content in order to keep television relevant and current alongside rapidly evolving technologies. This shift also reflects a recent trend in viewing habits, with more and more individuals using services like Hulu and Netflix to "binge watch" television. As audiences are increasingly watching entire seasons (or, at times, series) in marathon viewing sessions over a period of days or weeks, the nature of television storytelling is beginning to adapt to accommodate these habits.

The quality and popularity of original programming from paid subscription cable networks such as HBO (*Game of Thrones, Boardwalk Empire*) and Showtime (*Dexter, Homeland*) has led to an increased sophistication in programming from a number of basic cable channels such as AMC (*Mad Men, Break Bad*) and F/X (*Nip/ Tuck, The Americans*). With Netflix's recent addition of original programming, (*House of Cards, Orange is the New Black*), expanded options in media and entertainment speaks to not only the relevance of television in popular culture, but also to the promise of more nuanced and complex programming on network television. These series provide a more refined level of entertainment by taking the time to develop the plot and storylines, making for more compelling narratives. This extended format also lends itself to greater character development, leading to multidimensional characters that move away from stereotypical depictions of masculinity and femininity. Higher production values, along with big name actors making the move to the small screen from film, mean that television is positioned to become even more sophisticated in the coming years. While the effects of these shifts on broadcast television remain to be seen, there is reason to be optimistic that the increase in options, alongside more media-savvy audiences, will create a climate of improved diversity in television programming.

Questions for Class Discussion

1. Use the Internet to look up some clips from television series such as *The Goldbergs, I Love Lucy*, or *Maude*. How is early television programming different than television today? In your opinion, is television programming today more or less progressive?
2. Should the National Association of Broadcasters have a code of conduct for television today? Why or why not? What types of "codes" or "values" might be addressed? How might this be different (or not) from our current ratings system for television?
3. Watch local or national television news broadcasts. When gender is discussed, what is said? How is gender presented via the way the broadcasters look, dress and present themselves?
4. What types of careers are highlighted and/or showcased on television today? Is there a gendered component to these depictions?
5. How real is reality television? What does this type of programming tell us about the "reality" of today?

References

Douglas, S. J. (2010). *Enlightened sexism: The seductive message that feminism's work is done*. New York, NY: Time Books.

Everything is coming up Rosie [Television series episode]. (2013). In Green, N. (Executive Producer), *The real housewives of New Jersey.* NJ: Bravo.

Lauzen, M. N. (2012). *Boxed in: Employment of behind-the-scenes and on-screen women in the 2011–2012 prime-time television season.* Informally published manuscript, Center for the Study of Women in Television and Film, University of San Diego, San Diego, CA.

Lear, N. (1972). *Network censorship and creativity.* Statement to the senate subcommittee on constitutional rights, Washington, D.C.

Lorre, C. (Writer), & Schiller, R. (Director). (2004). Just like buffalo [Television series episode]. In Aronsohn, L. (Executive Producer), *Two and a half men.* Hollywood: Columbia broadcasting system.

Mulvey, L. (1975). Visual pleasure and narrative cinema. *Screen, 16*(3), 6–18.

National association of broadcasters. (1951). *Code of practices for television broadcasting*, Washington, DC.

Chapter 6

Popular Movies that Teach:
How Movies Teach about Schools & Genders
Adam J. Greteman & Kevin J. Burke

Introduction

The frame is central to film. How a filmmaker frames a shot and edits those frames together influences what the audience sees, how what is seen comes to be known, and much more. The frame limns the visual field drawing the eye and the "I" into the film's action, its story, and what it hopes the viewer will take from the film. Of course, as film theorists and critics have shown, there is never one thing a viewer takes from watching a movie. Viewers make meaning of visual culture (e.g., film, television, video games, Internet memes), but what meaning(s) they make is not known beforehand nor can it be predicted. Rather, meaning (e.g., of what it means to be a boy or a girl or neither) emerges within a complex web of visual cues, past experiences–both traumatic and joyous–contextual variables and much more. Meaning is, in part, a surprise. Film then, in framing, sets up the viewer much like someone who might be framed for a crime. The film frames the moving images in the hopes of setting up the viewer to follow along in some desired way, feeling a particular emotion or thinking about some particular issue.

In the current chapter we seek to think through the ways in which films–popular films–have framed both gender and education. Particularly, we engage how gender is manifest in movies that take education (schooling) as their setting and subject. We focus on gender and education because it is in schools that children are often subjected to gendered norms, contest those norms in various ways, and become educated individuals on what it means to be a boy, a girl, or with the growing visibility of transgender youth, transgender. Additionally, it is in "school" that students–perhaps you our reader–learn or are learning about and through film. As this is an introductory text most likely being used in a school setting, it seems appropriate then to think about

A. Trier-Bieniek et al., (Eds.), Gender & Pop Culture, 121–149.

how film itself represents school spaces, not only gender, as part of the process of learning about these issues.

Our chapter will do two separate types of readings of popular film. First, we will look at how an exemplary popular film from each decade starting in 1960 through 2000 is situated within the history of education. The films we use are *To Sir, with Love* (1967), *Grease* (1978), *Ferris Bueller's Day Off (1986), Hairspray* (1988), *Dangerous Minds* (1995), and *High School Musical* (2006). In this first reading we want to illustrate how popular film exhibits mainstream ideas about schools and their relationships to other dimensions of social life. How, we will ask, has popular film represented the purpose(s) of education, the role of students and teachers, and discussed, through its medium, the state of public education? Second, we look at a more familiar way of reading popular film in relation to representations of gender. In what ways has popular film over the last five decades framed gender roles for young adults and provided viewers with ways of creating gender norms both in and outside of schools? Such topics are too large to offer a comprehensive argument since five decades of film offers a vast archive on representations of gender and school, so our approach here is to offer an introductory engagement to thinking through gender, education, and film by looking to exemplar films from each of the five decades. This allows us to provide an initial reading of the history of gender and education in popular films set in high schools while also providing a methodological approach to reading popular film.

Our purpose: Popular film, gender, and education

It is the impact of film (real and imagined) that concerns us in this chapter. We do not, in introducing film theory, gender, and education seek to convince you that film has a nefarious purpose to "dumb down the masses" or "white-wash history"–although films might be read in such a way–nor do we seek to convince you that film does nothing but entertain with a pleasurable purpose to "make 'em laugh"– although films might be read in such a way as well. Rather, we want to engage popular film to teach lessons about gender and education. To read films in various ways, drawing on various film and educational theorists, is to provide a heterogeneous way of engaging film and its contents and discontents. Film, for instance, can be read to expose its underlying ideology and how it builds upon racist, sexist, homophobic, etc. ideas (see Giroux & Pollock, 2010 for this approach). Or film might be read to show a different side–be that film's technical components (see Elsaesser & Hagener, 2009 for this approach) or its contribution to the development of a subculture (see Dean, 2009 for this approach). In this chapter then we will be reading a select film from each of the last five complete decades (1960s - 2000s) that will provide our "flashpoints" for thinking gender, film, and education. In doing this, we will offer a history of education and a history of gender–questioning if and showing how things have changed. We offer our reading not to expose underlying ideology or engage technical aspects of film, but to show how we might use film to think about our own experiences in the world as gendered subjects within a milieu of popular culture.

We focus on popular films from each decade because it is the popular film that the "masses" spend money and time on to see, either in the theater or at home. While popular film and culture have precarious positions in the academy, it is the popular that provides space and time to develop a critical acumen for reading the moving image. Bickford (2008) challenges the oft spoken "emancipatory" possibilities of popular culture while recognizing the importance of popular culture in contemporary 21st-century education. She writes that while "popular culture in education may afford equal opportunity to participate through wider accessibility" such participation is on "unequal grounds" (p. 46). The unequal grounds of participation highlight the challenges of inclusion, yet also rely on a quantitative conception of inclusion. Bickford's conceptualization of democracy seeks "truly inclusive democratic participation" that rests on, within political theory, the deliberative model of democracy. What this means is that for Bickford, the purpose of engaging popular culture, particularly film, is to cultivate habits of critical thinking while expanding "interpretive possibilities" that allow more voices to be included in deliberations (p. 66). She writes, "We need to be mindful of the myriad, contradictory, and changeable ways that power is exercised within popular culture to make our attempts at inclusivity more effective" (p. 67). Yet, we are unconvinced that the democratic potentials of film rest on a quantitative numbers game. Instead, we move slightly putting "inclusion in question" to follow instead the path of equality (Bingham & Biesta, 2010).

Bickford, while focusing on inclusion implicitly, relies on the presence (and eventual overthrow of) hierarchy. Following the work of Jacques Rancière, however, we presume an equality of intelligence that does not rest on the implicit hierarchy of Bickford and other critical thinkers, a hierarchy that still requires an intelligent teacher to "teach" students how to be "mindful." Judith Halberstam (2010) follows the insights of Rancière to develop her take on popular culture and how the popular, if thought through critically, might be read to teach rather queer lessons. There is, in fact she asserts, no need to follow some teacher. Rather, there is only the recognition of being in a relationship with others of equal intelligence in attempts to find one another's way in the world. For Rancière, teachers (including us, the authors) must recognize we have nothing to teach so that students rather than learning to follow, in fact, learn how to lead their own scholarly lives. So, we offer our engagement here as an introductory opportunity to think through and about education and gender using popular film as our grounding object. Don't follow us; lead with your own readings.

Traditional schools certainly teach all kinds of lessons. One helpful frame for approaching schooling comes in the form of examining curriculum critically. Educational scholars have long distinguished between and among the explicit, hidden, and null curricula. The first of these is that which is explicitly taught in classes (think subject matter); the second of these, from Longstreet & Shane (1993), makes reference to the barely submerged technologies of learning that shape a student's day: disciplinary expectations, organizational techniques, behavioral demands, etc. The null curriculum (Eisner, 1994) is that which is explicitly not taught. One might consider recent laws in some states that disallow teachers from discussing homosexuality in classes. Here we have a combination of that which cannot be 'taught' (that homosexuality exists, say) and is thus nulled, and that which is hidden in the curriculum (that being gay is somehow so abject as to be spoken of). The central point to take from these distinctions is that curricula all around us are teaching lessons whether we know it or not. The lessons of popular culture, taking our cue from Rancière, Halberstam, and others of a similar ilk ask us to give up following the pied piper and repeating his lessons in order to lead ourselves and our readers through a possible adventure of film that dissents from seeing popular film as either dumb or as liberatory in order to see it as both/and OR neither/nor OR something completely different.

We turn to the lessons of film then, popular film to be exact, to explore potential lessons, leaving open space for critique that furthers our lessons in directions unforeseen. How do *To Sir, with Love* (1967), *Grease* (1978), *Ferris Bueller's Day Off (1986), Hairspray* (1988), *Dangerous Minds* (1995), and *High School Musical* (2006) offer popular representations of schools and genders through the technologies of film, and in doing so allow us to learn not simply about gender or education or film, but about the constellation of effects and affects such issues bring about? How does our decade-by-decade examination of film illustrate the time of gender, the time of education, the time of film? After all, as Mary Ann Doane (2002) writes, "What the new technologies of vision allow one to see is a record of time" such that "the cinema would be capable of recording permanently a fleeting moment, the duration of an ephemeral smile or glance" (p. 3). Glances and smiles, affects and relations, violence and intimacy all come to be influenced by and influence difference–in this chapter particularly gender and the lessons viewers come to learn from and with this "time-based media" of popular film. Why, you might wonder, do we treat two films from the 1980s? The simple answer is that this was the decade when we as authors first came to consciousness in and through film and so perhaps we see this era as more formative and significant than it really is. Such are our frames, we fear, but we still find the movies interesting and perhaps representative.

On theorizing and seeing film

There is a long tradition of film criticism that engages gender. Feminist film theorists have exposed and re-thought the "male gaze" (Mulvey, 1975; Snow, 1989); worked through the lessons of the femme fatale (Doane, 1991); brought forward transgender bodies in film (Halberstam, 2005); and challenged the overwhelming sexism that exists in representations of the gendered body in horror (Clover, 1992), action (Tasker, 1993), and pornography (Williams, 1989). Additionally, educational scholarship has grappled with the pedagogical potential and problems of film. This work ranges from examining the educational film and its "mode of address" (Ellsworth, 1991; 1999) to the political issues of popular film (Kelly & Caughlin, 2011; Sealey, 2008), and the ways film, with particular attention to Disney, distorts history (Walker & Rasamimanana, 1993; Giroux & Pollock, 2010). We do not want to regurgitate this work, but mention it here to recognize the importance of such work in developing our own understanding and engagements with film, education, and the representations of gender. Additionally, such work provides a starting point for students to more fully explore film, gender, and pedagogy after the initial lessons this book provides.

Art Critic John Berger (1978) begins *Ways of Seeing* writing:

> Seeing comes before words. The child looks and recognizes before it can speak. But there is also another sense in which seeing comes before words. It is seeing which establishes our place in the surrounding world; we explain that world with words, but words can never undo the fact that we are surrounded by it. (p. 1)

You began and will continue reading this chapter through the words in front of you. But while reading, your eyes will go elsewhere and see the surrounding space. You will see the screen of your computer and how it is framed. You will see the tabletop and your lap. You will see your hands turning the page. But, you will read the word and the words you are reading are attempting to, just as film does, frame ways of thinking about (putting words to) your experiences with the moving image–in this case–popular films. Seeing (images) and reading (words) combined help orient us to the world. You might, in reading this chapter, realize that as you should watch these films that you should see them and figure out if you would put the same words to them as we do. This would be a good task in developing your own vocabulary for thinking through the representations of gender (or race, or sexuality, or so-on-and-so-forth) and education while also further orienting yourself to the world(s) in which you live, learn, and work.

We are, in the 21st century, no longer easily amused nor surprised by the moving image. Its history, while short, is long enough for it to now be normalized. People no longer leap out of the way of the on-coming train like they did in the early days of film (see Scorsese's *Hugo* for a popular representation of this part of filmic history) because the moving image is all around us. We live and breathe the moving image, literally watching it on handheld devices as we shuttle to and fro. And in seeing the moving image as we ourselves move about the world we are experiencing and receiving lessons. These lessons are not pre-determined, nor are they always tied up to intense intellectual problems. Sometimes such lessons are lessons in pleasure and release. Film is, after all, particularly with regard to popular film, a pleasurable medium that we use for entertainment and to "escape" the real world of moving objects and subjects. We become immersed within the medium and lose ourselves to the imagined worlds of film. Even as entertainment though, such experiences with popular film teach us while we teach film via our money.

The history of education through film: Lessons from the school body

Film has a history. Our purpose here is not to provide such a history but to use the six films mentioned above as historical flashpoints that allow us to think about and through gender and education. Merging histories of education and gender we want to illuminate the relationship between film as a medium and its representations of gender and education while providing readers with a method of reading film. As this is a text that seeks to "introduce," our chapter does not seek to offer a comprehensive engagement with film theory, gender, or education, but rather to offer a jumping-off point to further engage such issues.

Film as a medium started with an impetus to educate. Orgeron, Orgeron, & Streible (2012) note "Indeed, cinema's roots in the work of such scientific investigators, lecturers, and visual experimenters as Eadweard Muybridge and Etienne-Jules Marey would indicate that this capacity to education was part of the original impetus for the medium" (p. 9). Film has quite the history with education, but it is theatrical cinema that dominates film studies, including our own

127

chapter here. Indeed it is less the educational film that holds sway in contemporary education than the popular, theatrical film. As hooks (2008) argued such media is the (explicit?) curriculum of today and so we begin our own approach to reading popular film merging work in film theory, educational history, and pedagogical studies to offer, what are, we hope, interdisciplinary lessons on gender, film, and education.

Public education, generally, is a rather remarkable social institution. Its history is complex but its idea simple. How, in the emerging democracy of a place like the United States, do a people become educated? History shows how who gets defined as "people" impacts who has access to education, and so it makes sense that public schools remain a prominent and important social institution for understanding culture, nation, and humanity. This social institution has been, and continues to be, asked to do different, competing things. Educational historian David Labaree (1988) in his work on public education draws attention to three main purposes of education: preparing students for the work force (social efficiency), preparing students to move up the social ladder (social mobility), and preparing students to participate in the world (democratic citizenship). These purposes at different times contradict and contest one another, but nonetheless provide an analytic scheme for seeing the complex challenges education faces. And amidst these three purposes we have bodies–students, teachers, staff, and administrators–that grapple with making sense of not only content, but also how to relate to the self, the other, and the (perhaps) drudgery of school-time.

Various historians have offered more complete pictures of the history of American education (e.g. Urban & Wagoner, 2009; Labaree, 2010; Spring, 2010). For our purposes here, we begin with the 1960s to think through the constellation of issues relating to gender, film, and education. It is in the 1960s that social change is afoot as oppressed populations begin (or continue) their struggle for rights and recognition. Coming off of the Supreme Court's decision in *Brown vs. Board of Education* (1954), it is the public school that in the 1960s is challenged to help the transformation of American society. At this time, the Civil Rights, Women's Rights, American Indian Movement, Mexican American Movement, and Gay and Lesbian Movement, in different ways, challenged the educational establishment. In the United

States, the 1960s saw the student uprisings associated with Vietnam, the growing argument for bilingual education, the establishment of policies (e.g., Affirmative Action, Title IX) related to gender and racial equity, and President Johnson's war against poverty. Popular films in education from this moment on arguably never stray from using these issues to pull at the heartstrings or making "pathetic" (in the sense of pathos, rather than hopeless) appeals while teaching various lessons about the state of education. And it is to these films that we turn to offer both a reading of popular film for its representation of educational history, followed by the representation, and history of gender within popular films set in high schools.

To Sir, with Love

With the War on Poverty emerging in the 1960s, *To Sir, with Love*, while set in Britain, illuminates the challenges of poverty and the lessons from the Coleman Report that peer groups mattered. As Urban and Wagoner (2009) put it, "Poorer students performed substantially better when put into classes with higher-achieving students from more advantaged backgrounds" (p. 360). *To Sir, with Love*, while integrated racially, portrayed an economically homogenous group of students. Mr. Thackery (played by Sidney Poitier) had to teach his students lessons that were missing from their poor lives; these ruffians showed up late, in tattered clothes smudged in filth and smelling of poverty. Mr. Thackery–a Black American who had been educated as an engineer–becomes the figure who, like his students, has faced and continues to face challenges and struggles with the social world. But he has persevered and, rather than engaging the impossible structural issues of racism, sexism, and classism, he presents his students with rather practical ways to "get on" in the world. He teaches them the (middle-class) standards of being male or female and the standards it takes to get a job, echoing the eventual turn to curricular standards in education that emerges with real force in the 1990s.

Thackery's lessons romanticized becoming normal and sophisticated as he denigrated the students' culture and approach to one another. The purpose of schooling we see in this 60s flashpoint is to grapple with difference (primarily racial and economic) but to do so by preparing students for jobs they can acquire. These students are not going to be the leaders of the free world, but they will be prepared by Mr. Thackery to become workers who know the social cues and norms to engage in modes of production. And this purpose is fulfilled by the benevolent and disadvantaged figure of Mr. Thackery who through his own personal experiences "straightens" the hoodlum students up and becomes their Black savior. They graduate, having learned the lessons of school and he is left with the love they have given him.

Grease

While *To Sir, with Love* offers an example of a long list of teacher-as-savior films (*Dangerous Minds* which will be discussed later offers a similar story), it would seem that by the late 1970s the excess of the 1960s and early 1970s was giving way to the conservatism that emerges in the 1980s. Ronald Reagan (echoing his British counterpart, Margaret Thatcher), in his return to conservatism, himself noted that the two decades before his presidency were plagued by excess and a decline in morality. Grease is the word then and it is with the musical *Grease* that the unruly student gets his and her day in the spotlight. Teachers take the backseat as the cinematic audience is treated to a 1950s fantasy of "bad kids."

   Grease, released in 1978, highlights excess, both through its genre as a musical and its fantasy of a return to the 1950s. This return to the 1950s operates, we argue, in two ways. It can be read simultaneously as engaging the turmoil and "badness" of students in the 1970s while also wishing for a return to the 1950s when badness was, well, really not that bad. This nostalgia of education as-it-used-to-be is prominent in the work of Lortie (1975, 2002) who notes that often teaching and school are held hostage to an "apprenticeship of observation" where social actors assume they know what is best for education because they have experienced school themselves. Missing of course is any trenchant analysis of the difference between experiencing school as a student and administering at or teaching in a school; in the process contexts become homogenized. The ideas that emerge extensively in the 1960s regarding difference had yet to take hold in the 1950s and

White America could bask in the White high school dance and car culture that 20-plus years later is inevitably not as bad as it has become by the late 1970s, as the world continues to grapple with or makes sense of the student protests, race riots, and severe challenges to the neoliberal ideas that emerged in the 1960s.

Depending on how we want to read *Grease,* then, we are able to see that reading film depends on the purpose of one's argument. Viewers inevitably make meaning of film and that meaning relates to prior knowledge. *Grease,* released in 1978, in the immediate temporal presence of the 1970s speaks to the audience's cultural understanding of contemporary 1970 education. Yet, the film, set in the 1950s, allows the viewer to fantasize about a historical moment they 1) may have been a part of which allows the film to operate through nostalgia of "happy days" (the television equivalent of *Grease* that aired from 1974-1984) and 2) for the viewer to superficially project the "happy days" on the "bad days" that were 'present' in the late 1970s (remember that the 1970s saw two oil crises one in 1973 and one in 1979 that adds another layer on the idea of "grease"). The misbehaving students of the film operate simultaneously as students that were not as "bad" as students are today while also reminding us of the better days before the energy crisis of the 1970s. But, additionally for our purpose, the film also represents the state of public schools in the 1970s, particularly gender relations because of the film's temporal release in the 70s. Indeed the transformation of Sandy (played by Olivia Newton-John) from insipid bobby-soxer to leather-goddess is softened in its devilish import by the musical camp that outlines the film itself. All is well, in the end, because of the very real un-reality of a world where the bad kids sing their way through their delinquency and their delinquency turns out to be far less worrisome than the delinquency of the 1970s.

Hairspray

Yet, nostalgia can operate in a different way allowing the horrors of the past (as envisioned by critical thought) to be shown in a different light, empowering the different "other" rather than positioning the "other" as always victim. It is with John Waters' 1988 *Hairspray* that we see a take on the tropes of *Grease* yet in a way that is reparative and reads the past and educational possibilities. The teacher-figure is primarily absent from these films, as the focus remains on the students as the wheels of change. Tracy Turnblad (played by Ricki Lake), one of the key protagonists of the film, is simply unruly in Waters' nostalgically comedic engagement with the shift from the 1950s to the 1960s. In Baltimore and amidst calls for desegregation, Tracy is sent to "special education" where she meets like-minded dancers who also happen to be all African American. Special education in the film highlights special education's normative intentions as the "queer" bodies (non-White and "pleasantly plump") are put together to make mainstream classrooms safe for "normal" students. Engaging the "generational struggle" between parents and children, Waters' film highlights the coalitional politics established by dancing, illuminating for the viewer the ways in which different marginalized populations' struggles are intertwined.

It is in *Hairspray* where the fat White female student and African American students merge their powers to counter the racist, segregationist policies of their/our time. And this film emerges in US history as the coalitional politics of the queer movement are in full force, fighting the homophobic and segregationist political responses to the AIDS crisis. But Waters (2010) operates through humor noting "If we can laugh at the worst things that happen to us because of our sexuality, we'll be the strongest minority of all, proud to be illegal, proud not to be like everybody else. Instead of 'act up', I'm for 'act bad.' Let's embarrass our enemies with humor." Waters' film utilizes the politics of desegregation in the 60s to offer commentary on the politics of the 80s' refusing to "act up" to instead "act bad," to refuse to abide by the police order of the parental generation. His nostalgic return to the 1960s illustrates the political agency of youth at a time when queer youth once again were under attack by the normative regimes of a particular political administration. And this is done, queerly, to resist the growing calls for normalizing gay subjects. School, we see, is represented as a space of normalization, where much is pathologized, but Waters twists the lesson to show the need for students to act bad in order to challenge the injustices and normalizing techniques of the school.

Dangerous Minds

The 1990s see a return to the teacher-as-savior popular (education) film. With *Dangerous Minds* (1995) a whole new generation (not privy to the popularity of *To Sir, with Love*) sees the plight of a White female teacher trying to teach the unruly poor Black, Hispanic and White students of Los Angeles. Based on LuAnne Johnson's life as a school teacher, this film provides the viewer with a morality tale of a teacher going into foreign territory to, as seen in *To Sir, with Love,* provide love for students who have gotten very little love from schools. Set in the second-largest school district in the United States, *Dangerous Minds* emerges at a time when education writ large is facing the challenges of failure. Coming out of the 1980s and the inflated rhetoric of *A Nation at Risk,* this film helps illustrate the risks our nation faces, including our nation's (White, female) teaching force. Unable to control a classroom and in a school that seems on the verge of falling apart we see that it is the White female teacher who, like Sidney Poitier before her, brought standards to her kids. Teaching her students the basics and eventually winning them over, the film speaks again less to the broad social, cultural, and political issues of the 1990s choosing to hone in on a particular story that comes to re-affirm the belief that the "teacher" matters and that "teachers" can make the difference, despite the overwhelming poverty, racism, sexism, and lack of opportunity that students, in schools like that represented in the film, face.

We see in the film, when we can situate it historically, the growing arguments for "better teachers" that are able to get even the "worst" of students to learn. And learn her students do, so much so, that the film ends with the students teaching their teacher a lesson. This lesson is the one that gets LuAnn to stay for another year because she is, as the student's note "their light." The teacher–despite the odds, the lack of resources, and the reality of paying for things in her classroom out of her own paycheck–is appealed to, to stay. Had she left, she and the film would have failed but instead it ends with the promise that a teacher, giving herself over completely, can change the lives of her students. This, of course, is not in itself a bad message. However, when situated within the broader context of American public education the film normalizes the idea that a public school teacher can do more with less echoing the arguments from the Coleman Report of the 1960s. She can change lives without the resources argued for by critical educational scholars.

Perhaps more so, however, the film inadvertently highlights the need for alternatives to public education. After all, it is the 1990s and public education is in the midst of a growing assault against what critics of public education call its "monopoly." As market-based arguments for education come more to the forefront through arguments about vouchers and charters, *Dangerous Minds* comes to illustrate the failing of a public school despite the success of one classroom teacher. As Urban and Wagoner (2009) write, regarding the mixed success of the educational reforms of Ronald Reagan and George Bush Sr., "they did succeed, however, in curtailing and sometimes reducing federal educational spending, in raising concern over moral education and school violence, and in sustaining a nationwide momentum for school choice plans" (p. 401). And these reform agendas have not left education since, as seen in the market-based policies of Bill Clinton, George W. Bush, and now Barack Obama. We will return to this history in our conclusion.

High School Musical

Yet, while the minds of youth can be dangerous as can public education we see a shift from the teachers-as-savior films to high school as musical fantasy in *High School Musical (HSM)*. Originally a made-for-TV movie, *HSM* shows a happy multicultural "urban" school where teachers and students get along and succeed with all the pesky issues of poverty, racism, and lack of opportunity no longer visible. The dream of multiculturalism seems to have come truc in this Disney-fied musical fantasy about contemporary American public schools. Similar to *Grease* in genre and *Hairspray* in focus on student agency, *High School Musical* takes place in a high school but the disciplinary curriculum is nowhere to be seen. Instead, the film highlights the social aspect of education in the first decade of the 21st century. Situated in the age of the Internet and the growing ubiquity of online learning, *HSM* more so than the other films here, completely ignores learning school lessons. The film is less about 'knowledge' (the epistemological project of education) and more about relationality or how people relate (the ethical project of education). The film provides evidence of a shift away from a focus on school learning in schools. School is neither dull nor exciting to these musically-inclined students. Rather it is the backdrop for socializing and coming-into-presence as students struggle to admit their multiplicity of desires, seen most aptly in the musical number "Stick to the Status Quo" where the students reveal their other desires (e.g., a jock that likes to cook; a nerd that likes to break-dance; a stoner that plays the cello) and are told they should "stick to the status quo." Yet, the secrets they share reveal simultaneously how Disney has watered down the challenges of meeting in schools and allowed the genre of musical, connected to the realm of fantasy, to remove us from the challenges of 21st- century education.

The viewer is left with "feel-good" goose bumps as the film ends: catchy music meant to make school, finally, trendy and cool. School has become, as we see in this film, less about engaging the systemic issues of inequality or the content students should learn, and more about highlighting successful socialization. Schools can, in fact, be successful and students can, in fact, graduate, although with what content we are unsure. No child has been left behind in this musical as the viewer is shown the struggles of high school students who even if trying to go against the status quo are not beaten or bullied, but are instead embraced for their differences. The film might, we see, illustrate through its fictionalized status what becomes documented in *2 Million Minutes* (Compton, 2008). This educational documentary illustrates how American high schools students are falling behind their peers on the global scene with regards to test scores. Instead, the viewer sees in this documentary what viewers also saw in *HSM*, which is that American students spend much less time doing school work while spending extensive time being busy with extra-curricular activities, jobs, and socializing. David Labaree writing on *2 Million Minutes* argues:

As we have seen, American schools are not terribly effective at turning out graduates with a deep command of the academic subjects in the elementary and secondary curriculum. Our test

135

scores internationally are at best in the middle of the distribution, which shows that other school systems are consistently more effective at teaching this material. But it is not clear that accumulating this kind of academic knowledge is particularly useful. For during the same period in the latter twentieth century that U.S. test scores were mediocre, U.S. economic development was stellar. (pp. 218-219)

High School Musical, then, might be seen as singing its way to pose the question if school matters for content or if it is the other aspects of adolescents' lives that provide a much more pleasurable and perhaps even relevant educational experience? Charles Bingham (2011) argues that "Relationality is much more central to the educational endeavor than what we learn or how we learn it," exposing and exploring the affective bonds of education (p. 517). While we could offer a reading that challenges *HSM* for any number of reasons, we can also, as we have done above illustrate how it–both through its genre as musical and its content–illustrates the affective and relational challenges of education in an age where knowledge is ubiquitous.

We see through a brief engagement with these five films then the ways education itself has been framed and reframed through popular film in order to illustrate particular ideas or components of the educational endeavor. With this, we move to how popular films about schools also teach us about gender, its history, and the way gender "goes to school."

Gender: A brief (insufficient but interesting) tour of theory and history

Jean Baudrillard (1994), in an early (and prescient) theoretical treatment of 'reality' television suggests that much of how we view the world through the scrim that becomes media is rooted in the notion of simulacra, a copy of something that never existed. Edward Soja (1996) uses something similar when he writes of Thirdspaces; for our purposes it's useful to think about something like Epcot Center: here you have a simulacrum of various nations, all thrown together in one space that comes to represent a kind of homogenized and sanitized reality that stands in for cultural authenticity. Important for our quick and dirty foray into gender theory, though, is the notion that for Baudrillard (1994) this simulated 'reality' is "a question of substituting the signs of the real for the real" (p. 2). Or "everywhere socialization is measured by the exposure to media messages. Whoever is underexposed to the media is desocialized or virtually asocial" (p. 80). At this point, then, it's less important if you have seen the specific movies we are analyzing here than it is that you have seen movies at all (and reality television and other forms of media) because the notion of coming-to-be that we are proposing is about being exposed to a form that then subjects us to messages which we take as some form of the real (and thus act accordingly in response, rejection, acquisition and/or interpellation). The idea is that, in some sense, movies both react to eras and create them; as such teachers and schooling as reflected and constructed in the various movies above are run through by discourses of gender and possibility, sexuality and improbability that are historically specific. We need to touch just briefly on discourse and then we'll dig into the ways in which theories about gender have (been) changed (by) us along the way. We use movies as emblematic of this work, and particularly movies that are centered in or on schools, most especially because schooling is the great socializing agent in American society; it is, too, a form of media. Popkewitz (1997) argues that the kind of citizens a society wants can be found in the curriculum perpetuated in its schools. We would argue that, to a degree, this can be extended to the movies it makes popular about its schools and in particular about how those movies address gender.

Discourse

Fendler (2010) argues that Michel Foucault considered discourse to be everything that is accessible with the individual mind. That which is accessible, of course, is always filtered by our experiences and the institutions (like schools, say) that in/de/reform the ideologies that we encounter in our daily existence. Here we are entrenched in the post-structural, third wave of feminism that sees the subject constructed through language, though not reduced from its materiality as a result (Butler, 1993, p. 5). This allows us to better understand the notion that a "feminist critique ought also to understand how the category of 'women,' the subject of feminism, is produced and restrained by the very structures of power through which emancipation is sought" (Butler, 1990, p. 4). You will notice that we have made a quick shift from discourse to power here. This is not an elision of duty in explaining discourse because "the juridical structures of language and politics constitute the contemporary field of power; hence there is no position outside this field, but only a critical genealogy of its own legitimating practices" (p. 7). Yes, you say, but so what? The point here is to help you note that in contemporary gender theory, all that we see of what it means to 'be' a man or woman or cisgender or transsexual or anything that can be categorized (even while resisting definition) comes from the discourses that surround and define us and indeed delineate what gets to be a category. Schools institutions that alter and affix those definitions and categories and movies are cultural markers that both transmit notions of power and possibility while also challenging these very notions. It's all very slippery of course, but that's the fun of studying this sort of thing. For now, though, let's think about history again in relation to the possibility of presenting (as) a gender. The goal of this section, in the end, is to give you the analytical tools to do your own analyses of film (and other texts) for the ways in which gender might be read into, out of, and through them.

Simone de Beauvoir (1989) is most well known in the cultural zeitgeist for her simple (but not simplistic) assertion that "one is not born, but rather one becomes a woman" (p. 301). The same, of course, can be said of the process of 'becoming' a man. Vital for us here, though is the idea of performativity. Outlined by the sense that "as a shifting and contextual phenomenon, gender does not denote a substantive being, but a relative point of convergence among culturally and historically specific sets of relations" (Butler, 1990, p. 14), gender is, then, (to quote another very famous line) "the repeated stylization of the body, a set of repeated acts within a highly rigid regulatory frame that congeal over time to produce the appearance of substance, of a natural sort of being" (p. 33). So in a performative sense, we may well 'perform' a gender (as on film) through the ways that we walk or talk or dance or dress, but these performances are caught up in a cultural web of discourse that makes those actions intelligible for the readers (our friends and families and enemies, etc.). We can choose our actions, but those choices are always already constrained by what is available to us based on our own socialization (and imagination) and our audience then can choose to read us from a perhaps limited range of possibility as well. Which means that, as we look back on films about schooling, we are being affected not only by the visual cues in the movie, but also by our own histories about what is possible in school and what is probable or likely in terms of how gender (in this case in particular) should look or act or present. This isn't something we ever get to the bottom of; we just need to try to account for these experiences in our readings as much as possible. Fair enough? OK. Onward.

Masculinities

Early gender research didn't talk much about men. Much early moral and psychological work was done on and with men in mind as they were assumed to be the universal norm. Men didn't, in other words, have gender while women, in an inferior sense, did and because to be male meant to be more rational and more highly formed, that which was considered normative was male (and straight and White). Much of this was rooted in ancient Greek notions (from Aristotle, among others) that women were just malformed men(!) So, first and second wave feminist work wrote and spoke and protested against the hegemonic power that was maleness through an assertion that women were equal in their humanity and then explicitly different in it. The study of masculinities came later to the game of critical research. Generally speaking it was RW Connell with the book *Masculinities* (1995) who started looking at the ways in which third-wave and post-structural accounts of gender might actually be used to expose and interrogate what it means to be and become a man. There are other accounts that are roughly contemporary here including Mac an Ghaill's *The Making of Men* (1994) and Harris' *Messages Men Hear* (1995) which suggest that there was something of a boomlet in the middle nineties in examining the becoming of masculine agency. These tomes, however, might have been in direct response (if not rebuttal) to Robert Bly's (1990) book *Iron John* which suggested a primitive essence to manhood that could be recreated through retreats into nature by way of hooking back into the primal (and often violent) maleness that was a part of the collective unconscious of manhood. We mention these books to suggest the start of the outlines of a field of masculinity studies (as well as for further reading should you be interested, dear reader) but also as a way toward examining shifts in masculinity as read through the movies previously examined. Connell (1995) notes that ultimately "it is the group that is the bearer of masculinity, in a basic way" (p. 107). If we are to believe that, then it's worth looking at the ways in which males act in groups in schooled settings: What are the conditions of their actions as set and de/limited by school policies, by social norms?

In this sense, we can think about the confrontations between Sidney Poitier and his erstwhile students through the first hour and change of *To Sir, with Love* as rehearsals of certain kinds of masculine agency and the enacting of stereotype. Willis (1981) writes about working-class British students who set their identity against authority (in the form of schooling and particularly teachers) who symbolize bourgeois ideals they don't see as possible for themselves, but also as an exercise of resistance to the kind of docile acquiescence to the broader (and conservative culture) that actively devalues their dying brand of (factory) work. It's interesting to note, in particular, that Poitier, in eventually winning over his charges through the belittlement of their cultural norms and the conversion of his students to a more regimented and conciliar style of learning, is a Black American man teaching in England. The point being, of course, that such a movie would not have been possible if set, at the time, in the southern United States. In this sense, the studio has taken the charge out of menacing Black masculinity, long a symbol of the emasculation of the White, southern male (Pinar, 2001) by placing the character into the much less well-defined (for American audiences) and thus more generic, London 'slums.'

In *Grease*, it's worth noting the performances put on by the male characters both in public and in private, in same-gendered and cross-gendered spaces. Pascoe (2007) writes about the specter of the fag, which outlines much of heteronormative (and homophobic) interaction between and among males in high school and beyond. Fag discourse, she notes, "is central to boys' joking relationships" (p. 60) through which "boys discipline themselves and each other" (p. 54). Cameron

(2006) observes something similar in college-aged men where "'gay' refers in particular to insufficiently masculine appearance, clothing and speech" (p. 66). One way to avoid the specter of the fag, of course, is to 'prove' through sexual prowess, that one is imminently heterosexual. Kimmel (2008) notes "Guys hook up to prove something to other guys. The actual experience of sex pales in comparison to the experience of talking about sex" (p. 206). We need only, then, think about the ways in which the song 'Summer Nights' tells us not only a great deal about the imagined masculinity of fifties rebel culture, but also of the coming to a close of sexual enlightenment and free love in the seventies. As both gender-segregated groups sing (and dance) in choreographed ways celebrating (and interrogating) Danny's and Sandy's reminiscences about romantic engagement in the halcyon light of faded summer irresponsibility, we get two emergent stories all rehearsed in school spaces: the outdoor cafeteria and the football stands. Note that as each character is urged to 'tell more' (hooking up, after all, being about the story), Sandy sings of innocent times flouncing along the beach and holding hands while Danny is goaded to tell his peers if he got "very far" sexually. While Sandy wryly sings of flirting, Kenickie, in a different space, wants to know if "she put up a fight," a troubling allusion to potential rape which Danny accedes to slightly by alluding to her getting "friendly down in the sand." Note the fixing of two very different ways of talking about "loving" in gendered spaces, but note, too, the ways in which the school remains the background for these tales of sexual "enlightenment."

Pascoe (2007) writes of the "unofficial sexuality curriculum" (think of the hidden curriculum mentioned above) in high school, which requires adults to be both patently disinterested and highly interested in the sexual lives of their students. Dating rituals are rehearsed at dances, appropriate clothing is mandated, often based on the limitation of skin (for girls generally), and adults are required to affix a disapproving gaze on student bodies that are at once sexualized for the sake of de-sexualizing them. The point is: school is where the rehearsal of sexual narratives happens, and particularly in *Grease*, this happens in song in one of the most iconic numbers in American theater and film, and the viewer is positioned as observer to either approve or disapprove, simulating the gaze of teachers and parents in various spaces.

In *Ferris Buehler's Day Off* we get something of a different message, for (and through) the young men involved at the center of the action: Ferris and his recalcitrant friend, Cameron. Adams (2008) reminds us that "masculinity has long been defined by what it is *not*" (p. 8) and thus often what is defined as preferred in popular culture is "associated" in contrast to "overcivilization and emasculation" (p. 11). Kimmel (2012) traces various waves of culturally acceptable forms of masculinity in mainstream American society but, generally speaking, concludes that culture has long devalued what we might call the fop, the fey, the metrosexual. Because the danger of the abject is that the boundaries of difference might fail to prove ontological, improper performances of gender must be properly devalued, if not punished. Indeed because "masculinity" is "increasingly an act, a form of public display...men felt themselves on display at virtually all times" (p. 75). And the best way to perform properly is to "learn early to mask one's vulnerability behind displays of toughness" (Messner, 2002, p. 51) and cleverness: to dare and to rebel. And so it is that we have our hero, the intrepid puck, Ferris (and his beautiful girlfriend) juxtaposed against Cameron, the bummer, the ill, the recalcitrant man who thinks of *consequences*. He is physically and mentally frail, cowed by his sinuses and a depression about his family situation while Ferris alights atop the day through his pluck, his moxie and his derring-do. The message is fairly clear, even though Cameron achieves something of a catharsis with the destruction of his father's ultra-modern house and his vintage car, that men ought to be the impish Ferris rather than the timid Cameron. Sloan (as with Ferris' shrewish sister) does not give us much to go on which is no accident in this film about male bonding through the avoidance of school. What could we possibly learn, after all, in Ben Stein's classroom? Anyone? Anyone?

The teacher-savior

To look at *Dangerous Minds* and *High School Musical* we'll step away from the masculinities literature and further into more works by feminists of the second and third wave. The point of the shift is not to say that these two movies have less to do with the enactment of masculinities, but to demonstrate, as noted in the introduction, that lenses and approaches matter for how we frame our viewing. A purposeful shift here is to signal how one might think about doing different kinds of gendered readings of films about schools.

Michelle Pfeiffer's character in *Dangerous Minds* comes from (and has spawned) a long line of teacher-saviors, generally White and female, bent on altering the terrible lives of inner-city and minority youth. The paternalism (perhaps maternalism) of this sort of movie is addressed in a number of places, but we want to focus on the notion that a film like this is both activist and deeply conservative. Though it may well demonstrate something like Lorde's (1984) "confrontation teaching" (p. 97) it still maintains a fairly traditional vision of what happens in schools: White women teach, poor and Black students from deficit-riddled homes resist until they realize that the teacher *cares* for them. The vision is a limited one whereby schooling (and the ministrations of a single heroic teacher, who simulates the White mother) becomes the instrument for salvation of students who otherwise would not have a chance. Or, if we think about it more broadly we can use Steinem; (1994) "economic systems are not value-free columns of numbers based on rules of reason, but ways of expressing what varying societies believe is important" (p. 204). In this sense, then, we can think about the social situation of the mid-nineties in the inner cities of major metropolises in the US. At the time, in the grips of the crack epidemic and suffering through the gradual demonization of the welfare queen of Reaganite (and later Clintonian) fevered imaginings, it became incumbent on schools to do more with less about the greatest travesties in the public eye. Enter the reincarnation of the republican mother (Rury, 1992), charged with investing the morals of the wider society into the youth, through schooling. Here Pfeiffer is certainly a sexier version than the young women called to serve in the Progressive Era but the implication remains; in a hard world, the White woman can best civilize (and save) the lowly savage (within).

In *High School Musical* something very different is being rehearsed. A precursor to a show like *Glee*, this heterotopic space (Foucault, 1986) is emblematic of a new "epoch of simultaneity…an epoch of juxtaposition" (p. 22) where crisis heterotopias (in this case schools, but particularly movies about schools) "are privileged…or forbidden places, reserved for individuals who are, in relation to society and to

143

the human environment in which they live, in a state of crisis" (p. 24). Note the safety of the choir room in *Glee*, where our resident freaks (single mothers, ostentatious gay boys, well-coifed male teachers, etc.) can let various flags fly, such it is, through song and dance in *HSM*. The very notion of theater as a gay space is blown up in an effort to show a sort of ecumenical high school experience where all difference is flattened out through choreography and song. Impossible, of course, in this version of the world, is a chance to stop and talk about the inner issues that might be affecting various characters. Why is it so odd to think a 'nerd' would want to break-dance, for instance? What makes that notion queer? As long as there's a beat to it, and pretty faces in front of it, the movies tells us, it matters little; just sing your way through and all will be well. If you can't grin and bear it in song, there's something likely wrong with you.

Conclusion, or, what's film got to do with it?

Education and gender, like film, are complicated and complex fields of study. The purpose of this chapter has been to offer an introductory way of reading popular films to think about how they (popular films) can be read to engage and learn about the complex history of gender and education. Of interest in this chapter has been how these popular films speak to, and about, the history of education and the history of gender in diverse and interesting ways. There are, of course, many other ways each of these films could be read and other popular films from each decade that would tell a slightly different story about the history of gender and education. That is a task you might take up; to slightly re-frame our focus here to tell a different story about education and gender as expressed through the medium of popular film.

We hope in providing an interdisciplinary reading that merges the history of education, film, and gender studies that we have provided a productive chapter for you to begin thinking about interdisciplinary scholarship that draws upon the popular and artistic, broadly construed. In the current decade, we can look to films like *Won't Back Down* or the documentary *Waiting for Superman* to see the continued use of popular film to document educational reform, history, and the role of gender in such debates. What these two films offer is an opportunity to see the continued assault on public education. Couched in language of choice and social mobility these films return us to the school as a space of knowledge acquisition and training ground for the nation's economic success. And this is done through a focus on women's roles in education and the plight of marginalized populations–read Black, Hispanic, and poor White families–to have the chance to succeed. However, as David Labaree argues, public schooling is a zero-sum game and as such someone has to fail (2010). Who fails has perhaps not changed much over the years, however popular film reveals, in what is seen and unseen, the complexity of education and gender and for those who might continue this project issues of race, class, religion, and much more.

Questions for Class Discussion

1. If you were to 'read' your experiences in schooling as a film, what instances related to gender, stand out? How can you make sense of these considering the kind of analysis we have done in the chapter?
2. Take another "identity category" (e.g., race, class, sexuality, religion) and work through a film you have seen recently thinking about how "x" is framed. What are problems the film presents? What are different ways of reading such a presentation?
3. Think across multiple identity categories and multiple films, discuss trends or common themes that you see in popular films representations of, for instance, Chicana, upper-class lesbians, White working-class men, straight Black men, Native American women? Who do you see represented more? Less? And what are the implications of such findings?

References

Adams, J. R. (2008). *Male armor: The soldier-hero in contemporary American culture*. University of Virginia Press.

Baudrillard, J. (1994). In S. F. Glaser (Trans.), *Simulacra and simulation*. Ann Arbor: University of Michigan Press.

Beauvoir, S. de. (1989). In H. M. Parshley (Trans.), *The second sex*. Vintage.

Berger, J. (1972). *Ways of seeing*. New York, NY: Penguin.

Bickford, A. L. (2008). Popular culture and the politics of revolutionary education. In K. S. Sealey (Ed.), *Film, politics, & education: Cinematic pedagogy across the disciplines*. New York, NY: Peter Lang.

Bingham, C. (2011). Two educational ideas for 2011 and beyond. *Studies in the Philosophy of Education, 30,* 513–519.

Bingham, C., & Biesta, G. (2010). *Jacques Rancière: Equality, emancipation, education*. Boulder: Paradigm Press.

Bly, R. (2004). *Iron John: A book about men* (Reprint.). Da Capo Press.

Bordwell, D., & Thompson K. (2010). *Film/Art: An introduction.* (9th ed.). New York, NY: McGraw Hill.

Butler, J. (1993). *Bodies that matter: On the discursive limits of sex.* New York, NY: Routledge.

Butler, J. (1999). *Gender trouble: Feminism and the subversion of identity* (1st ed.). New York, NY: Routledge.

Cameron, D. (2006). *On language and sexual politics* (1st ed.). New York, NY: Routledge.

Clover, C. J. (1992). *Men, women, and chain saws: Gender in modern horror film.* Princeton, NJ: Princeton University Press.

Connell, R. W. (2005). *Masculinities* (2nd ed.). CA: University of California Press.

Dean, T. (2009). *Unlimited intimacy: Reflections on the subculture of barebacking.* Chicago, IL: University of Chicago Press.

Doane, M. (1991). *Femmes fatales: Feminism, film theory, psychoanalysis.* New York, NY: Routledge.

Doane, M. (2002). *The emergence of cinematic time: Modernity, contingency, the archive.* Cambridge: Harvard University Press.

Ellsworth, E. (1991). I pledge allegiance: The politics of reading and using educational films. *Curriculum Inquiry, 21*(1), 41–64.

Ellsworth, E. (1999). *Teaching positions: Difference, pedagogy, and the power of address.* New York, NY: Teachers College Press.

Elsaesser, T., & Hagener, M. (2009). *Film theory: An introduction through the senses.* New York, NY: Routledge.

Fendler, L. (2010). *Michel Foucault* (1st ed.). Bloomsbury Academic.

Ferguson, A. A. (2001). *Bad boys: Public schools in the making of black masculinity.* Ann Arbor: University of Michigan Press.

Foucault, M. (1986). Of other spaces. *Diacritics, 16*(1), 22–27.

Ghaill, M. M. A. (1994). *Making of men.* Open University Press.

Giroux, H., & Pollock, G. (2010). *The mouse that roared: Disney and the end of innocence.* (2nd ed.). Lanham, MD: Rowman & Littlefield.

Halberstam, J. (2005). *In a queer time and place: Transgender bodies, subcultural lives.* New York, NY: NYU Press.

Harris, I. M. (1995). *Messages men hear: Constructing masculinities* (1st ed.). Taylor & Francis.

Kelly, S., & Caughlan, S. (n.d.). The hollywood teachers' perspective on authority. *Pedagogies, 6,* 46–65.

Kimmel, M. (2009). *Guyland: The perilous world where boys become men* (1st Reprint). Harper Perennial.

Kimmel, M. (2011). *Manhood in America: A cultural history* (3rd ed.). US: Oxford University Press.

Labaree, D. (1988). *The making of an American high school.* Binghampton, NY: Vail-Ballou Press.

Labaree, D. (2010). *Someone has to fail: The zero-sum game of public schooling.* Cambridge: Harvard University Press.

Longstreet, W., & Shane, H. (1993). *Curriculum for a new millennium.* Boston, MA: Allyn and Bacon.

Lortie, D. (2002). *Schoolteacher* (2nd ed.). Chicago, IL: University of Chicago Press.

Messner, M. A. (2002). *Taking the field: Women, men, and sports* (1st ed.). University of Minnesota Press.

Mulvey, L. (1975). Visual pleasure and narrative cinema. *Screen, 16*(3), 6–18.

Noguera, P. (2003). The trouble with black boys: The role and influence of environmental and cultural factors on the academic performance of African American males. *Urban Education, 38*(4), 431–459.

Orgeron, D., Orgeron, M., & Streible, D. (2012). *Learning with the lights off: Educational film in the United States.* New York, NY: Oxford University Press.

Pascoe, C. J. (2007). *Dude, you're a fag: Masculinity and sexuality in high school.* Berkeley, CA: University of California Press.

Pinar, W. F. (2001). *The gender of racial politics and violence in America.* Peter Lang Publishing.

Popkewitz, T. S. (1987). *The formation of school subjects: The struggle for creating an American institution.* Falmer Press.

Sealey, K. S. (Ed.). (2008). *Film, politics, and education: Cinematic pedagogy across the disciplines.* New York, NY: Peter Lang.

Snow, E. (1989). Theorizing the male gaze: Some problems. *Representations, 25,* 30–41.

Soja, E. (1996). *Thirdspace: Journeys to Los Angeles and other real-and-imagined places.* Cambridge, MA: Blackwell.

Spring, J. (2010). *American education.* (15th ed.). New York, NY: McGraw-Hill.

Tasker, Y. (1993). *Spectacular bodies: Gender, genre, and the action cinema.* New York, NY: Routledge.

Urban, W. J., & Wagoner, J. L. (2009). *American education: A history* (4th ed.). New York, NY: Routledge.

Walker, S. S., & Rasamimanana (1993). Tarzan in the classroom: How educational films mythologize Africa and miseducate Americans. *Journal of Negro Education, 62*(1), 3–23.

Waters, J. (1981/2005). *Shock value: A tasteful book about bad taste.* New York, NY: Thunders Mouth Press.

Williams, L. (1989). *Hard core: Power, pleasure and the 'frenzy of the visible'.* Berkeley, CA: University of California Press.

Willis, P. (1981). *Learning to labor: How working class kids get working class jobs* (Morningside.). Columbia University Press.

Films

Birtel, M., Chilcott, L., & Hindmarch, E. (Producers), & Guggenheim, D. (Director). (2010). *Waiting for superman* [Motion Picture]. United States: Electric Kinney Films, Participant Media, & Walden Media.

Bruckheimer, J., & Simpson, D. (Producers), & Smith, J. (Director). (1995). *Dangerous minds* [Motion Picture]. United States: Hollywood Pictures, Simpson/Bruckheimer Films, Via Rosa Productions.

Carr, A., & Stigwood, R. (Producers), & Klieser, R. (Director). (1978). *Grease* [Motion Picture]. United States: Paramount Pictures.

Clavell, J. (Producer & Director). (1967). *To sir, with love* [Motion Picture]. United Kingdom: Columbia Pictures.

DeVito, D., Shamberg, M., & Sher, S. (Producers), & LaGrevenese, R. (Director). (2007). *Freedom writer's diary* [Motion Picture]. United States: Paramount Pictures, Double Feature Films, & MTV Films.

Hughes, J., & Jacobson, T (Producers), & Hughes, J. (Director). (1986). *Ferris Bueller's day off* [Motion Picture]. United States: Paramount Pictures.

Johnson, M. (Producer), & Barnz, D. (Director). (2012). *Won't back down* [Motion Picture]. Walden Media & Gran Via Productions.

Schain, D. (Producer), & Ortega, K. (Director). (2006). *High school musical* [TV Movie]. United States: Disney Channel.

Talalay, R., Buchthal, S., & Waters, J. (Producers), & Waters, J. (Director). (1988). *Hairspray* [Motion Picture]. United States: New Line Cinema.

Chapter 7
Gender, Sport and Popular Culture
Emily A. Roper & Katherine M. Polasek

Introduction

Sports are forms of popular culture deeply rooted in modern society. Within this chapter, we will discuss the meaning of sport and the importance of studying sport from a sociological perspective. This chapter also includes: (a) a discussion of women's involvement and history in sport from the late 1800s to present, with attention directed toward the barriers that have kept women from participating in different forms of physical activity, (b) an overview of first and second wave sport media research and the televised sports manhood formula, and (c) a brief examination of future directions within sport.

Defining Sport

Most people have an understanding of what constitutes sport, but that definition varies greatly depending upon culture and geographic location. As Pfister (2013) stated, "When writing about sport, one has to address the challenge of meanings and translations as the term is defined differently depending on country and culture" (p. 163). Within North America, sport carries varied meanings. Sport Sociologist Jay Coakley (2009) defined sport as "well-established, officially governed competitive physical activities in which participants are motivated by internal and external rewards" (p. 6). Using this definition, there are a range of physical activities that constitute sport including youth organized soccer leagues, local charity running races, master's cycling, club gymnastics, pee wee football, collegiate swimming, high school wrestling, and Olympic snowboarding.

However, not all sports are created equal in terms of popularity and recognition; there are a number of factors that determine whether an activity will become important in the social and cultural life of a particular society. According to Coakley (2009), the North American

A. Trier-Bieniek et al., (Eds.), Gender & Pop Culture, 151–173.
© *2014 Sense Publishers. All rights reserved.*

sport culture is organized around a power and performance model which emphasizes the following characteristics: (a) strength, power, and speed, (b) competitive success achieved through hard work, personal risk, sacrifices, and playing through pain, (c) setting records and use of technology to monitor and improve the body, (d) a selection process based on physical abilities and success, (e) hierarchical authority structures, and (f) opponents as enemies. While most mainstream North American sport emphasizes the aforementioned characteristics, there are sport cultures that emphasize cooperation, personal empowerment, inclusive participation, democratic decision-making, and an ethic of care between sport participants. To those that subscribe to the dominant ideology of sport, a cooperative approach to sport is difficult to comprehend because most were socialized to believe that sport must be competitive, focused on strength, speed and power, and emphasize winning in order to be considered "real" and/or legitimate sport.

Coakley (2009) proposed an alternative approach to defining sport, which takes into consideration the ways in which people form ideas and beliefs about physical activities, and also allows for a broader acceptance of sport types. Using this alternative framework, the single definition of sport becomes obsolete; rather, the cultural differences in how sports are defined and interpreted are taken into consideration. Coakley uses the term *contested activities* to define those "activities for which there are no timeless and universal agreements about meaning, purpose, and organization" (2009, p. 10). For the purpose of this chapter, we will define sport broadly, to encompass a variety of contested activities ranging from elite sport to sport for all (including recreational physical activities). Such a broad definition is especially important in a chapter devoted to gender as women and girls' elite/organized sport opportunities have not always been widely available.

Sport as a Social Phenomenon

Sport is a pervasive part of U.S. society. Today, most people have participated in or watched, read about, and/or participated in discussions about sports. Sports have become integral parts of the social and cultural contexts in which we currently live. And, as such, they have meanings and influence that go well beyond scores and performance statistics (Coakley, 2009). As Karen and Washington (2010) suggested,

> Sports have assumed enormous importance in the modern world. The global attention paid to sport can be assessed not only in economic terms (total revenue generated from media, attendance, apparel, and equipment sales, etc.) and in time (total time spent watching, playing, reading about, etc.) but also in its impact on popular culture (advertising, journalism, movies). (p. 1)

Sport involvement has many benefits for its participants and for society. Parents often enroll their children in sport in order to provide them the opportunity to have fun, learn new sport skills, become physically fit, experience the excitement of competition, and make new friends. Sport provides examples of social integration, sacrifice, perseverance, good physical and mental health, hard work, courage, sportspersonship, and selflessness (Eitzen, 2012). However, despite the multitude of benefits associated with sport involvement, sport also warrants critical examination as it "shares with the larger society the basic elements and expressions of bureaucratization, commercialization, racism, sexism, homophobia, greed, exploitation of the powerless by the powerful, alienation, and ethnocentrism" (Eitzen, 2012, p. 11). Sport is worthy of critical examination by social scientists, not only because of the pervasive role it plays in society but also because of the great paradoxes (i.e., schools emphasize the personal and social benefits of sport participation but deny girls and women the same opportunities as boys and men), or contradictions, present within sport.

Gender and Sport

Gender and gender relations are central topics of study in the sociology of sport. From a historical perspective, sport has been a significant cultural practice in constructing and reproducing gender relations.

> From the beginning of modern sport, sport was a male preserve, and images of ideal masculinity for males were culturally

153

constructed through sports. The cultural script was that males validated their masculinity through athletic endeavors. Females had no place there; it could only make them masculine, like it makes males. (Eitzen & Sage, 2012, p. 313)

Today, despite the tremendous social change that has taken place over the past 40 years, sport still promotes and preserves traditional gender differences in many ways.

The first sociological analysis of women in sport began in the late 1970s. While much of the early research was atheoretical, researchers across many subdisciplinary areas (e.g., sport history, physical education, sport psychology, sport sociology) began to seriously examine the social and cultural conditions that influence women's sport experiences (Markula, 2005). Much of the research during the late 1970s and early 1980s focused on categorical differences between men and women. There was, however, a shift in the 1980s that pushed researchers to consider the complexities of power relations and social structures; during this time period, researchers began to focus on hegemonic power relations that dominate sport and how they affect women's sport experiences (Hall, 1996). By the 1990s, feminist researchers were continuing to establish sport as a site of male dominance. Their research also expanded to include analyses of media representations of physically active women, homophobia, compulsory heterosexuality, and women's physicality. Today, the field of feminist sport studies is evolving with advances in feminist theorizing and is continuing to further our understanding of the cultural and ideological practices at play in sport.

History of Women and Girls' Sport Participation

Sport provides a space in which women challenge stereotypes about physicality, can renegotiate concepts of femininity and masculinity, and demonstrate to their communities what they are physically and mentally capable of achieving. Promoting girls' and women's involvement in sports is an important tool in gender equality and women's empowerment and, more broadly, in development and social change. Understanding the history of women in sport, and specifically the barriers women have faced, is critical to appreciating how far women have come and how far women still have to go.

Prior to the 1870s, it was not deemed acceptable for women to participate in strenuous activities, or those that challenged gender norms; women were expected to stay indoors, guard their sexual purity, and hide their bodies. Some women, however, participated in varied forms of play activities that were recreational (non-competitive), informal (without rules), and emphasized physical activity. The emphasis of such activities was on maintaining the health of a woman, ensuring that she was capable of fulfilling her reproductive and domestic responsibilities (O'Reilly & Cahn, 2007).

In the late 1800s and early 1900s, physiological limitations associated with the female body dominated the way of thinking. Women's bodies were perceived to be weaker, more fragile and less capable of strenuous physical feats compared to men's bodies. For example, a woman was perceived to be in a "weakened" state during her menstrual cycle, and therefore, most forms of physical activities were deemed hazardous for women's health and well-being. It was during this time that the bicycle became a significant site of social resistance for women. Physicians, specifically gynecologists, questioned not only the appropriateness of a woman riding a bicycle, but also the potential harm caused to the female body. It was thought that riding a bicycle would threaten a woman's sexual purity and damage her reproductive capabilities. Women that rode bicycles during this time period were criticized for the "unladylike" effects of exercise – sweating, panting, and showing exhaustion. Despite these attitudes, more and more women were riding bicycles as a way to connect with the outdoors and free themselves from their domestic responsibilities within the home (Christie-Robin, Orzada, & López-Gydosh, 2012). As Christie-Robin, Orzada, and López-Gydosh (2012) explained,

> In the United States, bicycling tested time-honored social conventions, challenged gender roles and sparked controversies. It afforded women an independence that affronted the mores embodying US society for generations. A heated debate erupted over women cyclists' propriety. Women's bicycling costume was

another contentious subject. (p. 315)

Informal clubs also began to emerge for women interested in "ladylike" sports such as tennis, archery, and bowling. Women did not participate in intercollegiate sport until 1892 when basketball was introduced at Smith College. Intercollegiate and recreational sport opportunities slowly increased in the early 1900s, but came to an end by the depression in the 1930s. Wartime brought significant changes to women's role within the family. While women were once expected to stay at home and care for children and other domestic responsibilities, the 1940s thrust women into the work force. World War II also impacted women's place in sport with the emergence of the All-American Girls Baseball League (AAGBL) in 1943. Several major league baseball executives started the AAGBL in order to maintain baseball in the public eye while many of the men were away due to the war. Once the war was over, however, women were expected to return to their domestic responsibilities and forego their involvement in sport (O'Reilly & Cahn, 2007).

With the drive for Civil Rights in the 1950s and 1960s, feminist activism within the U.S. carried over to the athletic domain and broadened women's and girls' opportunities in sport. Women continued to challenge societal attitudes toward women's involvement in athletic pursuits. In 1966, Roberta Gibb became the first woman to run and finish the Boston Marathon, however, her time was disqualified because she was female. Then, in 1967, Katherine Switzer entered the Boston Marathon using only her initials "K. V. Switzer." Her entry in this male tradition received considerable notoriety when an image of Jock Semple, a race course official, attempting to physically remove Switzer from the race made national headlines. While Switzer finished the race, like Gibb, she was disqualified for being female. Despite her disqualification, Switzer and other women went on to challenge the Boston Athletic Association's all-male policy. Five years later, in 1972, women were permitted to enter the Boston Marathon.

In the early 1970s, growing challenges began to confront the patriarchal sport structure. In 1972, Title IX of the Educational Amendments was enacted by Congress and signed into law by Richard Nixon. Section 106.41 Athletics (a) reads:

No person shall on the basis of sex, be excluded participation in, be denied the benefits of, be treated differently from another person or otherwise be discriminated against in interscholastic, intercollegiate, club or intramural athletics offered by a recipient, and no recipient shall provide any such athletics separately on such basis.

When President Nixon signed the act, approximately 31,000 women were involved in college sports; spending on athletic scholarships for women was less than $100,000; and on average there were 2 women's teams at a college.

Title IX has had a tremendous impact on the sport participation rates of women and girls (Acosta & Carpenter, 2012). However, the impact was not immediate as challenges were consistently mounted against Title IX after its initial passage. As Messner (1988) stated, "Increasing female athleticism represents a genuine quest by women for equality, control of their own bodies, and self-definition, and as such represents a challenge to the ideological basis of male domination" (p. 197).

Also in the early 1970s, tennis icon and women's sport advocate, Billie Jean King was fighting for higher pay and professional treatment for women tennis players. Alongside eight other female tennis players, King organized the Virginia Slims Tour Circuit, a tour of tennis tournaments that were organized by and for women. Their goal was to increase the purses for female tennis champions and gain greater respect. In 1973, King was challenged to play Wimbledon champion, Bobby Riggs, in a tennis match dubbed the "Battle of the Sexes." With an estimated 48 million Americans watching on television, King beat Riggs, changing the way both men and women looked at themselves. As Ware (2011) stated, "In a single tennis match, Billie Jean King was able to do more for the cause of women than most feminists can achieve in a lifetime" (p. 7).

Prior to the 1990s, female athletes were almost invisible in popular culture; this however began to undergo a startling reversal in the early 1990s when Reebok, Nike, and other corporations began to produce advertisements with successful female athletes (Heywood & Dworkin, 2003). Such representation, as Heywood and Dworkin (2003) noted, made women feel "that they finally, after years of the self-doubt that comes with invisibility, were valued by the culture that had previously ignored [them]" (p. 3). During the 1990s, there was a "dramatic increase in the number of spectators, revenues and popularity for women's sports" (Christopherson, Janning, & McConnell, 2002, p. 171). The 1996 Olympic Games and the 1999 Women's World Cup were considered breakthrough moments in women's sport. Despite the unprecedented media coverage for the Women's World Cup in 1999, "reporters analyzed the games and the American Women's team through a gendered lens that highlighted and reinforced gender stereotypes about women" (Christopherson et al., 2002, p. 183).

Today's female athletes are playing a record number of sports in record numbers. Female athletes have more opportunities to participate in sport than ever before (Acosta & Carpenter, 2012). In 2012, 40 years after the passage of Title IX, there are approximately 200,000 female athletes participating in intercollegiate athletics (compared to 31,000 in 1972) and 8.73 women's intercollegiate sports teams (2.1 in 1972). The number of female head coaches of women's teams (3974) is also the highest ever (Acosta & Carpenter, 2012). The same type of growth can also be found at the high school level (NFHS, 2007). Just before passage of Title IX, there were 3,666,917 boys and 294,015 girls participating in high school athletics. In 2012, there were 4,494,406 boys and 3,173,559 high school girls (NFHS, 2007).

It is important to note that sport participation of women and girls will not automatically increase; persistent efforts are needed to ensure that gender equity is taken seriously. While the landscape of women's sport has significantly changed, societal barriers, stereotypes, and expectations continue to restrict their participation and experiences in sport. As Coakley (2009) suggests, sport worlds are usually organized to be male dominated, male identified, and male centered. Therefore, females participating in sport, regardless of their abilities, face obstacles due to comparisons to the male standard of what is "right" and "normal" in sport. Females are often judged according to the standards, orientations, and actions of males. Because men's sport is always perceived to be *bigger, faster,* and *stronger* it must therefore be more worthy of serious attention.

Gender Ideology in Sports

Sports are sites for reaffirming attitudes and beliefs about gender differences. The characteristics commonly associated with sport – strength, power, dominance, competitiveness, aggression – are socially defined as masculine traits/qualities. As a result, female participation in sport presents numerous challenges.

The ways in which girls and boys are taught to understand and physically use their bodies is quite different. Researchers have found that while boys are encouraged to experience and push their bodies and master complex patterns of skill development, girls are socialized to restrict and protect their bodies (Young, 1990). Girls learn early that they should take up less space and refrain from overly physical acts or run the risk of being perceived as less feminine. Research also illustrates that girls tend to play indoors more often and tend not to play team or competitive games, which limits their spatial experiences in outdoor settings (Greendorfer, 2002). While boys gain status and popularity as a result of their involvement in sport, girls who are physically aggressive, tough, strong, and/or display an overly competitive persona are often ridiculed, labeled as lesbians, and/or sexually harassed (Krane, 2001; Roper, 2013). Athletic adolescent females are often referred to as "tomboys," a term used to describe a female who engages in socially defined "masculine" activities. Such labeling works to establish sport involvement as an "abnormal" and anti-feminine component of female identity (Hall, 1996). It is during adolescence that such gender norms and expectations intensify, which in part explains the decrease in girls' sport participation during adolescence (Hasbrook, 1999; Shakib, 2003).

As previously noted, female participation in sport contradicts stereotypical notions of what it means to be "feminine." As a result, female athletes often find their sexuality is called into question just because they participate in sport. Kauer and Krane (2006) interviewed college female athletes about the perceived stereotypes surrounding women's sport, their reactions to such stereotypes, and any strategies they employed to cope with the stereotypes. The findings revealed that female athletes were commonly stereotyped as lesbians and masculine. To cope with the stereotypes, the heterosexual athletes described disassociating from their athletic identity (i.e., not wearing team athletic gear outside of the sport context) and emphasizing their heterosexuality (i.e., talking about their boyfriends) and femininity (i.e., wearing makeup, nails done). The lesbian and bisexual athletes described trying to conceal their sexual identity by using vague language, lying about their sexuality, or providing limited personal information. As Griffin (1998) suggested, "A lesbian participating in a hostile climate must be prepared to deny her lesbian identity and act in ways that lead others to believe that she is heterosexual" (p. 94). The fear of being labeled or identified as a lesbian has the potential to intimidate and limit all women in sport (regardless of sexuality) and forces many female athletes to go to extreme lengths to hide their sexuality or prove their heterosexuality (Griffin, 1998; Kauer & Krane, 2006). Consistent with Griffin (1998), female athletes involved in masculine sports use a variety of methods to "feminize" their appearance (e.g., wearing ribbons, wearing pink, growing their hair long). In addition, athletes have been found to engage in sexual activity (with men) as a way in which to prove their heterosexuality (Krane, Surface, & Alexander, 2005). These athletes, especially those who feel compelled to prove their heterosexuality, are particularly vulnerable to sexual harassment. Researchers also report that some female athletes will drop out of sport altogether or choose to participate in "feminine" sports to avoid the lesbian label (Griffin, 1998; Shakib, 2003).

As Eitzen and Sage (2012) suggested, "gender issues are not just about inequality, injustice, and sexuality involving females" (p. 331), researchers must also examine the role sports play in the social construction of masculinity and the respective consequences for males. Traditional gender role prescriptions have perpetuated problems for both males and females (Eitzen & Sage, 2012). While sports privilege men over women, they also privilege some men overs others (Coakley, 2009). As Coakley suggested,

Men's sports have always been key sites for celebrating and reproducing dominant ideas about heterosexual masculinity. Playing certain sports has been a rite of passage for boys to become men, and male athletes in contact and power sports are held up as models of heterosexual manhood in society. (p. 267)

Sport plays an important role in male social development and is considered to be one of the key sites for men to demonstrate their dominance and masculinity (Messner, 2002). The hyper-masculine sport culture often adheres to the most socially accepted form of masculinity – hegemonic masculinity (Anderson, 2008). Hegemonic masculinity is commonly associated with the attributes found in mainstream, team sport – strength, dominance, aggression, intimidation, and (hyper) heterosexuality (Anderson, 2008). By demonstrating physical and psychological attributes associated with success in athletic contests, boys gain status in most adolescent and preadolescent male groups. Boys who are more artistic, attracted to traditionally "feminine" sport forms, or uninterested in sport, however, are forced to find alternate ways to claim their masculinity or face being labeled gay or effeminate (Anderson, 2008; Messner, 2002). For example, men involved in dance are often faced with stereotypical assumptions regarding their sexuality. Polasek and Roper (2011) examined the ways in which male ballet and modern dancers negotiated the "gay stereotype" associated with men's involvement in dance. The dancers were found to employ a variety of methods to challenge the stereotypes associated with men in dance. To combat the pervasive stereotype, several of the dancers, both heterosexual and gay, described working to present an overly "masculine" image when outside of the dance space. The participants described wearing stereotypically masculine clothing (e.g., baggy, less fashion conscious), talking about their girlfriends when around strangers, and disconnecting from their career as a dancer (i.e., not wearing dance clothing outside the dance space and not talking about their dance career). The participants also described companies that actively discriminated against men that were openly gay, some even being known as having a 'no gays' policy. These findings, while clearly homonegative, are particularly interesting considering the meaning and significance of dance – especially ballet and modern – within the gay community.

Mass Media Coverage of Female Athletes

Popular culture is distributed across many forms of mass media (e.g., newspapers, television, radio, magazines, books, blogs, and social media). We study popular culture in order to learn about a culture and its values and ideals. The mass media plays a significant role in the transmission of dominant cultural values, especially in the perpetuation of images of gender difference and gender inequality in sport. As Kane (1988) stated:

> The mass media have become one of the most powerful institutional forces for shaping attitudes and values in American culture. Mass media portray the dominant images or symbolic representations of American society. These images in turn tell audiences who and what is valued and esteemed in our culture. How female athletes are viewed in this culture is both reflected in and created by mass media images. Thus, it becomes critical to examine both the extent and the nature of media coverage. (p. 89)

Despite considerable progress in terms of women and girls' sport participation and availability of better sport programs, the media has failed to improve the amount and quality of sport media coverage of female athletes.

A considerable amount of research has investigated the portrayal of female athletes in popular sports magazines (Bruce, 2013; Fink & Kensicki, 2002; Weber & Carini, 2013), newspapers (Kaisur & Skoglund, 2006; Toft, 2011), television coverage (Messner, Duncan, & Cooky, 2003; Messner & Cooky, 2010), children's literature (Roper & Clifton, 2013) and digital media (e.g., Facebook, blogs, media guides) (Clavio & Eagleman, 2011). Within what is now referred to as the "first wave of sport media research" (Kane, LaVoi, & Fink, 2013), researchers documented the marginalization of female athletes and women's sport through content analysis of visual and written texts. This research focused on *how* and *how often* female athletes are portrayed. The findings from this 30-year body of research, revealed that coverage of female athletes, regardless of medium, has consistently deemphasized the athletic accomplishments and athleticism of females, and focused primarily on femininity and heterosexuality (Fink & Kensicki, 2002) whereas male athletes are presented in an array of narratives that highlight their athletic abilities, strength and competence. As Kane (2011) suggested, "over the past three decades we have amassed a large body of empirical evidence demonstrating that sportswomen are significantly more likely to be portrayed in ways that emphasize their femininity and heterosexuality rather than their athletic prowess" (p. 28).

Despite increased sport opportunities, especially since the 1970s, women continue to hold only a marginal place in media coverage of sport, often referred to as the "symbolic annihilation" (Tuchman, 1978) of the female athlete. Through this omission, the media sends the message that female athletes and women's sports are less important than male athletes and men's sport.

Kaisur and Skoglund (2006) analyzed the column inches and the feature photos that were "above the fold" on the front page of the sports section on two U.S. newspapers from 1940 to 2005. Findings indicated that coverage of female athletes actually declined over time and never exceeded 10%. Toft (2011) examined 80 newspapers in 22 countries and found that athletic women were featured in only 9% of articles. Within *Sports Illustrated*, one of the premier sports magazines, sportswomen have been historically ignored. Lumpkin (2009) examined the representation of female athletes in feature articles in *Sports Illustrated* from 1954 to 1987. The findings revealed that 9.7% of feature articles pertained to female athletes or women's sport and written descriptors characterized the female athletes in blatantly sexist terms. Fink and Kensicki (2002) found that only 10% of the photographs in *Sports Illustrated* from 1997 to 1999 featured women athletes. Weber and Carini (2013) examined *Sports Illustrated* covers from 2000 to 2011 and found that women athletes appeared on only 4.9% of covers. In fact, women were featured on the covers from 1954 to 1965 at a higher percentage (12.6% vs. 4.9%) than 2000 to 2011.

On television, coverage of female athletes and women's teams is decreasing. Messner, Duncan, and Cooky (2003) examined the media coverage of women's sport on three local (Los Angeles) network affiliates and one national (ESPN) sports news broadcasts for six weeks in 1999 to determine the quality and quantity of televised coverage of women's sport. This study expanded on earlier studies in 1990 and 1994. "In the 1990 and 1994 studies, we noted that female athletes rarely received coverage on the televised sport news. The new study reveals only a slight increase in the proportion of sports news devoted to coverage of women's sport and women athletes over

163

the 10-year time period" (Messner, Duncan, & Cooky, 2003, p. 39). In 2010, Messner and Cooky (2010) reexamined gender in televised sports in news and highlight shows. The central aim of their study was to compare the quantity and quality of TV news and highlight shows' coverage of women's versus men's athletic events from 1989 to 2009. Their findings indicated that women's sports received only 1.6% of time on the three major networks and 1.4% on ESPN's *SportCenter* in 2009. These findings represent a significant decline in coverage since 2004, when 6.3% of the airtime was devoted to women's sports on the three networks and 2.1% on ESPN's *SportCenter*. Moreover, 100% of *SportCenter's* programs and sports news shows in the sample led with a men's sports story which are most often considered to be the stories with the highest production values.

When female athletes are represented in the mass media, there are a number of consistent themes that emerge. The focus is often taken away from the female athlete's athletic accomplishments and abilities and directed toward her domestic responsibilities (e.g., mother), relationships with men (e.g., daughter, wife, girlfriend), and appearance. Photographs of athletic females are less likely to depict them in action/motion and often the clothing they are photographed in does not represent their involvement in sport. Those female athletes that are represented are often those involved in "feminine" sports and those women whose appearance could be characterized as socially attractive. As Kane and Buysse (2005) summarized, females are more likely than males to be "portrayed off the court, out of uniform, and in passive and sexualized poses" (p. 215).

In 1990, Duncan examined print media coverage surrounding the 1984 and 1988 Olympic Games. She examined both content (i.e., physical appearance, poses and body position, facial expressions, emotional displays, and camera displays) and context (i.e., visual space in which the photo appears, caption, surrounding written text, and the title and substantiative nature of the article in which the photo appears) of sport photographs in popular illustrated magazines with large circulations in North America (i.e., *Life, Sports Illustrated, Newsweek, Time, MS.*) Duncan found an overemphasis on physical appearance, poses that resembled soft pornography, and camera angles and body positioning that emphasized smallness and submissiveness.

Similarly, Fink and Kensicki (2002) found that when female athletes were represented in *Sports Illustrated*, they were depicted as passive, out of the sport context, and focused on their "feminine" appearance (i.e., hair styled, wearing makeup, feminine clothing). Furthermore, 65% of the female athletes represented were from sex-appropriate sports. Weber and Carini (2013) also found that when featured on the cover of *Sports Illustrated*, women athletes often shared the cover with a male, were non-athletes, were involved in "feminine" sports, and/or were represented in highly sexualized images. Weber and Carini also acknowledged the paucity of female athletes of color on the cover of *Sports Illustrated*, with only 11 (of 716) covers depicting sportswomen of color. Like print media, when female athletes were portrayed on television, the emphasis was placed on their physical appearance and domestic roles. They were also typically sexually objectified and much of the attention focused on those participating in gender neutral or gender appropriate sports (Messner & Cooky, 2010).

As a reflection of the growth associated with women's sport during the 1990s, a number of women's sport magazines emerged in the 1990s. The goal of these magazines was to tap into the growing interest in women's sport. *Women/Sport* was first published in 1997, but was terminated after only four issues. *Sports Illustrated for Women* lasted only 20 months, ending in 2002 (Weber & Carini, 2013). The lack of interest and/or funding were the reasons cited for why both magazines were discontinued (Hardin, Lynn, & Walsdorf, 2005). Fink and Kensicki (2002) analyzed *Sports Illustrated for Women* from 1997 to 1999 and found that although female athletes were represented and stories highlighted their involvement in sport, the female athletes were still portrayed in stereotypic narratives. Even within a publication geared towards women, the female athletes were still presented in non-action shots, athletes were feminized, and an emphasis was placed on their non-sport roles and responsibilities.

In the "second wave of sport media research," research focused on digital media, the inclusion of intersectional variables (e.g., race, ethnicity, sexuality and gender), and examination of audience reception. For 30 years, sport media research focused on how often and how female athletes were represented in the media. More recently, an emerging body of work has been devoted to how consumers interpret media texts. What this research has found is that the practice of "sex sells" is an ineffective way in which to market and promote women's sports to its target audience (Kane, LaVoi, & Fink, 2013). "Female fans, female athletes, dads with daughters, families with girls and girls themselves – the core demographic for women's sports – react negatively to hypersexualized images of sportswomen" (LaVoi, 2013, p. 52).

While minimal research examining digital sport media exists, there are a handful of studies that have examined gender within these new sport mediums. Clavio and Eagleman (2011) examined portrayals of female athletes in 10 popular sports blogs and attempted to determine whether the same trends found in traditional media research were present in this new sport medium. Their findings indicated that female athletes and women's teams received minimal coverage, and when females were included, they were typically cheerleaders, dancers, or models portrayed in a hypersexualized manner. The results point to a continuation of the symbolic annihilation and objectification of females in this new sport medium. Research examining Twitter and Facebook using a critical feminist analysis is limited to date. While their study was not focused on gender, Wallace, Wilson, and Miloch (2011) found that both the National Collegiate Athletics Association (NCAA) and the Big 12 athletic department Facebook pages emphasized men's sports. The tweets, retweets, posts, and "likes" of men's sports far exceeded those for women's sport. Institutional athletic websites have also been found to marginalize in other ways. Calhoun, LaVoi, and Johnson (2011) examined intercollegiate athletic websites for the presence or absence of family narratives in online college coach biographies. The findings indicated a near absence of explicit LGBT coaches and their families and an overwhelming emphasis on heternormative frames. Of the 1,855 coaches in their study, only two identified as openly gay in their online biography.

Also within the second wave of sport media research, researchers have encouraged an intersectional analysis of how multidimensional identities of race, sexuality, gender, and class are constructed within sport media. One example of the use of intersectional theory is the work of Cooky, Wachs, Messner, and Dworkin (2010) in which they examined the mainstream print news media's response to Don Imus' discussion of the 2007 NCAA women's basketball championship game between Rutgers and the University of Tennessee. During the *Imus in the Morning Show*, Imus and his colleagues referred to members of the Rutger's women's team as "hard core hos" and "nappy headed hos." Cooky et al. (2010) concluded that the mainstream media reproduced monolithic understandings of social inequality and failed to address the intersecting nature of oppression for women in sport.

The trivialization of female athletes in the media is significant for a number of reasons. The marginalization and objectification of female athletes sends a hegemonic message that female athletes' accomplishments are not as important or impressive as those of male athletes. This message is especially significant for young girls who need confident, strong female athletic roles models in order to get involved and maintain their involvement in sport. The trivialization also affects the way in which gender, racial, and class groups are perceived by society. As Clavio and Eagleman (2011) suggested, "When certain frames become more prominent in the media, they have the ability to create more prevalent viewpoints or stereotypes in society" (p. 296).

Televised Sports Manhood Formula

While sport media research has focused primarily on the representation of women and girls in sport, there is growing research that points to the problems associated with the ways in which masculinity is represented in sport media. Boys and men are regular consumers of televised sports (Messner, Dunbar, & Hunt, 2000) and, as such, researchers have examined the types of messages and values being presented. Findings suggest that televised sports in particular, consistently presents boys and men with stereotypical messages about race, gender, and violence. This narrow definition of masculinity is commonly referred to as the televised sports manhood formula (Messner, Dunbar, & Hunt, 2000). Messner, Dunbar, et al.'s (2000) examination of 23 hours of sport programming (e.g., *SportsCenter*, Extreme sports on ESPN, NBA play-off games, Monday night football, MLB on TBS) and 722 commercials during a single week in 1999 found 10 distinct themes that make up the televised sports manhood formula. These themes included the following: (a) White males are the voices of authority, (b) sports is a man's world, (c) men are foregrounded in commercials, (d) women are sexy props or prizes for men's successful sport performances, (e) whites are foregrounded in commercials, (f) aggressive players get the prize; nice guys finish last, (g) boys will be (violent) boys, (h) give up your body for the team, (i) sports is war, and (j) show some guts. The ramifications of these messages being transmitted to boys and men are that "if consumed uncritically, males learn to view females as not fully human which decreases the likelihood of successful intimate and professional relationships with women, and an adoption of the belief that to be successful in sport, health and well-being are secondary" (LaVoi, 2013, p. 51).

Future Directions

It has been suggested that full gender equity will not be achieved in sport without changes in how people think about masculinity and femininity (Coakley, 2009). Today, "dominant sport forms in society are currently based on a two-category gender classification model, which leads to the conclusion that girls and women are by definition inferior to boys and men" (Coakley, 2009, p. 271). Dividing sports along masculine and feminine lines encourages and allows women and men to accept physical limits that have been placed on them. Within recent years, more and more women and girls are participating in sports deemed "masculine" or alternative. Their participation in such sport forms is challenging conventional definitions of femininity and physicality. One example is the growing popularity of women's flat track roller derby (Finley, 2010). Women's involvement in sports such as roller derby are providing scholars in feminist sport studies the opportunity to explore the dynamics through which alternative femininities are being constructed and reinforced within a social context.

In addition to new ways of thinking about femininity and masculinity, there is also a need for development of new sport forms that allow for fresh ways of "doing" sports. Such sport programs/ forms should: (a) promote lifetime sport participation and emphasize combinations of competition and partnership, (b) facilitate an ethic of care between teammates and opponents, (c) increase opportunities for gender-nonconforming people, and (d) allow for a shared experience amongst diverse participants (Coakley, 2009, p. 270). In changing the way sport is defined, organized, and played, we not only broaden the opportunities available to women and men, but also attempt to break down restrictive boundaries on what is considered "real" or legitimate sport.

Questions for Class Discussion

1. Bring in two to three current visual images of female athletes portrayed by the mass media. Compare the techniques used in the social construction of the images.
2. Sports such as skateboarding, snowboarding, and BMX biking, often labeled "alternative" sports, have gained status and popularity within our popular culture. Discuss the role(s) women and girls' play in these emergent sports.
3. Women are participating in increasing numbers in sports historically defined as masculine. With over 562 teams and 60 leagues, Women's Flat Track Roller Derby is growing in popularity. Derby has been argued to be the "most violent sport organized and owned by women. The skaters talk about 'kicking ass' and crowds shout 'kill, kill'" (Finley, 2010, p. 369). Examine the Women's Flat Track Derby Association's (WFTDA) website (http://wftda.com/leagues) and discuss the ways in which gender is constructed in each team name and team logo/mascot.

References

Acosta, V., & Carpenter, L. (2012). *Women in sport: A longitudinal, national study.* Retrieved September 24, 2013, from http://www. acostacarpenter.org/

Anderson, E. (2008). Being masculine is not about who you sleep with.... Heterosexual athletes contesting masculinity and the one-time rule of homosexuality. *Sex Roles, 58,* 104–115.

Bruce, T. (2013). Reflections on communication and sport: On women and femininities. *Communication and Sport.* doi: 10.1177/2167479512472883

Calhoun, A. S., LaVoi, N. M., & Johnson, A. (2011). Framing with family: Examining online coaching biographies for heteronormative and heterosexist narratives. *International Journal of Sport Communication, 4*(3), 300–316.

Christie-Robin, J., Orzada, B., & López-Gydosh, D. (2012). From bustles to bloomers: Exploring the bicycle's influence on American women's fashion, 1880–1914. *The Journal of American Culture, 35*(4), 315–331.

Christopherson, N., Janning, M., & McConnell, E. D. (2002). Two kicks forward, one kick back: A content analysis of media discourses on the women's world cup. *Sociology of Sport Journal, 19*(2), 170–188.

Clavio, G., & Eagleman, A. N. (2011). Gender and sexually suggestive images in sports blogs. *Journal of Sport Management, 7,* 295–304.

Coakley, J. (2009). *Sport in society: Issues and controversies* (10th ed.). New York, NY: McGraw-Hill.

Cooky, C., Wachs, F., Messner, M., & Dworkin, S. (2010). It's not about the game: Don Imus, race, class, gender and sexuality in contemporary media. *Sociology of Sport Journal, 27,*139–159.

Duncan, M. C. (1990). Sports photographs and sexual difference: Images of women and men in the 1984 and 1988 Olympic Games. *Sociology of Sport Journal, 7,* 22–43.

Eitzen, D. S. (2012). *Fair and foul: Beyond the myths and paradoxes of sport*. New York, NY: Rowman and Littlefield Publishers.

Eitzen, D. S., & Sage, G. H. (2012). *Sociology of North American sport* (9th ed.). Cary, NC: Oxford University Press.

Fink, J. S., & Kensicki, L. J. (2002). An imperceptible difference: Visual and textual constructions of femininity in Sports Illustrated and Sports Illustrated for Women. *Mass Communication and Society, 5*(3), 317–339.

Greendorfer, S. L. (2002). Socialization processes and sport behavior. In T. Horn (Ed.), *Advances in sport psychology* (pp. 377–401). Champaign, IL: Human Kinetics.

Griffin, P. (1998). *Strong women, deep closets: Lesbians and homophobia in sport*. Champaign, IL: Human Kinetics.

Hall, A. (1996). *Feminism and sporting bodies: Essays on theory and practice*. Champaign, IL: Human Kinetics.

Hardin, M., Lynn, S., & Walsdorf, K. (2005). Challenge and conformity on contested terrain: Images of women in four women's sports/ fitness magazines. *Sex Roles, 53*, 105-117.

Hasbrook, C. A. (1999). Young children's social constructions of physicality and gender. In J. Coakley & P. Donnelly (Eds.), *Inside Sports* (pp. 7–16). London, UK: Routledge.

Heywood, L., & Dworkin, S. (2003). *Built to win: The female athlete as cultural icon*. Minneapolis, MN: University of Minnesota Press.

Kaiser, K., & Skoglund, E. (2006), *Prominence of men and women in newspaper sports coverage as an indicator of gender equality pre- and post-Title IX.* Paper presented at the annual meeting of the Association for Education in Journalism and Mass Communication Convention, San Francisco, CA.

Kane, M. J. (1988). Media coverage of the female athlete before, during and after Title IX: Sports Illustrated revisited. *Journal of Sport Management, 2*, 87–99.

Kane, M. J. (2011). *Sex sells sex, not women's sports*. Retrieved from The Nation: http://www.thenation.com/article/162390/sex-sells-sex-not-womens-sports#axzz2Wbuy16qm

Kane, M. J., & Buysse, J. (2005). Intercollegiate media guides as contested terrain: A longitudinal analysis. *Sociology of Sport Journal, 22*, 214–238.

Kane, M. J., LaVoi, N. M., Fink, J. S. (2013). Exploring elite female athletes' interpretations of sport media images: A window into the construction of social identity and selling sex in women's sports. *Communication and Sport,* 1–31. doi:0.1177/2167479512473585

Karen, D., & Washington, R. E. (2010). *The sport and society reader*. London, UK: Routledge.

Kauer, K., & Krane, V. (2006). Scary dykes and feminine queens: Stereotypes and female collegiate athletes. *Women in Sport and Physical Activity Journal, 15*, 42–55.

Krane, V. (2001). We can be athletic and feminine, but do we want to? Challenging hegemonic femininity in women's sport. *Quest, 53*, 115–133.

Krane, V., Surface, H., & Alexander, A. (2005). Health implications of heterosexism and homonegativism for girls and women in sport. In L. Ransdall & L. Petlichkoff (Eds.), *Ensuring and health of active and athletic women and girls* (pp. 327–346). Reston, VA: National Association for Girls and Women in Sport.

LaVoi, N. M. (2013). Gender and sport media. In E. A. Roper (Ed.), *Gender relations in sport* (pp. 39–52). The Netherlands: Sense Publishing.

Lumpkin, A. (2009). Female representation in feather articles published by Sports Illustrated in the 1990's. *Women in Sport and Physical Activity Journal, 18*(2), 38–51.

Markula, P. (2005). *Feminist sport studies: Sharing experiences of joy and pain.* Albany, NY: State University of New York.

Messner, M. A. (1988). Sports and male domination: The female athlete as contested ideological terrain. *Sociology of Sport Journal, 5,* 197–211.

Messner, M. (2002). *Taking the field: Women, men, and sports.* Minneapolis: University of Minnesota Press.

Messner, M., & Cooky, C. (2010). *Gender in televised sports: News and highlights shows, 1989–2009.* Los Angeles, CA: USC Center for Feminist Research.

Messner, M. A., Dunbar, M., & Hunt, D. (2000). The televised sports manhood formula. *Journal of Sport and Social Issues, 24,* 380–394.

Messner, M. A., Duncan, M. C., & Cooky, C. (2003). Silence, sports bras, and wrestling porn: Women in televised sports news and highlight shows. *Journal of Sport and Social Issues, 27*(1), 38–51.

National Federation of State High School Associations. (2007). 2005–2006 NFHS high school athletics participation survey. Retrieved July 16, 2010, from http://www.nfhs.org/ 2006/09/participation_in_high_school_sports

O'Reilly, J., & Cahn, S. (2007). *Women and sports in the United States: A documentary reader.* Boston, MA: Northeastern Press.

Pfister, G. (2013). Developments and current issues in gender and sport from a European perspective. In E. A. Roper (Ed.), *Gender relations in sport* (pp. 163–180). The Netherlands: Sense Publishing.

Polasek, K. M., & Roper, E. A. (2011). Negotiating the gay male stereotype in ballet and modern dance. *Research in Dance Education, 12*(2), 173–193.

Roper, E. A. (2012). Gender, identity and sport. In S. Murphy (Ed.), *The Oxford handbook of sport and performance psychology*. Oxford University Press.

Roper, E. A., & Clifton, A. (2013). Representations of physically active girls in children's picture books. *Research Quarterly for Exercise and Sport, 84,* 147–156.

Shakib, S. (2003). Female basketball participation. *American Behavioral Scientist, 46,* 1405–1422.

Toft, D. (2011, October 3). *New sports press survey: Newspapers focus narrowly on sports results.* Retrieved from Play the game: http://www.playthegame.org/knowledge-bank/articles/new-sports-press-survey-newspapers-focus-narrowly-on-sports-results-5248.html

Tuchman, G. (1978). Introduction: The symbolic annihilation of women by the mass media. In G. Tuchman, A. Daniels, & J. Benét (Eds.), *Hearth and home: Images of women in the mass media* (pp. 3–38). New York, NY: Oxford University Press.

Ware, S. (2011). *Game, set, match: Billie Jean King and the revolution in women's sports.* Chapel Hill, NC: University of North Carolina Press.

Wallace, L., Wilson, J., & Miloch, K. (2011). Sporting Facebook: A content analysis of NCAA organizational sport pages and Big 12 conference athletic department pages. *International Journal of Sport Communication, 4,* 422–444.

Weber, J. D., & Carini, R. M. (2013). Where are the female athletes in Sports Illustrated? A content analysis of covers (2000–2011). *International Review for the Sociology of Sport, 48*(2), 196–203.

Young, I. M. (1990). *Throwing like a girl and other essays in feminist philosophy and social theory.* Bloomington, IN: Indiana University Press.

Chapter 8
Gender and Technology:
Women's Usage, Creation and Perspectives
Cindy Royal

Introduction

Computer technology has an active and pervasive presence in the lives of most Americans, and its influence grows worldwide. We use computers and mobile devices in an array of personal and professional settings, and the vast network of the Internet provides new ways to seek and share information with family, friends, acquaintances, and strangers on a scale that has never before been experienced. But the online world, just as it simulates real world experiences, mimics its gender implications and can also create new ones. On one hand, technology can be the great equalizer, providing voice to the voiceless in a setting where one's identity can remain anonymous and potentially fluid. But it can also perpetuate and extend sexist attitudes, stereotypes, and violence. The promise of a gender-free online existence has morphed into a space where identity is transparent and can dictate one's usage and potential with technology.

Technology itself covers a broad range. The Internet is the most ubiquitous incarnation with millions using social networking sites to communicate and share. But the computer industry also offers a place where gender issues magnify those of the workplace in general. These images of technology play out as the media makes decisions about who to cover and who to ignore.

Historical Context

Gendered uses have always been an outcome and driver of technology. Women's use of the telephone for social purposes changed the device from a business tool to the family's hub of socializing (Fisher, 1994; Marvin 1990). And television's place as the center of family life

A. Trier-Bieniek et al., (Eds.), Gender & Pop Culture, 175–189.

influenced the advertising market in the 1950s, geared toward women's role as homemaker (Spigel, 1992).

While it is little known, the early days of computing were actually pioneered by females. Ada Lovelace is considered the first programmer. The daughter of the English poet Lord Byron, Lovelace worked with Charles Babbage on his Analytical Engine in the mid-19th century. Her notes are regarded as the first computer algorithm and the precursor to modern computer programming (Fuegi, J & Francis, J, 2003). During World War II, university women with mathematical skills were recruited for "computer" positions, leading the statistical efforts stateside while many men were fighting the war. Their contributions in doing ballistic and trajectory calculations were considered instrumental in the war's outcome. Later women were recruited to provide the programs to test the Electronic Numerical Integrator and Computer, or ENIAC, the world's first general-purpose computer. Their roles, however, have been marginalized in history, having not been included in press releases, photos, or celebrations around the ENIAC introduction (Erickson, 2010). Fifty years later, several women associated with the project were finally given their due by being inducted into the Women In Technology Hall of Fame in 1997 (Brown, 1997).

Over time males began to dominate technology-driven fields. The early innovators of the Internet were all men in privileged university or government positions. And, as computer companies IBM, Microsoft, and Apple began to flourish in the 1970s and 1980s, the idea of the male coder became standard. Female voices and perspectives were missing from these early stages of development. It was not until computers became household items, much like the telephone and television, that women began to use them en masse. And now, with the perpetuation of mobile devices and social networking, women's use of technology equals and often exceeds that of males. But even with women's greater usage, their numbers have not yet been better represented in technology positions and companies.

Embracing Geekdom

It is an unusual contradiction to rationalize the geek stereotype with the traditional macho, male stereotype (Kendall, 2011). Those who work with computers are often considered to be less strong or athletic. Their edge is seen as "brains over brawn." But the power narrative has switched from "only the strong will survive" to "the geeks will inherit the earth." Men embraced the geek stereotype because it became evident that this was a path for the creation of wealth in a modern society, thus flipping the power dynamic. Several conditions have contributed to this shift:

• The move to a service economy
• Competition from more females in the workplace
• The propagation of computer technology in society
• The gainful nature of computer programming as a career

Women, however, have not embraced the same level of interest in the geek stereotype. Whether through socialization or the dynamics of the developing geek subculture, women have not been able to enjoy the same benefits with technology. In recent years, women's usage of social media has risen, but their numbers in computer science programs and within the tech industry have not grown, thus limiting their ability to influence technology's outcomes.

Gender and Social Media

In the first nationwide poll conducted by the Pew Internet & American Life Project in 2000, significantly more men (49%) than women (44%) were Internet users (Fallows, 2005). Over the years, the proportion of men and women who went online drew closer, and by 2005, their usage was almost equal. Some 80% of men and 76% of women now use the Internet, and the numbers grow as more gain access through the usage of smartphones and tablets (Zickuhr & Smith, 2012).

The rise of social networking, with its characteristics of communication and sharing, also has increased women's usage of technology. A Pew Internet study found that women were more likely than men to use social networking sites. While 67% of all users participate in social networking, 71% of women versus 62% of men did so (Duggan & Brenner, 2012). A Comscore study (Abraham, Morn & Vollman, 2010) echoed these results, showing women as the majority of social networking users who spend 30% more time

177

on sites than men. Mobile social network usage is 55% female, 45% male (Nielsen, 2010). Usage patterns can differ by the type of social networking site used. Women are more likely to use Pinterest, a social pinning site much like a virtual bulletin board (25% women vs. 5% men). Women are also more likely to use Instagram (16% vs. 10%) and Facebook (72% vs. 62%), are equally likely to use Tumblr (6% for both males and females) and close in their usage of Twitter (15% vs. 17%) (Duggan & Brenner, 2012). These statistics show a preference for sites with a visual component that offer the ability to communicate and share. Men, however, are twice as likely to use Reddit, a social news site which has a strong technology focus and has also been criticized for its unfriendly environment toward women (Duggan & Smith, 2013; North 2011) Men are also more likely to contribute to content on Wikipedia, the online, crowd-sourced encyclopedia (Antin, Yee, Cheshire & Nov, 2011).

The case of Pinterest provides a lens into women's motivations online. Women make up more than 80% of Pinterest users and, as mentioned above, 25% of female Internet users are on the site (Duggan & Brenner, 2012). The top 10 pinners are all women, each with more than 5 million followers (Meredith, 2013). Food/Drink is the most popular category with the most popular pin being a recipe for garlicky cheese bread. Women have migrated to Pinterest in ways that seem to reflect traditional female roles, using it to share and express interests in fashion, homemaking, food, and weddings. Some of the reason for women's increased usage on visually-oriented sites like Pinterest is that women are simply more socially inclined than men, the difference being that men generally view social media as a tool–a means to gain information or access entertainment–while women more often use it to interact with others and build a community online. Women are more likely to "like" or "follow" a brand and are less likely to display opinions on social media (Sawers, 2012). Pinterest has emerged as an important site to reach the female demographic from a marketing perspective, but also offers women a space to create and connect.

Social media can also provide a cause for concern for women by providing a platform for the publishing of violent imagery or stalking, bullying, and shaming of young girls and women. Violent depictions and abuse can lead to hate crimes against females and generally negative attitudes in society. As a result of peer pressure and other societal pressures, some young women have put themselves in compromising situations by publishing suggestive photos, making inappropriate comments, or sending messages with sexual content (called "sexting"). Young people do not yet comprehend the long-term effects and ramifications of their online behaviors (Martinson, 2013). This applies to boys as well, who also explore sexuality using social media. Responsibility for resolving these issues falls on a number of parties–the social media companies themselves, government, and individuals who feel empowered to speak up against these actions.

Gender and Computer Science

While usage levels show some progress, those involved in the creation of technology are still often men, as are most of those who rise to the top of technology companies. Women are not equally represented in computer science programs at colleges and universities, and therefore not able to secure positions that require these skills. This is a long-held problem that many universities have tried to counter with special programs and incentives to encourage women to enter and complete computer science degrees (Margolis and Fisher, 2002). But the numbers continue to decline. Currently only 12.9% of computer science degrees are awarded to women (Zweben, 2012).

Some blame the nerd stereotype for this difference. In a University of Washington study, women who read articles debunking stereotypes of computer science majors were more likely to express an interest in computer science than those who read articles that supported the stereotypes. "These stereotypes are inconsistent with the female gender role, the qualities that are considered appropriate for women," said Sapna Cheryan, a UW assistant professor of psychology. "It's inconsistent with how many women see themselves and how they want others to see them" (Armstrong, 2013). Others place blame on the lack of proper introduction before college, pressure from peers, and general societal expectations, which are difficult to counter once students reach the university level (Furger, 1998). Girls and boys seem to diverge in their interest in science and math in middle school. Socialization with computers at home and in having female role models can also influence interest later in life.

179

In some cases, women just don't feel that technology is their realm. The computer science culture can be discouraging to women, who may be unable to receive the proper level of support to be successful in a computer science program. The result is that women are systematically veered away from careers that can be gainful, challenging, and productive, and technology platforms lose women's perspectives early in the development process.

But computer science programs are no longer the only place to receive technology education. The mission of computer science departments is on high-level computing standards that are often deemed abstract concepts. The rise in the "learn-to-code" movement touts that everyone should have some programming literacy, and special programs have cropped up around the country to focus on Web development education: places like MakerSquare in Austin (themakersquare.com), Starter League in Chicago (starterleague.com), and Dev Bootcamp in San Francisco (devbootcamp.com). Many of these programs have incentives for women to join, including scholarships and discounted tuition. Organizations like Code Academy (codeacademy.com) and SkillCrush (skillcrush.com) offer online coding courses that can be taken anywhere. And as technology becomes more a part of every aspect of life, in the ways we communicate and connect with others, so does its training become a part of more academic disciplines. Journalism, art and humanities programs are stepping up technology training to provide students with long-term technology skills that will be necessary to their future as communicators. Courses in Web design, content management systems, Web frameworks, and mobile development creep into curricula as programs recognize their relevance to storytelling and communication careers (see advanced.cindyroyal.net, digitalninjasdsu.wordpress.com and www .utapps.com).

Tech companies like Facebook, Google, Apple, and Twitter are still dominated by males, particularly in engineering and programming positions. Women hold only about 20% of computer science jobs. This is despite the fact that women hold 60% of all bachelor's degrees and make up 48% of the workforce overall (Fisher, 2013). A small percentage of chief information officers are female and 30% of American tech executives polled by Reuters said their IT groups have no women at all in management (Casserly, 2012). And for women starting their own businesses, females only receive 4.2% of venture capitalist funding (Nisen, 2013).

There are exceptions. Virginia Rometty heads IBM and Marissa Mayer left an executive position at Google to become the CEO of Yahoo. Meg Whitman heads Hewlett Packard. Sheryl Sandberg is the chief operating officer of Facebook. In her book *Lean In*, Sandberg tackles the issues of women's representation at the higher levels of companies. "While women continue to outpace men in educational achievement, we have ceased making real progress at the top of any industry," says Sandberg. Her advice is for women to "lean in" to their careers and not readily accept being sidelined, understand likability-based biases, and to come to grips with the commitments and sacrifices of a professional career. "I believe that if more women lean in, we can change the power structure of our world and expand opportunities," says Sandberg. "Shared experience forms the basis of empathy and, in turn, can spark the institutional changes we need" (Sandberg, 2013, p. 5). Sandberg's critics have indicated that her approach places too much of the blame and the responsibility on women to change, and not enough on the institutions and culture that created these discrepancies (Lombrozo, 2013). But the book has generated attention and discussion of important issues around barriers and challenges that women face in the workplace.

Technology and Gender in Media

The media often perpetuates gendered stereotypes of technology. The television show *The Big Bang Theory* depicts a group of socially inept nerds. The somewhat disturbing image of the "brogrammer" or computer programmer with frat house sensibility has recently emerged (Gross, 2012; El Nasser, 2012). News articles and advertisements focus on the male programmer, and technology publications either ignore or objectify women on their pages. Technology conferences have been criticized for a dearth of female speakers and some have been called out for their use of "booth babes" or provocatively dressed women staffing trade show booths, and for the treatment of female attendees (Lang, 2013). This can create a hostile environment for women, one in which they feel out of place or isolated, thus discouraging their participation.

In March 2013, Adria Richards of tech company SendGrid tweeted about a conversation she overhead during the Python Conference (PyCon), an annual convention for the discussion and promotion of the Python programming language in the United States, and posted photos of two male attendees:

"Not cool. Jokes about forking repo's in a sexual way and 'big' dongles. Right behind me #pycon."

The interaction, now referred to as "Donglegate," resulted in one of the males being fired by his company. Richards herself became the target of hate, threats, and a denial-of-service attack on her website. At best, the interaction could have been considered juvenile and immature. But this type of discourse, when rampant in a "grown-up" culture, can serve to alienate and isolate females who hope to gain entry into a professional peer group. Richards herself was ultimately let go by SendGrid because of the negative attention brought about by her tweet. When women speak up about this treatment, they are often met with threats, violence, and in this case, unemployment that may serve to silence others.

In September 2013, gender-related incidents were at the forefront of another technology conference. A mobile application known as Titshare was introduced by Australian developers during a hackathon at the TechCrunch Disrupt conference in San Francisco. The application was billed as a humorous look at photos of men staring at women's breasts. Additionally, the conference also provided a platform for Circle Shake, an app that simulated masturbation. These incidents reinforce the belief that technology is a man's world and women don't have a place in it, or at least a place in which they will be respected. The conference organizers were quick to address the issues after a slew of online criticism decrying the sexist and juvenile nature of the presentations and the presence of a young girl in the audience, who was in attendance to present her own application.

The Case of *Wired* Magazine

The magazine, *Wired*, long considered the tech industry's leading authority on technology and culture, has provided some of the most insightful, provocative, and important coverage of the evolution of the technology industry and its roles in our lives over the years. But, *Wired* has defined its target demographic as men with advertising and editorial content in a similar vein to GQ and Maxim. Its cover images over the years reflect a male-dominated view of technology. In its 20-year history, women have only been featured for their contributions to technology in three issues, two of them coming before 1996 (scholar Sherry Turkle and musician Laurie Anderson). When women are featured, it is usually in an objectified manner for the roles they play in television and film or as anonymous or anime characters. You can see all of *Wired*'s cover images at www.wired.com/wired/coverbrowser. In the rare case when a woman of note, like Martha Stewart, was featured on the cover, it was to represent a theme issue (in Stewart's case the issue had a "How To" theme). The editorial coverage of Stewart in the magazine was limited to a superficial interview about her tech usage and not her business achievements or the technology strategy of her media empire.

In November 2010, *Wired* featured a close-up of breasts on its cover, to depict a story about tissue re-engineering. This prompted me to write a blog post "breaking up" with *Wired* (http://tech.cindyroyal.net/an-open-letter-to-wired-magazine). Growing tired of their depiction of or lack of women in the magazine, I felt less comfortable in recommending their content to my students, the majority of whom are female. I felt the magazine was contributing to a technology culture that was becoming increasingly unfriendly toward women.

My "break-up" post prompted a strong outcry. More than 20,000 people viewed the post which generated more than 300 comments, the majority of which were in favor of my position, that *Wired* objectifies and ignores women on its covers. *Wired*'s editors got involved, and while they were prepared to justify that one cover and how it represented the concept of tissue re-engineering, they were unable to address the pattern of women on their covers throughout the history of the magazine. I was ultimately invited to be part of a brainstorming session, via conference call, with the *Wired* editorial team. While none of my suggestions were accepted, the exercise did result in *Wired* featuring the first woman engineer on their cover, Limor Fried, in April 2011. Sadly, no women technologists have been featured on the cover since (although actress Alison Brie of *Mad Men* and *Community* was provocatively featured to depict an article on network ratings). Since then, *Wired* has featured Andy Samberg, Jeff Bezos, Marc Andreessen, Mythbuster host Adam Savage, Steve Jobs, Bre Pettis, hacker Kim Dotcom, Bill Hader and Jimmy Fallon, in addition to a few unidentified men and some cartoon males. In that time Sheryl Sandberg of Facebook wrote an important book on women and careers, Marissa Mayer became CEO of Yahoo and Meg Whitman became CEO of Hewlett Packard. These achievements, however, have not yet merited a *Wired* cover.

Other magazines that focus on technology have decided to take a different tact. Since 2002, Fast Company, a business culture publication, has featured women on its covers and has used editorial content to focus on women's issues. Chloe Sladden, head of media at Twitter, Marissa Mayer while she was still at Google, and Gina Bianchini as the co-founder of Ning are just a few of the women in technology to grace their covers. Their League of Extraordinary Women and Most Influential Women in Technology issues regularly feature high-achieving women. Fast Company editor Robert Safian has made a commitment to feature women on covers. "Silicon Valley and the tech community are not as diverse as they should be," Safian said, "and not enough attention has been paid to people who are diverse and worthy of attention" (Tenore, 2010).

Conclusion

The issues discussed in this chapter indicate that gender manifests across a wide range of technology issues and activities. While women's usage of social media is increasing, their representation as developers of technology and as leaders in technology programs remains low. It is important to recognize individuals and organizations that are actively seeking change in the industry.

She++ (sheplusplus.stanford.edu) is an organization founded by two Stanford technology students, Ellora Israni and Ayna Agarwal, that started with a conference in 2012 and led to the creation of video depicting their goals and the issues of women in technology. The video has been hosted at numerous screenings across the country. The video refers to the "Rosie the Riveter moment" in that "women are the great, untapped bench" in technology, clearly stating the potential in numbers and encouraging the tech industry to take notice. The video features high school students, recent computer science graduates, female technology CEOs, academics and venture capitalists, and inspires with strong personal stories and reflections.

Numerous groups have emerged across the country to support women in programming. Girls Who Code (girlswhocode.com), Women Who Code (women whocode.com), and Girl Develop IT (girldevelopit. com) are just a few of the meetups that provide mentorship, training, and a welcome venue for women to find their place in technology. Organizations like GirlStart in Austin, Texas provide science, technology, engineering, and math workshops to empower girls to study technology. Women in Technology (womenintechnology.org) and Women in Technology International (witi.org) are professional associations that provide support, professional development, and networking to women in technology careers.

Technology will only serve to become a more pervasive part of our lives. As the role of data emerges in the ways we communicate and share, more people who understand coding and technology issues will be necessary. A range of perspectives will also be necessary to provide the proper insight and innovation that is needed to appropriately represent the array of interests that engage with technology.

There are many other areas that are affected by technology. Video games represent another male-dominated industry and serve as a platform for gender stereotypes, sexist attitudes, and violence against women. But this area also holds much potential as women make up 47% of its users. Women gamers over the age of 18 make up 30% of the market, which exceeds that of boys 17 and under (Entertainment Software Association, 2012). Ignoring this demographic will be at the peril of the industry.

Much progress has been made in women's usage of technology, but as this chapter depicts, there is still much work to be done. Women are missing opportunities for gainful and challenging careers by not seeking technology education and experience and the result is technology platforms that don't have a broad representation of perspectives. But the culture of many technology organizations and institutions is not welcoming to women's contributions. What will be required is women's realization of the potential they have with technology as well as the industries' acceptance of women's contributions. Different approaches to technology education that occurs outside of traditional computer science programs may be necessary to attract non-traditional participants. But the increased usage of technology by women for the purposes of creativity, creation, development, sharing, connection, and communication is a positive development that will have lasting effects on the future.

Questions for Class Discussion

1. Why do you think women have not been interested in computer science careers?
2. What do you think are the barriers to women in technology? Are they cultural, institutional, individual? What actions or activities might make technology of more interest to women?
3. What images come to mind when you think of someone who works with computers? Where do you think these images originate?
4. What can computer science programs do to recruit and retain more women? Discuss the ramifications of the computer science discipline remaining male dominated.
5. Why do you think women are more interested in using Pinterest? What aspects of the platform have caused its strong appeal to women? Why do you think men have not adopted Pinterest? What are the elements of a platform with broad appeal?
6. Look at the way that gender is represented on technology websites and publications. Why do these representations exist? What effect do you think these representations have on women's usage of technology?

References

Abraham, L. B., Morn, M. P., & Vollman, A. (2010). *Women on the web: How women are shaping the internet.* Comscore. Retrieved from http://www.comscore.com/Insights/Presentations_and_Whitepapers/2010/Women_on_the_Web_How_Women_are_Shaping_the_Internet

Antin, J., Yee, R., Cheshire, C., & Nov, O. (2011, October). *Gender differences in Wikipedia editing.* In Proceedings of the 7th International Symposium on Wikis and Open Collaboration (pp. 11–14). ACM.

Armstrong, D. (2013, June). *More women pick computer science if media nix outdated nerd stereotype, University of Washington.* Retrieved from http://www.washington.edu/news/2013/06/25/more -women-pick-computer-science-if-media-nix-outdated-nerd-stereotype

Beck, V. S., Boys, S., Rose, C., & Beck, E. (2012). Violence against women in video games a prequel or sequel to rape myth acceptance? *Journal of interpersonal violence, 27*(15), 3016–3031.

Brown, J. (1997, May). *Women proto-programmers get their just reward.* Retrieved from Wired: http: www. wired.com/print/culture/ lifestyle/news/1997/05/3711

Casserly, M. (2012, May). *How women in tech are losing from top to bottom.* Retrieved May 14, 2013, from http://www.forbes.com/sites/ meghancasserly/2012/05/14/women-in-tech-are-losing-from-top -to-bottom

Duggan, M., & Brenner, J. (2013). *The demographics of social media users–2012.* Retrieved from Pew Research Center's Internet & American Life Project: http://www.pewinternet.org/Reports/2013 /Social-media-users.aspx

El Nasser, H. (2012, April). *Stereotype of computer geeks fades and nerds are cool.* Retrieved from http://usatoday30.usatoday.com/ tech/news/story/2012-04-10/techie-geeks-cool/54160750/1

Entertainment Software Association. (2012). *Essential facts about the computer and video game industry.* Retrieved from http://www. theesa.com/facts/pdfs/ESA_EF_2012.pdf

Erickson, L. (2013). *Top secret Rosies: The female computers of WWII High Definition video documentary.* Retrieved from topsecretrosies. com

Fallows, D. (2005). *How women and men use the Internet.* Retrieved December 28, 2005, from Pew Internet & American Life Project: http://www.pewinternet.org/Reports/2005/How-Women-and-Men Use-the-Internet/04-Demographics/01-Background.aspx

Fisher, A. (2013, May). *Why are there still so few women in tech?* Retrieved from http://management.fortune.cnn.com/2013/03/11/women-science-tech

Fisher, C. S. (1992). *America calling: A social history of the telephone to 1940*. CA: University of California Press.

Fuegi, J., & Francis, J. (2003). Lovelace & Babbage and the creation of the 1843'notes'. *Annals of the History of Computing, IEEE, 25*(4), 16–26.

Gross, D. (2012, May). *In tech, some Bemoan the rise of brogrammer culture*. Retrieved from http://www.cnn.com/2012/05/07/tech/web/brogrammers

Kendall, L. (2011). White and Nerdy: Computers, race, and the nerd stereotype. *The Journal of Popular Culture*, 44(3), 505–524.

Lang, D. (2013, June). *E3: Women that aren't 'booth babes' still Hard to find at video game trade show*. Retrieved from San Jose Mercury News: http://www.mercurynews.com/business/ci_23460978/e3-women that-arent-booth-babes-still-hard

Lombrozo, T. (2013). *Should all women heed author's advice to 'Lean In'?* Retrieved from NPR.org: http://www.npr.org/blogs/13.7/2013/03/31/175862363/should-all-women-heed-authors-advice-to -lean-in

Martinson. (2013, July). Tech weekly podcast: Violence against women in the digital realm. *The Guardian*. Retrieved from http://www.guardian.co.uk/technology/the-womens-blog-with-jane -martinson/audio/2013/jul/24/podcast-tech-weekly-women-digital-abuse

Marvin, C. (1988). *When old technologies were new* (p. 140). New York, NY: Oxford University Press.

Meredith, C. (2013). *What Pinterest reveals about women*. Retrieved from http://www.csmonitor.com/Innovation/Latest-News Wires/2013/0222/What-Pinterest-reveals-about-women

Nielsen. (2010, March). *For social networking, women use mobile more than men*. Retrieved from http://www .nielsen.com/us/en/newswire/2010/for-social-networking women-use-mobile-more-than-men.html

Nissen, M. (2013, March). *Venture capitalists don't respect female entrepreneurs* Retrieved from http://www.businessinsider.com/entrepreneurship-has-been-typed-as for-men-2013-3

North, A. (2011, September). *Reddit users find new way to be assholes.* Retrieved from http://jezebel.com/5839306/reddit-users-hit-a-new-low

Sandberg, S. (2013). *Lean in: Women, work, and the will to lead.* Random House.

Sawers, P. (2012, February). Men are from foursquare, women are from facebook, apparently…. Retrieved from http://thenextweb.com/socialmedia/2012/02/15/men-are-from-foursquare-and-women-are-from -facebook-apparently

Spigel, L. (1992). *Make room for TV: Television and the family ideal in postwar America.* University of Chicago Press.

Tenore, M. J. (2010). *Fast company editor: We want to have women represented on our covers.* Retrieved from Pew Internet and American Life Project: http://www.poynter.org/latest-news/top-stories/108375 /fast-company-editor-we-want-to-have-women-represented-on-our-covers/

Zickuhr, K., & Smith, A. (2012). *Digital differences.* Retrieved from Pew Internet & American Life Project: http://www.pewinternet.org/Reports/2012/Digital-differences/Main Report/Internet-adoption -over-time.aspx

Zweben, S. (2012). *Computer degree and enrollment trends from the 2011–2012 Taulbee survey.* Retrieved from http://cra.org/govaffairs/blog/wpconent/uploads/2013/03/CRA_Taulbee_CS_Degrees_and_Enrollment_2011-12.pdf

Chapter 9
Using the Lessons Outside of the Classroom:
In Other Words, Now What?
Adrienne Trier-Bieniek & Patricia Leavy

Let's return to our opening discussion about Merida from the film *Brave* and her short-lived Disney Princess makeover. One of the major takeaways from that example is that groups of people have the power to enact cultural change. The petition, started by *A Mighty Girl*, worked quickly to allow people to voice their concerns about the newer, sexier version of the character and, indeed, change Disney's marketing of Merida. As you start to consider what you can do to challenge gender stereotypes in pop culture, we hope you reflect on the lessons in this text. We conclude by briefly returning to the contributor chapters and harvesting their messages about how to challenge and change the culture. We then offer our own suggestions for how you can get involved online, on your campus, or in your community.

What lessons have we learned from the authors in this book?

While the chapters in this book each focused on analyzing gender portrayals within particular genres of pop culture, the authors of each chapter, in one way or another, made suggestions about how we can resist dominant pop culture constructions of gender. In Chapter 2 Scott Richardson addressed how boys and girls are impacted by pop culture, specifically music and marketing. His discussion of patriarchy and commodities as the allegorical cave demonstrates that we must first begin to change what we consider acceptable gender norms with our own product consumption. In the following chapter on advertising, Patricia Arend also suggests consumers can have an impact by demanding companies act in socially responsible ways. She further notes that media literacy and continued feminist critique are needed in order to combat the negative impact of advertising. In Chapter 4 on music, Adrienne Trier-Bieniek and Amanda Pullum emphasize

A. Trier-Bieniek et al., (Eds.), Gender & Pop Culture, 191–198.

the important role of consciousness-raising as a necessary precursor to social change. This theme is echoed in the following chapter on television as Jenn Brandt suggests audiences are becoming more media savvy which will continue to lead to more diversity in content (and the manner by which we receive that content). The relationship between consciousness-raising, savvy audiences, and activism is also touched on in Chapter 6 on film. Kevin Burke and Adam Greteman argue that in the instance of film and education, for example, we can use popular culture to learn about social inequalities in education and who in fact our schools are failing. Emily Roper and Katherine Polasek return our attention to the importance of challenging conventional definitions of masculinity and femininity so we can think about gender and sport differently and conceive of new ways of "doing" sports. Finally, Cindy Royal highlights the role of organizations in challenging stereotypes. She turns our attention to the organizations that are bridging the technology gap by helping women get into tech development.

What can be done?

As you have read through the chapters of this book you may find yourself wondering what else you can do to combat gender stereotypes in pop culture, or how you can raise awareness about the positive and negative portrayals of gender in film, music, television, advertising, social networking, or sports. Becoming aware of the connection between gender and pop culture opens the door to the development of activist agendas which can be used to combat sexism and raise consciousness. We hope that you have found some inspiration in these pages to go beyond your classroom and venture into your community. In addition to making careful consumer choices, and in effect impacting pop culture through your wallet, there are other ways you can make a difference. Here are some suggestions for getting involved.

Harness the Power of Social Networking

One of the easiest, cheapest, and quickest ways you can begin to raise awareness about the topics covered in this book is by logging on to social networking websites or starting a blog. Facebook has options for joining or creating a consciousness-raising group. Facebook is an easy way to share links to petitions, events, inspirational quotes, or stories that make others aware of the impact pop culture has on our lives. You can utilize their calendar to plan events or just amass a large following of people on your own page. Follow organizations which you know have a focus on social change or that seek to raise awareness about the issue you are most concerned with. A few examples of Facebook pages that are popular (as of this printing) are the *Ms. Magazine* page which features academic research and opinion pieces about gender and pop culture, among other topics. Another popular page which has a connection to an academic organization is *Sociological Images: Seeing is Believing.* Run by Lisa Wade, PhD, *Sociological Images* (and their related blog) presents a myriad of articles, images, and videos relating to gender and pop culture. Finally, one of the co-editors of this book runs the smaller page *Pop Culture Feminism* with the goal of re-framing the ways gender is presented in media. Bear in mind that many of the scholars mentioned in this book have an online presence as well. Twitter is also a great way to share links to just about anything electronic, especially if you are linking it to a blog.

Starting a blog is another easy way to raise awareness and actively share your perspective. Websites like WordPress or Tumblr offer quick sign-ups and give you most of the tools you need to start blogging. Treat your blog as you would any piece of writing that could be read by anyone around the world. In other words, be aware of your online footprint in terms of the content and quality of your writing. Once you have a blog, use Twitter and Facebook to help spread your work around. Find like-minded pages on Facebook to share your blog on and use the hashtag and @ options on Twitter to spread the word about your work. If you have a blog you are extremely confident with, look at websites like Feministing, xoJane and Jezebel to inquire about sharing your work with their audience.

Another way to harness the power of the Internet is to start petitions on websites like Change.org, iPetitions, or Care.com. As we saw with *A Mighty Girl's* petition for *Brave*, these are fast and simple ways to raise awareness and get others involved. Make sure your petition is clearly written and focuses on something that is current. Share your petition via email and social networking. If your blog, Facebook page, or petition needs external funding in order to continue to do the work you want, consider fundraising websites like Kickstarter or Indiegogo. Fundraising websites (including Paypal) can also be used to raise funds for local and national non-profit organizations. For example, the Rape, Abuse and Incest National Network (RAINN) has a section of their website dedicated to "RAINNmakers," people and groups who wish to help raise money for the organization.

Getting Involved Locally: On Campus

Another simple way to affect change is at the local level. If you are reading this book for a college or high school course you probably already have some great resources available to you through your school. Check out your campus's student-run organizations and find one that speaks to you. Also, find out if your campus has a women's center, multicultural center, or LGBTQ (lesbian, gay, bisexual, transgender, queer) center and seek out volunteer opportunities.

You can also considering hosting a campus screening of a film that addresses gender stereotypes and social inequality in pop culture. Structured film screenings are excellent ways to promote consciousness-raising, media literacy, and the kind of feminist critique many of the authors in this volume mentioned. You could use a commercial film or opt for a documentary like *Miss Representation, Tough Guise, Killing Us Softly 4, Born into Brothels, Wrestling with Manhood, Mon Vie en Rose,* or *Pink Ribbons Inc.* Even popular comedies like *Mean Girls* can go far with talking about gender and the impact of media and culture. After you watch the film, have a set of questions prepared which ask viewers to consider what scenes stood out to them and why, what made them uncomfortable while watching, and what they may have taken away from the film. Additionally, many of the documentaries we have mentioned have viewing guides and discussion questions available on their website.

Getting Involved Locally: Off Campus

You can also seek out non-profit and community-based organizations that are always looking for people to lend their time and talents.

National agencies like YWCA/YMCA, Girl Scouts, Big Brother/Sister and United Way usually have opportunities for people looking to get involved in their communities. If you are interested in gender and technology you can check out some of the organizations Cindy Royal listed in the conclusion of the last chapter. It may also be worthwhile to seek out local, more independent agencies in your community and see what their opportunities for volunteering are. When you approach these places, it is important to be professional and prepared to explain what motivates you to volunteer.

Consider getting involved with local or campus politics. This is a great way to learn about the political process while also being a part of creating policies which will affect people for many years. Look into websites like MoveOn.org, Political Action Committees (PAC's), or national organizations like NOW (National Organization of Women).

If you enjoy writing and blogging, consider getting involved with your local media. Find a local newspaper or website and inquire about writing op-ed's (opinion editorials) for them. One website which might help in learning how to write op-ed's, and how to send them for review, is The OpEd Project (www.theopedproject .org). This website will give you information on how to construct an op-ed and what editors are looking for, and it includes a list of major newspapers in the US.

Art as Activism

One of the most impactful ways people confront oppression, stereotypes, and inequality is through the creation of art. Art is a tool for resistance, consciousness-raising, education, and creating social change, as seen in the Trier-Bieniek and Pullum chapter on music. Visual art can be a powerful tool in this regard. For example, research shows that counter-stereotypical images are a highly effective way of fighting pervasive but subtle racial and gender bias (Vedantam, 2013). As you can imagine, we could write another book on the relationship between art, gender, and pop culture. For now, we suggest that if you are an emerging artist find a way to display your work in your community or online (please be weary of copyright and other intellectual property issues when you share your work online). Some of the most powerful works of art have started as Internet campaigns such as the NoH8 Campaign which photographed people in front of a white sheet with duct tape over their mouths and "NOH8" painted on their face/body. The photo series was originally developed as a reaction to the Proposition 8 vote in California which denied gay and lesbian people the right to marry. (This proposition was overturned by the U.S. Supreme Court in 2013.) Another popular campaign is "Dear World" which photographs people around the world with messages inscribed on their bodies. Each message is a hope for what they want the world to look like.

Final Message

We hope that this book contributes to future research and study in the area of gender and pop culture but, perhaps more importantly, we hope that this book has inspired you to look past typical representations of femininity and masculinity in culture and recognize that those depictions are socially constructed. When you interrogate pop culture texts, bear in mind that representations of gender are inextricably bound to representations of race, ethnicity, socio-economic class, and sexuality. Question and challenge those images and stories because they can be changed. Ask yourself questions like:

- What are the messages in this representation? What does it imply about gender, race, and/or sexuality?
- How does consuming this make me feel?
- Is this representation harmful to me? Is it harmful to others? How so?

As the writer and poet Audre Lorde (2007, p. 45) said, "It is axiomatic that if we do not define ourselves for ourselves we will be defined by others. For their use and to our detriment."

Activity

Create an Action Plan

The purpose of this assignment is for students to create an action plan which connects what has been done in the classroom with social activism. While the action plan in these pages is meant to be applied, it can certainly be hypothetical as well. When it has been presented as hypothetical, many students choose to skip the hypothetical aspect and go right into implementing their plan on campus or in the community. Generally, this assignment is done in groups.

Directions: The purpose of this action plan is to take one of the topics covered in class and connect it to something you can do to make a difference in the community. Using the worksheet below figure out an activity that you can do to raise awareness/raise contributions for/ volunteer time for. This can be anything from doing a fundraising drive to creating products to sell on campus or blogging about a chosen topic. Keep in mind that, with this assignment, details matter.

Action Plan Worksheet

Please use this worksheet to work out ideas for your action plan.

1. In small groups identify issues or problems at your school or in your community that you would like to see changed, addressed, or improved. These might relate to ending an unfair situation, reducing prejudice, promoting understanding or difference, or preventing hate crimes. Brainstorm what issues interest you. Include this brainstorm when you hand in your action plan.
2. From the above list, select the one issue that you consider most pressing and circle it. Then brainstorm a variety of projects you could undertake to address this issue. To get started, review the suggestions attached. What steps could you take to tackle your issue? Name at least three.
3. Within your groups, discuss and list the pros and cons of each activity. Then select one activity that you will undertake. List that activity along with how you would execute it.
4. List the steps you would need to take in order to execute your plan. Each group member should be assigned duties. Be specific here. What are the exact things you would need to do? If you are doing a play, for example: Would you need someone in charge of lighting? Finding a space? If you are doing a marathon, where would you get refreshments and food? Where would you hold it?

Examples of supplemental materials: Posters advertising your events, samples of items you decide to sell/give away, pamphlets you want to distribute etc.

5. Execute your plan and write up the results. What went well? What would you have changed? Be sure to relate your write-up to a reading done for class.

References

Lorde, A. (2007). *Sister outsider*. New York, NY: Random House.
Vedantam, S. (2013, July 19). *How to fight racial bias when it is silent and subtle*. http://www.npr.org /blogs/ codeswitch/2013/07/19/203306999/How-To-Fight-Racial-Bias-When-Its-Silent-And-Subtle

Further Reading

In this section we provide suggestions for further reading on the topics found in the book as well as those which focus on international studies of pop culture and gender.

Anderson, E. (2011). Updating the outcome: Gay athletes, straight teams, and coming out in educationally based sport teams. *Gender and Society, 25*, 250–268.

Baumgardner, J., & Richards, A. (2000). *Manifesta: Young women, feminism and the future*. New York, NY: Farrar, Straus and Giroux.

Beck, V. S., Boys, S., Rose, C., & Beck, E. (2012). Violence against women in video games: A prequel or sequel to rape myth acceptance? *Journal of Interpersonal Violence, 27*, 3016–3334.

Bessett, D. (2006). Don't step on my groove!: Gender and the social experience of rock. *Symbolic Interaction, 29*, 49–62.

Bordwell, D., & Thompson K. (2010). *Film/Art: An introduction*. New York, NY: McGraw-Hill.

Brown, E. H. (2008). Marlboro men: Outsider masculinities and commercial modeling in postwar America. In R. L. Blaszczyk (Ed.), *Producing fashion: Commerce, culture and consumers* (pp. 187–206). Philadelphia, PA: University of Philadelphia Press.

Brunsdon, C. (2007). *Feminist television criticism: A reader*. Oxford: Oxford University Press.

Burns, L., & Lafrance, M. (2001). *Disruptive divas: Feminism, identity and popular music*. New York, NY: Routledge.

Capella, M., Hill, R., Kees, J., & Rapp, J. (2010). The impact of violence against women in advertisements. *Sex Roles, 37*, 37–51.

Carter, B. A. (2013). Nothing better or worse than being black, gay, and in the band: a qualitative examination of gay undergraduates participating in historically black college or university marching bands. *Journal of Research in Music Education, 61*, 26–43.

Cowie, E. (1997). *Cinema and psychoanalysis*. Minneapolis, MN: University of Minnesota Press.

Dunham, Y., & Skorek, M. (2012). Self-enhancement following exposure to idealized body portrayals in ethnically diverse men: A fantasy effect of advertising. *Sex Roles, 66,* 655–667.

Elsaesser, T., & Hagener, M. (2009). *Film theory: An introduction through the senses.* New York, NY: Routledge.

Gengaro, C. L. (2009). Requiems for a city: Popular music's response to 9/11. *Popular Music and Society, 32,* 25–36.

Gibson, P. C. (2004). Introduction: Popular culture. In S. Gillis, G. Howe, & R. Munford (Eds.), *Third wave feminism* (pp. 137–142). New York, NY: Palgrave MacMillan.

Jamila, S. (2002). Can I get a witness? Testimony from a hip-hop feminist. In D. Hernandez & B. Rehman (Eds.), *Colonize this!: Young women of color on today's feminism* (pp. 382–394). New York, NY: Seal Press.

Javors, I. R. (2004). Hip-hop culture: Images of gender and gender roles. *Annals of the American Psychotherapy Association, 7,* 42–64.

Johns, M. L. (2007). *Third wave feminism and television: Jane puts it in a box.* London: I. B. Taurus.

Kilbourne, J. (1999). *Deadly persuasion: Why women and girls must fight the addictive power of advertising.* New York, NY: The Free Press.

Lemish, D. (2010). *Screening gender on children's television: The views of producers around the world.* New York, NY: Routledge.

Lotz, A. D. (2006). *Redesigning women: Television after the network era.* Chicago, IL: University of Illinois Press.

Lowe, M. (2003). Colliding feminisms: Britney spears, 'Tweens', and the politics of reception. *Popular Music and Society, 26,* 123–140.

Lugo-Lugo, C. R. (2001). The Madonna experience: A U.S. icon awakens a Puerto Rican adolescent's feminist consciousness. *Frontiers, 22,* 118–127.

Martine, B. (2013). *Difficult men: Behind the scenes of a creative revolution: From the sopranos and the wire to mad men and breaking bad.* New York, NY: Penguin Press.

Mehaffy, M. M. (1997). Advertising race/racing advertising: The feminine consumer (nation), 1876–1900. *Signs: Journal of Women in Culture and Society, 23*(1), 131–174.

Monk-Turner, E., Kouts, T., Parris, K., & Webb, C. (2007). Gender role stereotyping in advertisements on three radio stations: Does musical genre make a difference? *Journal of Gender Studies, 16*, 173–182.

Parkin, K. J. (2006). *Food is love: Advertising and gender roles in modern America.* Philadelphia, PA: University of Pennsylvania Press.

Travers, A., & Jillian D. (2011). Transgender inclusion and the changing face of lesbian softball leagues. *International Review for the Sociology of Sport, 46*, 488–507.

International Studies of Pop Culture

Assuncao, M. R. (2005). Brazilian popular culture or the curse and blessings of cultural hybridism. *Bulletin of Latin American Research, 24*(2), 157–166.

Caglar, A. S. (1998). Popular culture, marginality and institutional incorporation: German-Turkish rap and Turkish pop in Berlin. *Cultural Dynamics, 10*(3), 243–261.

Ezra, E., & Rowden, T. (2006). *Transnational cinema: The film reader.* London, UK: Routledge.

Frederiksen, B. F. (2000). Popular culture, gender relations and the democratization of everyday life in Kenya. *Journal of Southern African Studies, 26*(2), 209–222.

Fung, A., & Curtin, M. (2002). The anomalies of being faye (Wong): Gender politics in Chinese popular music. *International Journal of Cultural Studies, 5*(3), 263–290.

Huat, C. B. (2004). Conceptualizing an east Asian popular culture. *Inter-Asia Cultural Studies, 5*(2), 200–221.

Huq, R. (2003). From the margins to mainstream?: Representations of british Asian youth musical cultural expression from Bhangra to asian underground music. *Young, 11*(1), 29–48.

Karlin, J. (2002). The gender of nationalism: Competing masculinities in Meiji Japan. *The Journal of Japanese Studies, 28*(1), 41–77.

Kumar, S., & Curtin, M. (2002). Made in India: In between music television and patriarchy. *Television & New Media, 3*(4), 345–366.

Lee, L. (2008). Understanding gender through Disney's marriages: A study of young Korean immigrant girls. *Early Childhood Education*, *36*, 11–18.

Looseley, D. (2005). Fabricating Johnny: French popular music and national culture. *French Cultural Studies*, *16*(2), 191–203.

Makri-Tsilipakou, M. (2003). Greek diminutive use problematized: Gender, culture and common sense. *Discourse & Society*, *14*(6), 699–726.

Preiler, M., Kohlbacher, F., Hagiwara, S., & Arima, A. (2011). Gender representation in Japanese television advertisements, *Sex Roles*, *64*, 405–415.

Ratele, K. (2005). Proper sex, bodies, culture and objectification. *Agenda*, *2*(63), 32–42.

Ross, M. W., Mansson, S. A., & Daneback, K. (2011). Prevalence, severity, and correlates of problematic sexual internet use in Swedish men and women. Arch Sex Behavior, 41, 459–466.

Saldanha, A. (2002). Music, space, identity: Geographies of youth culture in Bangalore. *Cultural Studies*, *16*(3), 337–350.

Shin, E. H., & Nam, E. A. (2004). Culture, gender roles, and sport: The case of Korean players on the LPGA tour. *Journal of Sport & Social Issues*, *28*(3), 223–244.

Toth, C. (2008). J-Pop and performances of young female identity: Music, gender and urban space in Tokyo. *Young*, *16*(2), 111–129.

Vu, H. T., & Lee, T. (2013). Soap operas as a matchmaker: A cultivation analysis of the effects of south Korean TV dramas on Vietnamese women's marital intentions. *Journalism & Mass Communication Quarterly*, *90*(2), 308–330.

Zoonen, L. V. (2002). Gendering the internet: Claims, controversies and cultures. *European Journal of Communication*, *17*(1), 5–23.

About the Contributors

Patricia Arend, Ph.D. is an Assistant Professor of Sociology at Fitchburg State University. She received her PhD in Sociology from Boston College and has an MA in Sociology and Graduate Certificate in Women's Studies from Northeastern University. Her research focuses on the relationship between consumer culture and gender inequality. Specifically, she examines women's fantasies about weddings to explain the popularity of the traditional, white wedding in an era of growing gender and marital equality. She has published in journals including *Race and Society* and *Journal of Consumer Culture* and has co-edited a book titled *Culture, Power, and History: Studies in Critical Sociology*, which was published by Brill in 2006.

Jenn Brandt, Ph.D. is Director of Women's and Gender Studies and an Assistant Professor of English at High Point University. Brandt's work focuses on gender and cultural studies in literature, film, and television. Previous publications include articles on *Sex and the City*, *Nip/Tuck*, and *The DaVinci Code*. She has also been published in *The Journal of Graphic Novels and Comics*, *Critique: Studies in Contemporary Fiction*, and the forthcoming *Feminist Theory and Popular Culture*.

Kevin Burke, Ph.D. is Faculty Fellow with the Institute of Educational Initiatives at the University of Notre Dame. His interests center on curriculum theory and teacher education most particularly the ways in which gender and religion come to in/re/deform student possibility and teacher training. His first book, *Masculinities and other hopeless causes in an all-boys catholic school* (2011) is available through Peter Lang.

Adam J. Greteman, Ph.D. is an instructor of Art Education at the School of the Art Institute of Chicago and a contracted professor of Leadership at Creighton University. His work engages issues of ethics, sexuality, and education. He is currently working on a number of projects ranging a philosophical and historical analysis of the Marquis de Sade in educational philosophy to a co-authored book (with Kevin

J. Burke) on the ubiquity of "like" as an historical, philosophical, literary, and economic concept. His research has been published in *Educational Theory, Sex Education,* and *Educational Philosophy and Theory.* He also spends part of his time as a personal stylist in Chicago "teaching" the art of sartorial disguise.

Katherine M. Polasek, Ph.D. is an Associate Professor in the Department of Kinesiology at the State University of New York at Cortland. Dr. Polasek earned her doctorate in Kinesiology with an emphasis in sport and exercise psychology from Temple University and her M.S. in Kinesiology from the University of Illinois at Chicago. Her research focuses on gender and sport. Dr. Polasek's work has been published in *Women in Sport and Physical Activity Journal, The Sport Psychologist,* and *Research in Dance Education.* She also contributed to the book *Sports Around the World.* Dr. Polasek currently serves as a reviewer for *Athletic Insight* and *Research in Dance Education.*

Amanda Pullum is a graduate student in sociology and President's Dissertation Year Fellow at the University of California, Irvine. She studies social movements, gender, and labor unions, and she is especially interested in social movement strategy and tactics. Her past research focuses on the Tea Party movement, and her previous publications include chapters in *The Wiley-Blackwell Encyclopedia of Social and Political Movements* and *Democratizing Inequalities: Pitfalls and Unrealized Promises of the New Public Participation,* among others. Her dissertation, "The ABCs of Dissent: Teachers' Unions and Influences upon Strategic Choice," examines influences on strategic choice in teachers' unions as they work to oppose restrictions on public K-12 teachers' collective bargaining and tenure protections.

Scott Richardson is the author of *eleMENtary School: (Hyper) Masculinity in a Feminized Context,* and curriculum theorist specializing in democratic educational models and the intersections of gender, sexuality and schooling. He is currently an assistant professor of Educational Foundations, Women's Studies affiliate and co-director of the Sexuality & Gender Institute at Millersville University of Pennsylvania.

Emily A. Roper, Ph.D. is an Associate Professor in the Department of Health and Kinesiology at Sam Houston State University. Dr. Roper earned her doctorate in cultural studies with an emphasis in sport and exercise psychology from the University of Tennessee and her M.S. in sport psychology from the University of Toronto. Her research focuses on gender, sexual identity, and sport and has been published in *Research Quarterly for Exercise and Sport, Women in Sport and Physical Activity Journal, Sex Roles,* the *Journal of Applied Sport Psychology, The Sport Psychologist, Research in Dance Education,* and *Athletic Insight.* She has also contributed to several books including *Cultural Sport Psychology: From Research to Practice, Contemporary Sport Psychology,* and *The Oxford Handbook of Sport and Performance Psychology.* Dr. Roper's edited book, *Gender Relations in Sport,* is due for publication in late 2013. At the professional level, she has served as the Publications and Information Division Head for the Association for Applied Sport Psychology (AASP) from 2010 to 2013 and as an Associate Editor for *Athletic Insight.* She was the recipient of the 2001 AASP Dissertation of the Year Award and 2013 SHSU College of Education Researcher of the Year Award.

Cindy Royal is an associate professor in the School of Journalism and Mass Communication at Texas State University where she teaches Web design and digital media courses. She completed Ph.D. studies at The University of Texas in 2005. Her research interests include understanding the role of programming and data in journalism and the integration of technology in education. Her students have gone on to digital media careers at *The New York Times, Austin American-Statesman, Blackbaud, Spredfast, Homeaway, SXSW, T3* and more. Royal hosts a music blog at onthatnote.com and a tech blog at tech. cindyroyal.net. She writes for *Texas Music Magazine* and co-founded the Austin chapters of *Hacks/Hackers* and *Online News Association.* In 2013, Royal was accepted to the Knight Journalism Fellowship program at Stanford University to work on a platform to teach journalists how to code. More information on her background and activities can be found at cindyroyal com.

About the Editors

Adrienne Trier-Bieniek, Ph.D. is currently an assistant professor of sociology at Valencia College in Orlando, Florida. Her first book, *Sing Us a Song, Piano Woman: Female Fans and the Music of Tori Amos* (Scarecrow Press 2013), addressed the ways women have used Tori Amos's music as a means to heal after experiencing trauma. She has published in the journals *Qualitative Research* and *Humanity and Society*, is a contributor to *The Art of Social Critique: Painting Mirrors of Social Life* and has been a guest columnist for *The Orlando Sentinel*. She is the editor of the forthcoming books *Feminist Theory and Pop Culture* (Sense 2015) and *Fan Girls and Media: Consuming Culture* (Scarecrow Press 2014.) Adrienne has been a guest on NPR-WGVU, Power Talk Radio and has been interviewed by various media on the use of music as a tool for healing as well as gender stereotypes in pop culture. Additionally, Adrienne is regularly invited to college campuses and community organizations to speak about music, gender and pop culture. She has written for the *Gender & Society Blog, Feministing. com, Girl w/ Pen* and *The Survivor Manual*. She regularly contributes to organizations seeking advice or information on music and healing. Adrienne can be reached at www.adriennetrier-bieniek.com.

Patricia Leavy, Ph.D. is a public intellectual, independent researcher and novelist, formerly Associate Professor of Sociology and the Founding Director of Gender Studies at Stonehill College. Leavy's work is internationally known. She has emerged as a leader in the qualitative and arts-based research communities. She is the author of the arts-based feminist novels *American Circumstance* (Sense Publishers, 2013) and Sense's top-selling title to date, *Low-Fat Love* (2011). She has published a dozen nonfiction books. She is the author of *Fiction as Research Practice* (Left Coast Press, 2013); *Essentials of Transdisciplinary Research: Issue and Problem-Centered Approaches to Research* (Left Coast Press, 2011); *Oral History* (Oxford University Press, 2011); *Method Meets Art: Arts-Based Research Practice* (Guilford Press, 2009); and *Iconic Events: Media, Politics and Power in Retelling History* (Lexington Books, 2007). She is coauthor of *The Practice of Qualitative Research* (Sage Publications, 2005, 2011) and *Feminist Research Practice: A Primer* (Sage, 2007). She is the editor of *The Oxford Handbook of Qualitative Research* (Oxford University Press, expected Spring 2014) and the co-editor of *Hybrid Identities: Theoretical and Empirical Examinations* (Haymarket, 2008); *Handbook of Emergent Methods* (Guilford Press, 2008); *Emergent Methods in Social Research* (Sage, 2006) and *Approaches to Qualitative Research* (Oxford University Press, 2004). She is the editor for the *Social Fictions, Teaching Gender* and *Teaching Race & Ethnicity* book series with Sense Publishers and the Oxford University Press series *Understanding Qualitative Research*. She is regularly quoted by the national media for her expertise on pop culture, gender and other sociological topics and has appeared on national television programs. She is also a regular blogger for the *Huffington Post*. The New England Sociological Association named Leavy the 2010 "Sociologist of the Year" and she has recently been nominated for a Lifetime Achievement Award by the International Congress of Qualitative Inquiry and a Special Achievement Award by the American Creativity Association. She makes presentations and keynote addresses at universities as well as national and international conferences.

Please visit www.patricialeavy.com.

CPSIA information can be obtained at www.ICGtesting.com
Printed in the USA
LVOW07s0454051215

465439LV00007B/47/P